THE
School Network
Handbook

EDUCATION
DEVELOPMENT CENTER

Center for Online
Professional Education

© 2002 Education Development Center, Inc.

The School Network Handbook

EDUCATION DEVELOPMENT CENTER, INC.—
CENTER FOR ONLINE PROFESSIONAL EDUCATION

Director of Publishing
Jean Marie Hall

Acquisitions Editor
Mathew Manweller

Book Publishing Project Manager
Tracy Cozzens

Data and Communications Manager
Diannah Anavir

Administrative Assistant
Pam Calegari

Copy Editor
Larry Russell
Lynne Ertle

Cover and Book Design
Kim McGovern

Layout and Production
Tracy Cozzens
Kim McGovern

Illustrations
John Yarrow
Signe Landin

International Society for Technology in Education (ISTE)
480 Charnelton Street
Eugene, OR 97401-2626
Order Desk: 800.336.5191
Order Fax: 541.302.3778
Customer Service: orders@iste.org
Books and Courseware: books@iste.org
World Wide Web: www.iste.org

First Edition
ISBN 1-56484-191-X

About ISTE

The International Society for Technology in Education (ISTE) is a nonprofit professional organization with a worldwide membership of leaders in educational technology. We are dedicated to promoting appropriate uses of information technology to support and improve learning, teaching, and administration in K–12 education and teacher education. As part of that mission, ISTE provides high-quality and timely information, services, and materials, such as this book.

The ISTE Publishing Department works with experienced educators to develop and produce classroom-tested books and courseware. We look for content that emphasizes the use of technology where it can make a difference—making the teacher's job easier; saving time; motivating students; helping students who have unique learning styles, abilities, or backgrounds; and creating learning environments that would be impossible without technology. We believe technology can improve the effectiveness of teaching while making learning exciting and fun.

Every manuscript and product we select for publication is peer reviewed and professionally edited. While we take pride in our publications, we also recognize the difficulties of maintaining quality while keeping on top of the latest technologies and research. Please let us know what products you would find helpful. We value your feedback on this book and other ISTE products. E-mail us at **books@iste.org**.

ISTE is home of the National Educational Technology Standards (NETS) Project and the National Center for Preparing Tomorrow's Teachers to Use Technology (NCPT3). To learn more about NETS or request a print catalog, visit our Web site at **www.iste.org**, which provides:

> Current educational technology standards for K–12 student and teacher education

> A bookstore with online ordering and membership discount options

> *Learning & Leading with Technology* magazine

> *ISTE Update*, membership newsletter

> Teacher resources

> Discussion groups

> Professional development services, including national conference information

> Research projects

> Member services

About the EDC Center for Online Professional Education

The EDC Center for Online Professional Education, established in 1998, focuses on the use of technology, in conjunction with other means, to support ongoing communities of education professionals and to enhance teaching and learning in K–12 schools. Center projects focus on work with education leaders in the areas of school improvement, technology for teaching and learning, online professional development, mathematics education, and cultural diversity. The center is located in Newton, Massachusetts.

Grant Acknowledgment

The writing of this book was supported by the U.S. Department of Education, Office of Educational Research and Improvement, through the Northeast and Islands Regional Technology in Education Consortium; by the AT&T Foundation; and by the Education Development Center, Inc. Opinions expressed are those of the author and not necessarily shared by the funders.

Acknowledgments

Special thanks are due to John Yarrow, senior manager of Enterprise Architecture for Southwest Airlines, whose considerable experience in school systems, technical expertise, hard work, and good humor have left their mark on every page. John patiently discussed the management and technologies involved with school networks during dozens of hours of interviews, answered many questions by electronic mail, and reviewed the manuscript. In addition, John conceived all the network diagrams for the book and co-authored an earlier version of much of the material in the Appendices.

Thanks also to Shahriar Moin (Genome Therapeutics) for his work on this manuscript, including many excellent content and editing suggestions, and for demonstrating that one can manage technology both passionately and well.

Illustrations are by Emily Passman, Education Development Center, and Stephan Miller.

Finally, thanks to the many other people who provided counsel and technical information (in alphabetical order):

Jim Butler, Marcom Technical Resources

Jim Chace, coordinator of Technology Services, Acton-Boxborough (Massachusetts) Regional School District

Alan Epstein, director of Technology, Watertown (Massachusetts) Public Schools

Amy Fetherston, teacher, Washington High School, Milwaukee Public Schools

Michael Goldstein, founder and chief executive officer, Youth Tech Entrepreneurs, Malden, Massachusetts

Margaret Honey, Education Development Center

Sherry King, superintendent, Mamaroneck (New York) Public Schools

Glenn Kleiman, Education Development Center

Priscilla Kotyk, technology curriculum integration specialist, Acton-Boxborough (Massachusetts) Regional School District

Mathew Manweller, acquisitions editor, International Society for Technology in Education (ISTE)

Michael McDonald, network manager/technical coordinator, Acton-Boxborough (Massachusetts) Regional School District

Susan Metrick, Education Development Center

Robert Nelson, director of technology, Milwaukee (Wisconsin) Public Schools

Jean Pendleton, director of instructional technology K–12 for the Brookline (Massachusetts) Public Schools

Jeff Post, Education Development Center

Lee Pulis, senior scientist, TERC

G. David Rockwell, instructional technology coordinator, Beaufort (South Carolina) Middle School, Beaufort County School District

Lawrence Russell, editor, International Society for Technology in Education (ISTE)

Mary Skipper, director, TechBoston, Boston, Massachusetts

Bob Spielvogel, Education Development Center

Sarah Tate, assistant superintendent for operations, Mamaroneck (New York) Public Schools

Kris Yerby, Education Development Center

Contents

3. Traffic Regulators

4. Travel Operations Centers

5. Technologies for Long-Distance Networks

Appendixes

Glossary

Index

Introduction

What Is This Book About?

Illusions

A technology coordinator updates her computer inventory to include the long list of network hardware and software she has installed this year. Next year, she knows, there will be more computers, more breakdowns and upgrades—an endless round of technical challenges that feels overwhelming. A science teacher by background, she has no formal training in fixing computers. Every hour that she spends on these technology operations steals directly from time she should spend with teachers developing technology-rich curricula. How can she possibly juggle all these demands?

Across the city, a network manager enters the room that contains his district's network servers (shared computers). He thinks of the room as an orphanage—an odd lot of unruly equipment that arrived by donation or one-of-a-kind purchases when district money was available. He spends most of his time simply keeping the computers running—no easy feat when the equipment is so old and varied that instructions and parts are hard to come by. How can he learn enough about all this hardware and software to keep up?

In the next office, the assistant superintendent of technology spreads out network diagrams. Her network manager has annotated his recommended purchases. No matter how long she works in technology, she always feels a bit lost when trying to make these big decisions. How can she protect the interests of the community, administrators, teachers, and students? How can she learn enough to do this job?

Visions

A technology coordinator updates her computer inventory to include the long list of network hardware and software she has installed this year. Next year, she knows, there will be more computers, more breakdowns and upgrades—an endless round of technical challenges. But she also knows that next year she'll be in a better position to do the job. She and her students have just completed an industry-based curriculum that covered computer network management. They learned together about network communications, performing system upgrades, preventing viruses, and a whole host of other technical topics. The district hired the best students to be her technical assistants. She can hardly wait to see how much better things will run with a few extra hands, and how her students' confidence will grow as the district recognizes their contributions!

Across the city, a network manager enters the room that contains his district's network servers (shared computers). He thinks of the room as an orphanage—an odd lot of unruly equipment that arrived by donation or one-of-a-kind purchases when money was available. He has hope that one day things will be different. Last year he and colleagues in other schools researched best practices for selecting and managing critical network equipment. They found that the most successful school districts chose their critical equipment from a small number of well-respected vendors, and they kept that equipment up-to-date. The group presented their findings at a state technology conference, and that presentation helped persuade his director of technology to rethink the district's three-year technology purchase plan. Improving his network might take time, but the district has made a good first step.

In the next office, the assistant superintendent of technology spreads out network diagrams. Her network manager has annotated recommended wiring and other infrastructure changes for the coming year. No matter how long she works in technology, she always feels a bit lost when trying to make these big decisions. But partners at local technology companies have volunteered to work through the district's infrastructure planning. They've provided information on Ethernet installations, security equipment, and—critically—guidelines for managing consultants and technical staff. The partners don't always agree with each other (or with her network manager), but their conversations always yield a better conclusion than she could make on her own.

Realities

Making computer technology work well requires two kinds of knowledge: (1) technical knowledge about network components and operations and (2) knowledge about best practices for purchasing, installing, and maintaining equipment and managing personnel. The educators described in *Illusions* struggle to attain these types of knowledge, and their work is made difficult by that struggle. The educators in *Visions*—with no greater financial resources, time, or recognition—put both types of knowledge to work to make their technology infrastructures work successfully.

This book is a guide for both technical information and management practices in K–12 schools. It provides a detailed introduction in lay language to most of the technologies that compose school networks—Ethernet, wireless connections, routers, servers, TCP/IP (Transmission Control Protocol/Internet Protocol), security devices, and many other topics. It also provides suggestions for selecting staff and consultants, planning infrastructure purchases, implementing security systems, and many other management topics. This combination of technical information and technology management tools is designed to provide the reader with a firm basis for building school networks that can support powerful kinds of teaching and learning with technology.

Intended Audience

The School Network Handbook is intended for anyone interested in how network technologies work and, more specifically, how schools can efficiently manage their networks.

> **Technology coordinators, curriculum coordinators, librarians, and other specialists** who provide technical support will learn how desktop, laptop, and handheld equipment interoperate; how viruses or other destructive agents can be contained; how operating systems such as Windows XP or Macintosh OS X work, and the benefits and weaknesses of each; what Ethernet is; how the Internet is connected by TCP/IP (and what that acronym stands for); and many other topics.

> **Network managers** will learn about the similarities and differences of network operating systems such as Windows 2000 or Novell NetWare, and their relative merits; how to manage backup services; the ways routers, firewalls, proxy services, intrusion detection systems, and other security devices can be deployed; how virtual private networks work; the similarities and differences between ISDN (Integrated Services Digital Network), frame relay, leased lines, and other wide area network technologies; and many other topics.

> **Assistant superintendents of technology and directors of technology** can focus on the sections of the book that describe best practices for planning and managing well-run networks. They can also refer to the technical sections of this book to deepen their understanding of specific network technologies or answer particular technical questions as they arise.

Organization of This Book

Sections

Chapters 1 through 5 describe the technical details of how networks work. Chapter 1 introduces the three broad categories of computers on a network—clients, servers, and peripherals. Chapter 2 outlines Ethernet, Internet protocols, and other fundamental network communication standards. Chapter 3 describes switches, routers, firewalls, and other devices that interconnect networks or protect them from unwanted intrusion. Chapter 4 examines network operating systems such as Windows 2000, Windows XP, and Novell NetWare. Chapter 5 discusses very large networks called metropolitan or wide area networks. The appendixes include sections describing best practices for managing daily network operations, tips on long-term planning and management, acquisition and budgeting options, and a variety of other helpful information. The glossary defines technical terms used in this book.

Special Assistance

For assistance in understanding the technical complexities described in this book, look for sections marked like this, which summarize the most important concepts in simple language:

Technical Information Summary

For advice about purchasing and managing network components (rather than technical explanations), look for sections marked like this:

Practical Advice

For additional help in defining technical terms and concepts introduced in this book, consult the following Internet Web sites:

Dictionary of PC Hardware and Data Communications Terms (Schneir):
www.oreilly.com/reference/dictionary

PC Webopedia: **www.webopedia.com**

TechWeb Encyclopedia: **www.techweb.com/encyclopedia**

Whatis: **http://whatis.techtarget.com/**

Network Computing Glossary: **www.svisions.com/ml/net-glossary.html**

A Helpful Analogy

Network planners share many of the same concerns and responsibilities as individuals involved with designing transportation systems. Both are tasked with getting things to move from point A to point B quickly and safely. To do this, they must carefully plan their systems to match the needs of their respective communities and institute procedures that efficiently monitor and regulate the flow of traffic, whether it be automobiles or packets of data. Each technical chapter of this book, therefore, begins with a transportation system analogy as a way of illustrating how the chapter topic fits within the larger context of building and managing a computer network as a whole.

The School Network Handbook

Destinations on the Information Highway

CLIENTS, SERVERS, AND PERIPHERALS

A network is an information highway. Bits of information (data packets) travel back and forth along this highway and come to rest at specific destinations. These destinations generally fall into one of three categories—clients, servers, and peripherals. When printing a document, for example, a desktop or laptop computer (a client) sends stored bits of information that make up the document to a printer (a peripheral). Likewise, when a computer user is viewing a Web page, bits of information that make up the Web page pass from a Web server to a client desktop or laptop computer. This chapter focuses on the role and purpose of clients, servers, and peripherals within a network. Particular attention will be paid to their physical, or hardware, characteristics and how each is interconnected to the others.

Clients

A client is any networked device or program used directly by an individual to request services from or deliver them to a network. Clients are distinguished from peripherals and servers by the fact that their primary purpose on the network is to process and store information directly for individuals. For example, networked desktop and laptop computers are considered clients because individuals use them to access shared network resources.

Software programs such as Web browsers or FTP (File Transfer Protocol) programs are also referred to as clients because individuals use them to send and receive information to and from remote locations.

In client/server systems, individuals using client computers send inquiries to powerful servers (shared computers) that search, retrieve, and display information on behalf of the client and do so faster than the client alone could.

Schools across the country are currently experiencing a dramatic increase in both the number and variety of network clients readily available for educational use. Among the most important of these are desktop computers, laptops computers, and handheld devices.

DESKTOP COMPUTERS

Desktop Computers

The term *desktop computer* refers to a computer, or in some cases a workstation, that is typically used for home, school, or business computing. The capabilities of desktop computers include word processing, spreadsheet and database manipulation, document storage and retrieval, programming, graphic design, and multimedia development. Both desktop and laptop computers possess several basic components, including monitors, memory, and so forth.

Monitor, Keyboard, and Mouse (or Other Pointing Device)

A computer takes input from its keyboard, mouse, or other pointing device and sends its output (a picture of its work) to its monitor (video display).

Central Processing Unit

The central processing unit (known as the CPU or processor) supervises all of a computer's activities. When information in a spreadsheet is calculated or a word processor is used to move text, it is the CPU that performs the necessary calculations. The CPU also manages the functions of other components such as memory and disks that are involved in the operation. Processor capability is measured, albeit roughly, by the speed at which the CPU processes information. Modern processors operate between 500 megahertz (MHz) and 2 gigahertz (GHz), where 1 megahertz represents one million electrical cycles (alternations of electrical current) per second and 1 gigahertz represents one billion electrical cycles.

Common processor types include Pentium III and Pentium 4 (used in many home computers running Windows operating systems), PowerPC (used in Macintosh computers, among others), and AMD K6 (also used in many Windows PCs). Pentium III and Pentium 4 computers have largely replaced the older 386 (80386 chip) and 486 (80486 chip) processors.

Memory

Computers have several types of memory: read-only memory, random access memory, cache, and disks (hard disks, CD-ROMs, DVDs, etc.).

READ-ONLY MEMORY. The instructions required for starting a computer reside in a special type of memory called read-only memory (ROM). On Windows PCs, ROM is also referred to as BIOS (basic input/output system). ROM settings can be reconfigured using menus or control panels or upgraded through special programs provided by the manufacturer. ROM settings are generally not changed, however, unless the physical components of the computer have been altered (e.g., a new hard disk has been added) or the operating system software has been upgraded (e.g., moved from Windows NT 4.0 to Windows 2000).

RANDOM ACCESS MEMORY. Random access memory (RAM) provides temporary storage for information that computers need quickly. When a word processing document is opened, for example, its contents are copied from the computer's hard disk (permanent storage) to RAM—a portion is also displayed on the monitor. As the document is scrolled, the CPU draws contents from RAM to refresh the monitor's display. When the CPU has exhausted the contents of its RAM, it accesses the hard disk for additional information. (Drawing contents from RAM is faster than drawing them from the hard disk.) Likewise, when a document is changed, the changes are stored in RAM until explicitly "saved." When documents are saved, the CPU copies the corresponding contents of its RAM to the hard disk. "Unsaved" data stored in RAM are usually, although not always, lost if the computer crashes or loses power. RAM is measured in MB (megabytes, or million bytes). Most desktop and laptop computers commonly have between 64 MB and 256 MB of RAM. Generally speaking, the more RAM a computer has the faster it will run and the greater the number of application programs (such as Microsoft Word or AppleWorks) it will be able to keep open simultaneously. RAM is located on small, often removable (upgradeable) circuit boards whose shapes and sizes vary. These different physical characteristics are described by acronyms such as DIMM (dual in-line memory module), RIMM (Rambus in-line memory module), and many others. RAM packages use a variety of different strategies for storing and retrieving information. These technologies are referred to by an equally wide array of acronyms—SRAM (static RAM), DRAM (dynamic RAM), SDRAM (synchronous DRAM), or VRAM (video RAM), to name a few.

CACHE. A cache is a (relatively small) storage place that is used to hold temporary information for quick retrieval. A computer contains many different caches. For example, a computer stores caches of Web pages on its hard disk enabling it to retrieve pages more quickly from cache than from the Internet. A computer has a different cache for information it may need on a recurring basis. Sometimes this cache is built into the microprocessor itself. Termed level 1 (L1), this cache is extremely fast (about twice as fast as RAM). Optionally, a CPU may use a cache called level 2 (L2) on an associated chip. L2 cache is not quite as fast as L1 but it is still faster than RAM. A CPU examines L1 cache first to see whether it contains the desired information; if not, it then examines L2 cache, RAM, and finally the hard disk in turn to locate the information it needs.

Motherboard

The motherboard is a computer's main electrical circuit board. CPU, ROM, RAM, and cache are all located on parts of the motherboard, as are the components that control network and printer connections, video logic, mouse and keyboard circuitry, hard disk, and other necessary subsystems. On the motherboard, all of these components are interconnected by a series of electrical lines, or buses, through which they communicate. The motherboard contains a number of slots that are used to expand or upgrade its capabilities. The processor slot accepts new or additional CPUs; video slots accept small video circuit boards that connect and control the monitor. RAM slots accept additional memory. Expansion slots accept small circuit boards that add network connections, sound, and other capabilities. Expansion slots are often named for the type of bus they connect to on the motherboard. Common bus types include PCI (Peripheral Component Interconnect), ISA (Industry Standard Architecture), EISA (Extended Industry Standard Architecture), and IEEE 1394, also called FireWire. These standards specify the speed, the number of data bits (on-off signals) that transmit information, and the number and position of wires on the motherboard used for communication inside a computer. PCI provides fast connections on both Macintosh and PCs (personal computers using Intel 80x86 microprocessors), but older ISA slots are provided for backward compatibility on PCs (only).

Video

A computer's video system produces the images on the monitor. These images generally pass to and from the computer's motherboard along one of two buses—a Peripheral Component Interconnect (PCI) bus or an Accelerated Graphics Port (AGP), with the latter able to process video information faster. The video bus also includes brief stops at special memory called video RAM (VRAM). Video components are measured in terms of the VRAM they offer as well as the bus they use. Most modern computers offer AGP video (describing the bus) with 16–32 MB video RAM (the amount of VRAM).

Disks

Disks are storage devices used to permanently hold relatively large amounts of data. They come in a variety of configurations.

> **Hard disks** consist of a magnetic material that stores or retrieves information by electrical current. They provide the primary storage for most computers. Hard disks are divided into two common types—IDE/ATA (Integrated Drive Electronics/AT Attachment) and SCSI (Small Computer Systems Interface). Most computers use IDE/ATA hard disks, which are fast and inexpensive. Servers and high-end worksta-tions use SCSI hard disks, which offer greater expandability and more performance-enhancing features. Typically, a computer's hard disk stores critical startup and shut down information as well as data needed to operate peripherals such as a monitor, printer, or modem. Hark disks generally retain between 10 and 60 GB (gigabytes, or billion bytes) of information.

> **Floppy disks** store information electromagnetically like hard disks, only they store much less of it—approximately 1.44 MB.

> **CD-ROM, CD-RW (CD-ROM read-writeable), and DVD discs** store information optically using lasers instead of electromagnets. Optical discs (spelled with a "c" instead of a "k" by convention) are more durable, if slower, than magnetic disks. Data stored on optical discs are far less vulnerable to degradation caused by aging or environmental changes. CD-ROM and CD-RW discs store 650 MB of information, while DVDs store as much as 17 GB. All of these optical discs can be removed from the computer for convenient, portable storage.

> **Zip disks and super disks** store information electromagnetically like hard disks but are portable like CD-ROMs. These disks hold 100 MB and 250 MB of information, respectively.

Ports

A computer's internal components may connect to a variety of external devices such as monitors, keyboards, networks, and modems. These connections are made through a com-puter port (opening). If the computer uses an external modem (a device that connects the computer to the outside world by dialing or answering a telephone), it is likely to be con-nected to the serial port (sometimes also labeled COM1 or COM2). The keyboard and mouse may connect through a PS/2 port (on PCs) or Universal Serial Bus (USB) port (on PCs or Macintoshes). A printer may be connected by a parallel port, or it may use a USB. (A Universal Serial Bus is much faster than a parallel port and it allows many devices to be con-nected in a line.) SCSI ports connect external hard disks, scanners, tape drives, and other devices manufactured for the SCSI standard. Each of these connectors has different special-ties and capabilities, and each has a different shape. External devices such as modems or printers come with documentation that explains the type of port they require.

Input/Output

Input/output, or I/O, refers to subsystems involved with moving data to or from the computer. A mouse and keyboard are examples of input devices. Printers are output devices. Disks are both input and output devices.

LAPTOP COMPUTERS

Laptops

Laptop computers have roughly the same capabilities as desktops but are smaller, lighter, and have all their components (keyboard, monitor, and central processing hardware) in a single, portable case. Laptops are generally more expensive than equivalent desktop computers and sometimes require more maintenance, but they are becoming increasingly common in schools.

Advantages

Laptops have certain advantages over conventional desktop computers:

> Laptops are portable. Teachers can take laptops home or use them during planning periods outside their classrooms. Students can take laptops into the field to record data or observations. Some districts assign laptops to teachers permanently on the theory that laptop portability encourages their use.

> Laptops can run for two hours on average without electrical connections, easing the burden on classrooms in which the electrical infrastructure may be inadequate to support dozens of computers. Laptops must be plugged into an electrical outlet and recharged when battery power dwindles. Managing this recharge cycle can create considerable complexity. Some schools buy an extra battery for each laptop in order to recharge them at night.

> Multiple laptops can be gathered together and placed on a cart to form mobile computer labs. Mobile labs allow a school to gain a whole classroom that otherwise would have been used as its computer lab. The laptops in these mobile computer labs often use wireless network connections so that students can share work with each other or save work to the school network for easy retrieval later. (Of course, wireless connections are also available in desktop computers, but they are more frequently found in laptops.)

Disadvantages

Laptops also have disadvantages when compared with desktops:

> Laptop computers are more expensive than desktops and less expandable. It is usually more difficult and more expensive, for example, to add a new hard disk to a laptop than a desktop.

> Laptops are often more difficult to keep running smoothly and more expensive to repair.

> Laptops are easier to damage and harder to secure against theft or other malicious destruction.

> Typical student desks are not designed to accommodate laptops. This makes laptops more difficult for students to operate comfortably.

> Even though laptops cost considerably more, they traditionally lag behind desktops in terms of speed and storage capacity.

Laptops are able to connect to docks or replicators. A dock provides a way for laptops to add space for additional hard disks, Zip disks, sound cards (circuit boards that connect to speakers and provide good-quality audio), network connections, and peripherals. A replicator is a mini-dock, usually providing ports to connect to a network or keyboard, for example. Docks and replicators are useful to connect laptops to standard keyboards, monitors, and mice, which are sometimes easier to use than those built into the laptop. They also provide convenience. A dock or replicator can be connected permanently to a network and the laptop simply inserted into the dock whenever network connections are required.

HANDHELD DEVICES

Handheld Devices

Handheld devices, sometimes also called Personal Digital Assistants (PDAs), fit in the palm of your hand. iPAQ, Palm Pilot, and Visor are just a few of an ever-growing number of handhelds. When handheld devices first appeared on the market, their capabilities were limited to basic tasks such as keeping track of important engagements, creating to-do lists, storing personal notes, and maintaining address book information. Since their introduction, however, the power and versatility of these tiny computers have grown enormously.

Modern handhelds are able to send and receive electronic mail, display electronic books, download Web sites, and even create and exchange documents with other handheld devices using wireless connections. Handheld devices run spreadsheets, word processors, and databases like desktop computers and can be connected to keyboards for convenient data entry. Handhelds can also be used to collect data using special sensors and to graph and annotate those data.

Despite these capabilities, managing 20–30 handheld devices per classroom remains a difficult task. Protecting handheld units from theft or damage requires considerable effort. The software for each unit must be licensed and installed manually from a desktop or laptop (unlike desktop computers, for which software installations can be automated by using the network). Because they are small and operate on batteries, the permanent storage capacity of handheld devices is limited. Desktop or laptop computers must connect periodically to a handheld to copy its documents and software for safekeeping.

Handhelds are inexpensive (around $200 each) and hold enormous potential to provide truly ubiquitous computing. More information regarding the use of handheld devices in school settings may be found at the following Web sites: **www.pdaed.com**, **www.palm.com/education/**, and **www.k12handhelds.com**.

Thin Clients and Network Computers

Thin clients provide all the capabilities of full-fledged desktops at a fraction of the cost. Because they contain no moving parts—no hard drives, CD-ROM, or floppy drives—thin clients are cheaper to purchase and maintain, and are less prone to trouble than desktops. In fact, they contain just the bare essentials: a central processing unit, a network connection, a monitor, and memory. Thin clients can operate with so few parts because they have no permanent storage capability. Instead, they provide a conduit through which users may access network services such as storing information, delivering programs, and printing.

The term thin client is often used to refer to a variety of computers, including network computers, Windows terminals (sometimes known as Windows-based terminals), and Internet appliances.

When network computers start, they download their operating system and application software from a network server. Once downloaded, the operating system and application programs run on the network computer, using its CPU and RAM.

Unlike network computers, Windows terminals do not download and run programs; they do all their work using the RAM and CPU of a shared computer called a Windows terminal server. A Windows terminal server can, in fact, run software on behalf of a wide array of desktop computers, including Macintosh computers, old and new Windows PCs, and even UNIX workstations (a powerful computer often used by engineers). A Windows terminal server can be a good solution for Macintosh users who need to run just a few Windows programs or for older computers that need to run modern Windows software.

Internet appliances are inexpensive, limited-purpose devices designed specifically for delivering electronic mail, Web browsing, playing video on demand, or using other Internet-based services. In conjunction with a CD-ROM and Web site provided by the manufacturer, for example, an Internet appliance might provide lesson plans, word processing, instructional software, and electronic mail among many other options. Internet appliances place the processing burden on structures outside the school—on the Internet to carry the information and on the manufacturer's servers to deliver it.

Advantages

Thin clients have a number of advantages over standard desktops and laptops:

> Thin clients are relatively inexpensive to purchase.

> The software programs used by thin clients run from powerful, expensive, and robust servers that are much less likely to break down than standard desktops or laptops.

> Because software is centralized on the server, upgrades need to be installed just once (on the server rather than on each desktop or laptop). Software licensing is done just once also (although a fee is required for each client), eliminating the need to track licenses for each computer.

> Thin clients are mechanically less complex than full-fledged computers and therefore require less troubleshooting and support. Viruses cannot infect them. Students and teachers cannot damage them easily.

> Data are stored on the server, not on the thin client itself. This allows data to be backed up more easily and remain more secure than it would be if left on a desktop computer.

> Support staff can perform diagnosis and repair on a single machine—the server—rather than visiting individual classrooms or labs. Likewise, they can monitor the screens of each user to assist or to perform diagnostic services from a central location.

> Training improves in thin client environments because everyone uses the same brands and versions of programs. People are able to help one another more easily when they are familiar with each other's programs.

Disadvantages

The benefits of thin clients may be offset by other considerations. Thin clients have the following disadvantages over desktops and laptops:

> Thin clients require expensive servers with substantial memory, disk space, and processing speed. Even with these additional resources most thin client architectures do not serve video, graphic-intensive programs, chat, or Internet downloads well.

> Any disruption to the server or the network—cable outages, server malfunctions, or sudden traffic from too many terminals—will disrupt the operations of every thin client. For this reason, it is often necessary to provide redundancy at every level of the network (servers, software, power supplies, cabling, and other network hardware connecting the server and thin clients). The cost of implementing redundant components can reach hundreds of dollars per unit. Some of these increased costs recur each year in the guise of server software upgrades and network upgrades.

> Installing and managing a thin client system is more demanding than managing a local area network. Experienced personnel with specialized training are needed to run thin client servers.

> Many educational programs designed to run on desktop or laptop computers will not run successfully from servers in thin client environments.

> Thin client architecture may not provide as rich an experience for teachers and students as standard networks. Teachers using thin client computers (without hard disks) will be unable to install new software. Some educators argue that these constraints limit spontaneity and innovation. Teachable moments may be missed.

Strategies for Centralization

Some school districts limit the use of thin client architecture to only certain parts of their networks (e.g., libraries or administrative computing). Such selective implementation takes advantage of the strengths of thin client architectures while minimizing their weaknesses. Other school districts have taken an entirely different approach. Instead of using thin client networks, they minimize cost by using a suite of software tools to centralize and simplify network administration:

> Novell's ZENworks and Apple's Network Assistant give network administrators the ability to perform software installations and repair services from a central server.

> Security software such as Fortres 101 and FoolProof for Windows or At Ease and Macintosh Manager for Macintosh prevents unauthorized users from installing software or from saving their work to local disks. Many network administrators find that support calls diminish significantly when software installations are restricted and when all documents are saved to network servers (where they can be backed up and restored more easily).

> For computer labs and other public settings, software such as Deep Freeze for Windows PCs performs the invaluable service of erasing any changes made during the day and restoring computers to a known, stable state whenever they restart.

Servers

Servers are large, powerful computers that store information in a centralized location so that many clients may use it simultaneously. Additionally, servers make application programs available so that each client runs its programs from the server instead of from its own hard disk.

Servers

> ensure that printers are available to everyone on the network and that printing happens in an orderly fashion;

> provide virus protection to all clients on the network;

> make information available from central CD-ROMs;

> create nightly backups of important information;

> run scripts on behalf of users automatically at login (for example, to show daily announcements);

> provide a centralized location where information and application software can be stored, updated, and disseminated to clients;

> provide security by protecting sensitive data or by restricting the programs that users can access;

> monitor network traffic and warn of impending trouble;

> enable client computers to view or change information from shared databases such as student records, lesson plans, attendance information, or lists of Web links, while still ensuring that sensitive information can be seen only by authorized users;

> provide Web, e-mail, Internet filtering, or other services; and

> serve as the "brains" for thin client computers, running their programs and processing each keystroke and mouse movement on behalf of the clients.

Servers contain the same components as desktop computers, but the components are more powerful, durable, faster, and sometimes more numerous. For example, servers often include several very fast central processing units that work together to increase overall processing speed. (These servers are often referred to as "two-way," "four-way," or "eight-way" servers to define the number of central processing units they contain.) Servers include fast buses (connections between the central processing unit and other internal components) and multiple hard disks—most often configured to a standard called redundant arrays of inexpensive disks, or RAID. In most RAID arrays, each disk writes or reads data simultaneously, providing much faster throughput and greater security than a single disk might do. Most modern servers also include multiple network connections, cooling capabilities, and power supplies.

In large server-based networks, servers specialize in different tasks. For example, one or more may function as print servers. They receive the documents that client computers send to be printed, queue the documents in proper sequence for the appropriate printer, and notify clients if there are printing difficulties. People store documents on file servers and connect to application servers when they want to run programs such as Microsoft Office. Dynamic Host Control Protocol (DHCP) servers assign the unique network identification numbers required by each client to receive electronic mail, browse the Web, or participate in other Internet services. Web servers specialize in delivering Web pages; Internet filtering servers and proxy servers in filtering Internet content so that students can visit only appropriate sites; electronic mail servers in providing messages; and database servers in housing student records, instructional systems, payroll, or other large stores of information.

Two or more servers (performing the same function) can be clustered or joined together. Each clustered server can take over if another one fails. Work can be distributed among clustered servers to complete jobs quickly. Groups of clustered servers are often called server farms. They are commonly used for large databases, very active Web sites, or in other situations in which applications or large amounts of data must be served with great reliability.

Practical Advice

QUESTIONS TO ASK ABOUT SERVERS

What should you use your servers for?

Network servers store shared documents, provide virus protection, manage printers, and back up essential data.

Some application programs must be run from a server. For example, accounting, student records, and computer-based learning systems generally require servers to supply sufficient processing power and to protect the data from unauthorized access. Other application programs may operate either from a server or from a client.

Centralized model. Networks that run applications from centralized servers are easier to upgrade and service because network personnel can troubleshoot the entire system by visiting a single computer (the server). If the server fails, however, none of the client systems will function until the server is restored. The server must be upgraded as new clients are added to the network to ensure that the server remains responsive.

Decentralized model. Distributing application programs to each client computer incurs increased support costs. Network staff must service each machine to upgrade its software or to repair problems. Desktop management software (such as ZENworks from Novell, Inc.) can minimize these costs by distributing and troubleshooting client software from a central location. If application programs are provided from the server, plan to phase in each program one at a time, testing the server and network performance for responsiveness and stability after each new addition. Ask software manufacturers for configuration recommendations. When servers are overburdened, they do not always show obvious symptoms. Watch for slow performance or sporadic, unexplained malfunctions or crashes.

Should you specialize your servers?

Consider assigning specific tasks to specific servers if

> application programs on the network require large amounts of the server's processing power to run efficiently;

> the network is large and includes many different kinds of network services such as electronic mail, access to the Internet, Web publishing, Web filtering, and databases (accounting, student records, or computer-based instruction systems); or

> the network includes information that is extremely sensitive and would be best protected by occupying a server separate from all others (where unauthorized users could be denied complete access to everything on the server).

What should you consider when purchasing clients and servers?

Technology managers typically recommend purchasing top-quality desktop and laptop computers with enough processing speed, memory, and disk space to last three to five years. In the long run, computers built from top-quality components are less expensive and easier to maintain than computers made of cheaper but unreliable and nonstandardized components. Because maintenance accounts for 70–80% of the total cost of owning a computer, many managers maintain that the higher initial cost of purchasing a top-quality computer is offset by lower long-term support costs.

Many managers feel that they get a better return on investment if they purchase all clients from the same manufacturer. Likewise, they purchase servers from a reputable server manufacturer. Purchasing each kind of equipment from a single manufacturer reduces complexity and makes it easier for support staff and users to understand and maintain the equipment. Standardization also enables a network to use the manufacturer or vendor's equipment management software. For example, Compaq's Insight Manager warns of impending hard disk failures and tracks the versions of network operating system software on Compaq servers.

Additional savings can be realized by purchasing servers with redundant systems. Modern servers are equipped with multiple power supplies, fans, and network connections, as well as RAID disks. If one component fails, the redundant unit ensures that the server keeps working.

Purchasing multiple computers at once can often lead to significant savings. Many managers try to replace a certain percentage of their clients, servers, peripherals, and network connecting devices each year. They purchase the most powerful equipment they can afford in each purchase cycle. This pattern of incorporating new equipment at consistent intervals (known as evergreening) helps avoid the financial burden and the technical complexity that occurs if all equipment in a large installation must be replaced en masse.

Some technology managers negotiate service contracts or secure training for their staff as part of the purchase price of new equipment. For an additional fee, most vendors will offer on-site service contracts that guarantee repairs within a specified time frame. For some districts, short of staff and already overburdened with repairs, this type of vendor support is critical to maintaining reliable performance. Other districts, unable to afford the cost of such contracts, often certify their own staff to repair the vendor's equipment and assume the entire support burden internally.

How many servers should you purchase?

Plan to purchase at least one server if the intent of the network is to share information, devices, or Internet connections, and if the network

> includes more than a few clients;

> includes software such as accounting systems that must run from a server;

> contains clients running an older operating system such as DOS or Windows 3.1, as these systems are difficult to network unless they are connected to a server;

> connects all clients on the network to the Internet;

> allows clients to share resources such as printers or CD-ROMs; or

> includes sensitive information that must be protected from access by unauthorized personnel.

The actual number of servers that a particular network will need depends upon its network operating system software (e.g., Windows NT 4.0, Windows 2000, Novell NetWare, or Linux), its major shared applications (student records systems, accounting, Web servers, filtering), the tasks managed by each server, and the number of people using each server. Some network operating systems require many servers and others just a few. Some major shared applications require a server of their own to run reliably while others can share a server. Servers dedicated to a single, simple task such as printing can handle hundreds of users, while servers containing accounting or student records (database) information may handle only a fraction of that amount. Schools may house and manage their own servers or centralize servers in a district office to simplify management.

What if a server fails?

Servers perform critical tasks on a network. Whenever a device performs such critical tasks, planning must account for the time when (not if) its services are temporarily unavailable. Some sites agree that they can survive for a day or two without critical services. Other sites maintain a stock of server parts that fail most frequently—power supplies, hard disks, and memory chips—to shorten the crisis. Still others secure maintenance contracts and service agreements with vendors who provide repair services within a specified time frame. No matter what strategy is used, it is critical that district-level administrators define the maximum acceptable downtime for each piece of critical equipment on the network. With service agreements and sufficient financial resources in hand, network managers can make sure that hardware and network vendors provide the desired services.

Staff members are the single most important factor in determining whether a network experiences a minor service disruption or a major catastrophe. It is critical that staff members be competent and trained to manage and repair critical components even if an external repair service is also retained.

Peripherals

Peripherals are supplementary devices such as printers, fax machines, scanners, CD-ROM towers, external hard disk drives, external Zip drives, or external modems (among many possibilities) that work in tandem with clients. Monitors and keyboards are sometimes considered to be peripherals; for the purposes of this book, however, they are considered part of the client computer.

Connecting Clients, Servers, and Peripherals

Local Area Networks

Local area networks (LANs) connect hardware and software within one building or a few buildings in close proximity. There are two types of LANs: peer-to-peer networks and server-based networks.

Peer-to-Peer Networks

Although it is common to think of a network as having banks of servers and tens, if not hundreds of clients, in its simplest form, a network can consist of as few as two clients (and their peripherals). A small network such as this, consisting of just clients and peripherals (without servers), is referred to as a peer-to-peer network (or just peer network).

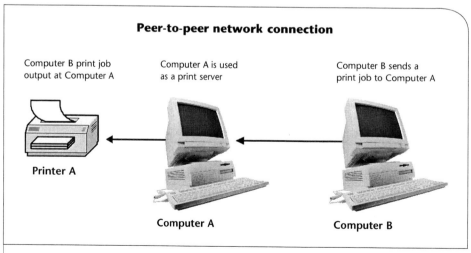

Peer-to-peer network connection

Computer B print job output at Computer A

Computer A is used as a print server

Computer B sends a print job to Computer A

Printer A

Computer A

Computer B

FIGURE 1.1

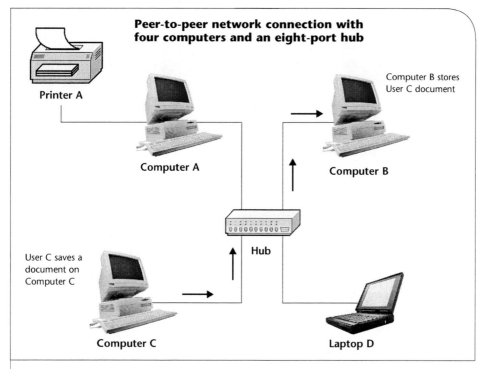

Peer-to-peer network connection with four computers and an eight-port hub

Printer A

Computer A

Computer B stores User C document

Computer B

Hub

User C saves a document on Computer C

Computer C

Laptop D

FIGURE 1.2

In a peer network, computers act as both clients and servers. Each computer is a client in the sense that it can view or change documents on other computers (if the owner of the other computer grants permission). Likewise, each computer is a server in the sense that other computers can access its documents or attached peripheral devices. Small offices or schools use peer networks, for example, to share printers and access documents.

Figures 1.1 and 1.2 show two peer networks. In Figure 1.1, two computers, A and B, are connected directly to each other. Computer A is attached to a printer that Computer B can use through the network. The network in Figure 1.2 is somewhat more complex. Four computers are connected to a hub (a device that repeats the signals of one computer so that other computers can hear them). In this case, the hub interconnects the computers so that any of them can use the printer connected to Computer A. In both diagrams, the computers can share documents as well as printers.

Peer networks are relatively easy to set up but they are practical on only a small scale. If more than a half dozen computers are connected to share information, peer networking does not provide sufficient power for reliable and efficient use. (Network traffic will slow to a crawl while the individual clients service each other's requests.) Peer networks also lack the security and orderly document management of server-based networks.

Server-Based Networks

Server-based networks differ from peer networks in that they include at least one powerful, shared server. Client computers depend upon this server for printing, access to large databases such as student information systems, and protection of sensitive information. Server-based networks can be complex to set up, but they provide all the services that a district might need.

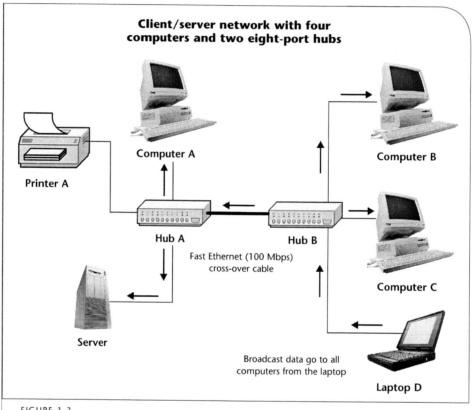

Client/server network with four computers and two eight-port hubs

Printer A

Computer A

Computer B

Hub A

Hub B

Fast Ethernet (100 Mbps)
cross-over cable

Computer C

Server

Broadcast data go to all
computers from the laptop

Laptop D

FIGURE 1.3

Figure 1.3 shows a server-based network in which all computers can store documents on the server and send them to the printer. The server manages this activity in various ways. It monitors each print job and queues the requests if more than one print job is submitted simultaneously. The server also provides a protected storage area for each computer and ensures that the user of one computer cannot view, change, or delete the contents saved by another.

It is possible to mix peer-to-peer and server-based networks. Schools might design their computer labs so that each desktop computer can share its documents directly with others. This peer network can be connected to the larger, server-based network as well, making each desktop in the computer lab also a client on the larger network.

Introduction to Metropolitan Area Networks and Wide Area Networks

Wide area networks (WANs) differ from local area networks because generally speaking they use different signaling and information-carrying technologies. WANs are optimized to carry information over longer distances, often operate more slowly than LANs, and are also more costly to implement per connection. In addition, WAN connections are often leased; they rarely belong to the organization whose parts the WAN connects.

Metropolitan area networks (MANs) are sometimes conceived of as a hybrid between LANs and WANs. MANs connect buildings over city-sized areas; the networks interconnecting school buildings in large districts are often considered MANs. MANs generally combine the technologies found in both LANs and WANs. Their infrastructures are sometimes leased and sometimes owned but always cover shorter distances than WANs.

Technical Information Summary

CLIENTS, SERVERS, AND PERIPHERALS

A **client** is any networked device or program used directly by an individual to request services from or deliver them to a network. They can include desktops, laptops, handheld devices, and thin clients (computers that are inexpensive and easy to maintain because they lack hard disks and floppy disks). While thin clients can reduce the total cost of owning client computers, they require an expensive and robust network infrastructure, shared servers, and considerable expertise to manage. They sometimes possess limited capability for multimedia software. Handheld devices show great promise, but only a small number of educational software programs are available for them. Tracking and configuring handheld devices also presents a management challenge.

Servers are powerful computers that store information for many clients to use simultaneously.

Peripherals are devices such as printers, fax machines, scanners, CD-ROM towers, external hard disk drives, external Zip drives, or external modems (among many possibilities) that are attached to a computer or network.

A **network** is created when computers (clients), servers, and peripherals are connected. Networks are generally divided into three categories: local area networks, metropolitan area networks, and wide area networks.

Local area networks are generally subdivided into two types: peer-to-peer networks and server-based networks. Peer-to-peer networks connect two or more clients and peripherals (but lack any servers). Server-based networks include at least one server and form the kind of local area network most commonly found in schools.

Highways and Rules of the Road

CABLES, WIRELESS CONNECTIONS, AND PROTOCOLS

In the introduction segment of this book, computer networks are likened to transportation systems. Instead of being composed of roads, however, computer networks are made up of cables and wireless paths that carry bits of information to their intended destinations. And just like the roads that make up real highways, cables and wireless paths in a computer network must be built according to careful specifications. To ensure that information gets to where it is going safely and efficiently, networks are constructed so that the flow of traffic obeys certain rules of the road. These rules of the road are known as network protocols. This chapter discusses the physical assembly and the protocols that underlie network technologies commonly found in schools—Ethernet and Internet connections.

The Open Systems Interconnect Reference Model

Before discussing the nuts and bolts of building networks, it is perhaps necessary to describe a simple model that clarifies network operations. This model, known as the OSI or Open Systems Interconnect reference model, divides network operations into seven component parts, or layers. Each layer describes one portion of the complex task of conveying data over a network. Conceiving of network operations in terms of the OSI reference model simplifies both network design and implementation. For example, manufacturers design equipment for tasks at a single layer; each piece of equipment performs its particular function and leaves other functions to other devices. Likewise, network software developers generally focus their software for tasks at a specific layer. Changes in the way the network operates at one layer—perhaps the speed at which it sends information and receives information (layer 1)—can be made without affecting network behavior at most other layers.

To better understand the OSI reference model, consider the process of sending an electronic mail message from the model's point of view. First, an electronic mail program creates a message. It then calls upon network software in the computer to prepare the data for network transport (layer 7 of the model) and to encode or encrypt the data (layer 6). The encoding software calls upon other software in the computer to initiate the network connection (layer 5), to divide the data into small packages (layer 4), and to assign the data's final destination address (layer 3). Finally, the small packages are enclosed in a wrapper appropriate for the local area network (layer 2) and placed onto the cable or wireless path (layer 1). At the recipient's end, the reverse happens. The data are picked up from the cable or wireless path (layer 1) and sent up through each layer in turn until the recipient reads the message.

TABLE 2.1: SIMPLE VIEW OF THE OSI REFERENCE MODEL

OSI Layer	Tasks Performed by This Layer
7 Application	Provides electronic mail, file, print, directory (ability to browse through network computers), and other services used directly from the computer
6 Presentation	Converts the data into a usable system format (Windows, Macintosh); also encrypts or compresses data
5 Session	Initiates and closes a network connection
4 Transport	Divides the network data into, or reassembles data from, small packages called packets appropriate for the internetwork journey; ensures that data arrive in the proper sequence and checks for data errors
3 Network	Manages network address information and ensures that data include a final destination address
2 Data Link	Rewraps (outgoing) packets into or unwraps (incoming) packets from small packages called frames appropriate for the local, physical network cabling (or wireless connections)
1 Physical	Manages the physical media (wires or wireless) and electrical signals

The exact manner in which network equipment operates at each layer is specified by stringent layer protocols. The OSI reference model layers define what tasks must be accomplished; layer protocols specify exactly how they will be accomplished. For example, one particular protocol—the Internet Protocol (IP)—specifies how to address a message for transmission across the Internet (layer 3). Transmission Control Protocol (TCP) specifies how Internet information will be checked for errors at its destination, and how it will be reassembled if necessary for the recipient (layer 4). There are one or more protocols for each layer of the OSI reference model.

Protocols ensure that the traffic proceeds in an orderly fashion from one computer to another, no matter how far apart they may be or what kind of computers they are. Both the sending and receiving equipment must use the same protocols for the transmission to be successful. If a network in Chicago uses IP and TCP to address its messages, then its recipient network in Springfield must also use these protocols to read them.

Protocols come in families. Each member of the family is responsible for a particular task and a particular layer of the OSI reference model. These families are formally referred to as protocol stacks. Each protocol stack is named for its most prominent protocol (family member). IP and TCP belong to one family sometimes known as the TCP/IP protocol stack.

Networks include many different protocol stacks, and each stack serves a different purpose. For example, two computers communicating over the Internet might do so using the TCP/IP protocol stack while two Macintoshes on a local area network might use a protocol stack called AppleTalk to communicate. To make matters more confusing, computers can (and often do) run more than one protocol stack simultaneously. A typical Macintosh computer is able to run AppleTalk as well as TCP/IP.

Details of the OSI Reference Model

Software that implements the TCP/IP protocol stack includes many different modules. Each module is responsible for one primary task at one layer of the OSI reference model. Different interconnecting devices such as hubs, bridges, switches, and routers each focus on tasks at specific layers of the OSI reference model. Table 2.2 describes the OSI reference model layers and some of the common software and hardware associated with each layer.

The OSI Reference Model in Action

One way to illustrate the connection between the OSI reference model and the way information travels across a network is to consider the following example. John in Chicago wishes to send an electronic mail message to his friend Mary in Australia. Here is what has to happen for John's mail message to reach Mary.

TABLE 2.2: DETAILS OF THE OSI REFERENCE MODEL

OSI Layer	Common Network Hardware & Software Associated with Layer	Tasks Performed by This Layer	Examples of Protocols Implemented by Hardware & Software*
7 Application	Provides electronic mail, file, print, directory (ability to browse through network computers), and other services used directly from the computer	Electronic mail, Web browsers	SMTP, FTP, HTTP, TELNET
6 Presentation	Converts the data into a usable system format (Windows, Macintosh); also encrypts or compresses data	(Same as above)	
5 Session	Initiates and closes a network connection	(Same as above)	
4 Transport	Divides the network data into, or reassembles data from, small packages called packets appropriate for the internetwork journey; ensures that data arrive in the proper sequence and checks for data errors	Software: TCP (has the same name as the protocol it implements)	TCP, UDP
3 Network	Manages network address information and ensures that data include a final destination address	Software: IP (has the same name as the protocol it implements) Hardware: routers, some switches	IP
2 Data Link	Rewraps (outgoing) packets into or unwraps (incoming) packets from small packages called frames appropriate for local, physical network cabling (or wireless connections)	Hardware: bridges, some switches	Ethernet
1 Physical	Manages the physical media (wires or wireless) and electrical signals	Hardware: hubs, network interfaces; unshielded twisted pair copper wire (a type of copper cable—abbreviated UTP), coaxial cable, optical fiber	Ethernet

See Table 2.3: Explanation of Terms

TABLE 2.3: EXPLANATION OF TERMS IN TABLE 2.2

Protocol	Full Name	Explanation
Ethernet	—	A common type of local area network
FTP	File Transfer Protocol	One set of rules (among many possible) that governs the way documents can be transferred between computers. FTP is used when starting programs such as Fetch or WS_FTP, or when addresses beginning with ftp://... are entered into a Web browser.
HTTP	HyperText Transfer Protocol	Another set of rules governing the way that documents can be transferred between computers. HTTP is used to view Web pages.
IP	Internet Protocol	The set of rules governing the way addresses are assigned to and read from information traveling across the Internet
SMTP	Simple Mail Transfer Protocol	The rules describing how electronic mail is sent to and read from the Internet
TCP	Transmission Control Protocol	The rules governing how data are divided into small packages called packets and checked for errors when transmitted; and how data are accurately reassembled by the recipient's computer. Internet communications such as electronic mail use TCP.
UDP	User Datagram Protocol	Very much like TCP, except that UDP does not check for errors after transmission (it leaves this work to higher-layer software) and is therefore faster. Internet communications such as multimedia transmissions use UDP.
TELNET	Terminal Emulation Via Network	Provides a way for a computer to access programs and files (log in to) from another computer

1. John's mail message passes through the application, presentation, and session layers.

John's electronic mail software assembles text and attachments, optionally applies special effects like encryption, and opens the network connection. As his electronic mail software executes these tasks, it follows rules described by protocols such as SMTP (Simple Mail Transfer Protocol). SMTP describes the proper way for electronic mail to be formatted for and transferred to the Internet. If his electronic mail software enacts these rules properly, then Mary's electronic mail program (obeying the same rules at the other end of the connection) will be able to decode the message successfully. By completing these tasks, John's electronic mail software fulfills the requirements of the application, presentation, and session layers (OSI layers 7, 6, and 5).

2. John's mail message passes through the transport and network layers.

When John's electronic mail software has finished its preparations, his message is then handed to the next layer of software—in most cases, a suite of programs grouped under the moniker TCP/IP (Transmission Control Protocol/Internet Protocol). Think of this suite like any other program on a computer except that TCP/IP works behind the scenes and manages network information.

Within the TCP/IP suite of software, or protocol stack, a software module called TCP appends a variety of information to the message. TCP encloses a number (called a port number) representing the software that sent or will receive the message. TCP also encloses error-checking codes calculated from the data in John's message. The TCP software on Mary's computer will validate the data by recalculating the error-checking codes to see whether the data still match the original calculations. In completing these tasks, TCP software follows the rules prescribed in the TCP protocol and fulfills the requirements of the transport layer of the OSI reference model (OSI layer 4).

When TCP has completed its work, it hands the message to another software module, called IP. IP, among other tasks, appends two numbers to the message—the Internet addresses of both John and Mary. For example, suppose John has a mailbox on his school network (ajones@myschool.k12.ma.us) and Mary has a mailbox on her school network (jsmith@mcsv.k12.sd.au). The two electronic mail systems—myschool.k12.ma.us and mcsv.k12.sd.au—have unique numeric IP addresses. The IP software looks up these addresses and appends them to the message according to the rules of the IP protocol. IP software fulfills the requirements of the network layer of the OSI reference model (OSI layer 3). The data, along with the additional address and error-checking information, are now called a packet and are sent onto the network interface.

3. John's mail message passes through the data link and physical layers.

After the TCP/IP software completes its tasks, it passes John's mail message to his computer's network interface and its associated software. (The network interface usually consists of a piece of hardware inside a computer that connects it by a cable to a network.) John's network interface adds new information to the message that enables it to travel on his physical network. His mail message, along with this additional information, is now called a frame and is placed on the network wire (or converted to infrared or radio waves if John is using a wireless network).

As the network interface executes these tasks, it follows rules described by protocols such as Ethernet, which establish the proper way for signals to be sent onto a computer cable. By following these rules, the network interface ensures that cable in John's local area network will be able to convey the signals accurately. By completing these tasks, the network interface fulfills the requirements of the data link and physical layers of the OSI reference model (OSI layers 2 and 1).

4. John's mail message travels across the Internet.

If John's electronic mail message was destined for a recipient on a network connected directly to his computer (that is, on the same segment of his local area network), then his message could be delivered directly. In this example, Mary lives in Australia (not part of John's local area network) and therefore the message must pass through one or more routers, devices that connect one network to another. (Routers maintain internal information about the location of remote destination networks and select appropriate paths for network traffic. They are most likely connected to a leased line—a private data line that is rented from a local telecommunications carrier—or other wide area communications line.)

In this case, the router discards the Ethernet information and encapsulates the rest of the data (including the IP and TCP information, as well as the original message) in the particular data link and physical protocol acceptable for the leased line connection. The router then forwards the message onto the Internet. Very often, a message will pass through many different routers, as well as physical and data link protocols, en route to its destination. Each router reads the destination address information enclosed by IP, selects the next leg of the journey, and repackages the data if necessary for the physical requirements of the next network on the path. Eventually, the message reaches the intended recipient.

5. John's mail message passes through the physical and data link layers a second time.

Once John's message reaches Mary's mailbox, it passes once again through the OSI layers, this time in reverse order. Mary's network interface accepts John's message in the form of electrical signals. Following Ethernet protocols, it decodes the signals, removes the additional information that was appended for the purposes of the physical network, and then passes the data to its TCP/IP software. By completing these tasks, Mary's network interface fulfills the physical and data link layer tasks (OSI layers 1 and 2).

6. John's mail message passes through the network and transport layers a second time.

Mary's TCP/IP software, following the TCP and IP protocols, checks the network address, ensures that there are no errors, and then removes the additional address and error-checking information and passes the data along to John's electronic mail software (fulfilling the network and transport layer tasks at OSI layers 3 and 4).

7. John's mail message passes through the session, presentation, and application layers a second time.

Finally, Mary's electronic mail software processes any special requirements (such as decryption) and informs her that she has mail (completing the session, presentation, and application tasks at OSI layers 5, 6, and 7). To do so, her electronic mail software follows protocols like those described by SMTP.

Technical Information Summary

THE OSI REFERENCE MODEL

The OSI reference model describes many different protocols, or standards of behavior, that are required for computers to communicate on a network. The OSI reference model divides these protocols into categories, or layers, based on the kinds of activities they perform. The lowest layers are called the physical and data link protocols. Protocols at these layers are responsible for placing outgoing signals onto a network cable or receiving incoming signals from it. The middle layers are called the network routing and transport protocols. The protocols at these layers are responsible for assigning addresses to outgoing information and checking incoming information for integrity. The upper layers are called the session, presentation, and application protocols. These protocols define how information must be prepared for its journey across the network, or how information arriving from the network must be prepared for use.

Each layer of the OSI reference model is associated with particular hardware and software on a network. For example, OSI layer 3 specifies that network information must include network addresses for the sender and the receiver that are unique across the entire network. To fulfill this directive, network software (such as Internet Protocol) and specific hardware (such as routers) collaborate to address the information and route it correctly to its destination. Other OSI layers involve different hardware and software components.

Physical and Data Link Layer Protocols

Physical and data link layer protocols define the way that data are converted to electrical signals, the manner in which these signals enter the cable or wireless connection, and the speed at which they travel. Local area networks use common physical and data link protocols such as Ethernet, Token Ring, Fiber Distributed Data Interface (FDDI), and LocalTalk. A wide area network is likely to use physical and data link protocols such as frame relay (data link), T1, ISDN (physical), Asynchronous Transfer Mode (ATM), FDDI, or Switched Multimegabit Data Service (SMDS).

The first step in creating a local area network involves choosing which physical and data link protocols to use. When purchasing equipment for a local area network, every network component must be compatible with the physical and data link protocols you have chosen. Most schools and businesses select Ethernet as the physical and data link protocol for their local area networks. Occasionally, schools use LocalTalk in addition to Ethernet. LocalTalk provides very slow connections for older Macintoshes only (roughly those produced before 1998), but it is inexpensive and easy to implement. Note, however, that LocalTalk is used less frequently every year, and in fact, the newest generations of Macintosh can no longer communicate by LocalTalk at all. (They use Ethernet or wireless networks.)

Ethernet

Ethernet was developed by researchers at Xerox's Palo Alto Research Center (PARC) in the 1970s to interconnect their client computers. It was subsequently standardized by the Institute of Electrical and Electronics Engineers (IEEE). Ethernet can deliver large amounts of data to clients; its equipment is widely available from many manufacturers and can be installed economically. For these reasons, Ethernet may be the most frequently used physical and data link protocol in the world.

Each computer, printer, scanner, or other device on a network becomes part of the Ethernet through its network interface. The network interface usually consists of a small circuit board inside the computer. Alternatively, it may be built into a computer's main circuit board (referred to as a motherboard). Each Ethernet network interface has a unique network address expressed as six groups of numbers separated by hyphens.

Here is one possible Ethernet address: **08-00-2B-A8-77-F4.**

Each group of two digits represents a number in base-16 (hexadecimal) format. For example, "08" represents the number 8, and "F4" represents the number 244. ("F" represents the number 15. "F4" denotes 15 x 16 + 4 x 1 = 244.)

There are many types of Ethernet networks. They are similar in many respects, most notably the way that data are divided up, packaged, and placed onto a network cable (that is, how frames are created). But they differ in speed, the kinds of cable they require, and other characteristics. The most common type of Ethernet is 100BaseTX, and many schools also now include its faster cousin, 1000Base-T.

10BaseT and 10BaseFL (IEEE 802.3)

10BaseT is an older though still common form of Ethernet. Using baseband signaling over twisted pair copper wire, 10BaseT sends information at a transmission rate of 10 megabits per second (10 million bits per second, or 10 Mbps). 10BaseFL also transmits at 10 Mbps but uses light signals over fiber optic cable instead of electricity over twisted pair copper cable.

In baseband signaling, a single frequency carries all the information on a cable (or wireless connection). Baseband signaling differs from broadband signaling (in which many different frequencies carry information on a cable simultaneously). Cable TV, cable modems, and digital subscriber line (DSL) modems employ broadband signaling. For technology planners, the important distinction between baseband and broadband is the different kind of equipment each type of signaling requires.

TABLE 2.4: COMMON TYPES OF ETHERNET

Name	Speed	Signal	Cable	Associated Acronyms
10BaseT	10 Mbps	Electrical	Unshielded twisted pair copper or UTP (a type of copper cable)	The 10BaseT and 10BaseFL are also termed IEEE 802.3 Ethernet (the number designates the IEEE working group that developed the standards).
10BaseFL	10 Mbps	Light waves	Fiber optic	IEEE 802.3
100BaseTX	100 Mbps	Electrical	Unshielded twisted pair copper	IEEE 802.3u (also called Fast Ethernet)
100BaseFX	100 Mbps	Light waves	Fiber optic	IEEE 802.3u (also called Fast Ethernet)
1000Base-T	1000 Mbps	Electrical	Unshielded twisted pair copper	IEEE 802.3ab
1000Base-CX	1000 Mbps	Electrical	Unshielded twisted pair copper	IEEE 802.3z
1000Base-LX	1000 Mbps	Light waves	Fiber optic	IEEE 802.3z
1000Base-CX	1000 Mbps	Light waves	Fiber optic	IEEE 802.3z

Note: Mbps is an abbreviation for "million bits per second."

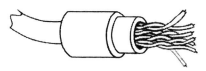

TWISTED PAIR COPPER WIRE

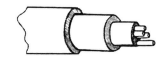

FIBER OPTIC CABLE

ST CONNECTOR

Twisted pair copper wire consists of a single cable that usually contains four individual pairs of wire with the strands of each pair twisted around each other to reduce signal interference from other pairs. The ends of the cable are fitted with RJ–45 connectors, a common type of connector that looks like it fits into an oversized phone jack.

Fiber optic cable consists of a glass or plastic core surrounded by a protective sheath. The ends of the cable are fitted with **ST** or **SC connectors**. Within fiber optic cable, light waves carry network information.

In most installations, 10BaseT carries signals between computers while 10BaseFL carries signals over longer distances, perhaps between buildings or between one local area network and another.

At 10 Mbps, these protocols offer sufficient speed to accommodate regular daily network operations including electronic mail, document sharing, and databases of modest size. A transmission rate of 10 Mbps means that Ethernet can theoretically send 10 million data bits of information per second (roughly equivalent to 1 million characters per second). However, their use in school networks is rapidly being replaced by the 100-megabit Ethernet protocols.

10BaseT and 10BaseFL Ethernet Standards for Data Format

Each Ethernet frame, or small package of data, carries portions of the data as well as the Ethernet addresses for the source and destination computers. (Ethernet addresses are distinct from Internet addresses.) Data on a network are associated with multiple addresses used for different purposes. Ethernet addresses are used to direct information within a local area network. Internet addresses are used to direct information beyond a local network, anywhere in the world. (An Ethernet address is more accurately called a media access control [MAC] address.)

Because an Ethernet frame has a maximum size of 1,518 bytes (characters), information must often be divided into many frames for its network journey. Within a frame, each byte, or group of eight on or off signals, carries a particular kind of information. Some bytes mark the beginning or ending of the frame while others carry address, error checking, or data information. For example, the destination address in an Ethernet frame begins eight bytes after the start of the frame. The Ethernet frame is quite different from frames used by other physical and data link protocols.

TABLE 2.5: A SAMPLE ETHERNET FRAME

Bytes

8	6	6	2	0–1500	4
Preamble	Destination Ethernet address	Source Ethernet address	Length of data field	Data field, including (for example) IP and TCP information as well as electronic mail or other data	Frame check

10BaseT and 10BaseFL Ethernet Standards for Sending Data

The Ethernet media access method defines the way computers on an Ethernet network share a cable (or wireless path) without interrupting and overwriting each other's messages. If Ethernet protocols are used, each computer that wishes to transmit information first listens to the network. If it hears that no other computers are transmitting, it attempts to send information. After it sends information, it listens to the network again to determine whether its transmission collided with (was distorted by) another computer transmitting simultaneously. If such a collision occurs, the computer attempts to retransmit after a specified waiting period. A certain number of collisions (as much as 10% of network traffic) is normal for an Ethernet network. This scheme is called Carrier Sense Multiple Access with Collision Detection (CSMA/CD).

10BaseT Ethernet Standards for Physical Media

The 10BaseT Ethernet protocol requires a cable consisting of two pairs of unshielded twisted pair (UTP) copper wires at or surpassing Category 3 for performance. Categories of Performance are defined by a loose consortium of the American National Standards Institute (ANSI), the Electronic Industries Association (EIA), and the Telecommunications Industries Association (TIA). There are seven current categories of performance, but only a few are in common use—Categories 3, 5, 5E, and 6.

TABLE 2.6: COMMON CATEGORIES OF PERFORMANCE

Rating	Type of Cable	Used for	Notes
Category 3	Unshielded twisted pair copper (UTP)	10BaseT	Category 3 cable is found in older network installations. It shouldn't be installed in newer ones.
Category 5	Unshielded twisted pair copper (UTP)	10BaseT 100BaseTX 1000Base-T	Category 5 cable is suitable for 100BaseTX Ethernet. If Category 5 cable is used for higher speeds such as 1000Base-T (Gigabit Ethernet), test the cable for undesirable electrical characteristics such as return loss and far-end crosstalk.
Category 5E	Unshielded twisted pair copper (UTP)	10BaseT 100BaseTX 1000Base-T	It is better to use Category 5E or higher for 1000Base-T (Gigabit Ethernet).
Category 6	Unshielded twisted pair copper (UTP)	10BaseT 100BaseTX 1000Base-T	Category 6 standards have not been finalized.

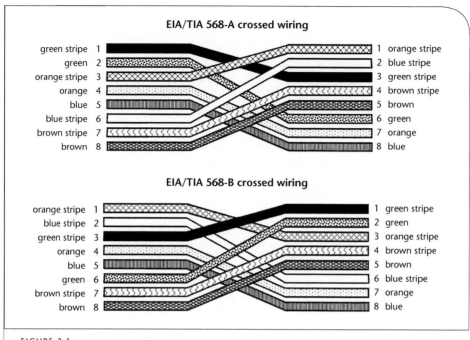

EIA/TIA 568-A crossed wiring

green stripe	1	1	orange stripe
green	2	2	blue stripe
orange stripe	3	3	green stripe
orange	4	4	brown stripe
blue	5	5	brown
blue stripe	6	6	green
brown stripe	7	7	orange
brown	8	8	blue

EIA/TIA 568-B crossed wiring

orange stripe	1	1	green stripe
blue stripe	2	2	green
green stripe	3	3	orange stripe
orange	4	4	brown stripe
blue	5	5	brown
green	6	6	blue stripe
brown stripe	7	7	orange
brown	8	8	blue

FIGURE 2.1

The 10BaseT Ethernet protocol defines how the pins in the RJ-45 connector must be connected to the four pairs of copper wires in the cable. (All four pairs should be connected even though only two pairs are used for 10BaseT. Connecting all pairs accommodates future upgrades that mandate use of all pairs.) There are several standard methods of connecting the pairs of wires to the pins, most commonly those defined by the family called ANSI/EIA/TIA 568-A and 568-B. (These standards also specify electrical and mechanical specifications and transmission requirements, and they evolve continuously. When installing cable, ask the installers which standards are most current and how they plan to test the cable to ensure its compliance.) The wiring schemes for ANSI/EIA/TIA 568-A and 568-B are functionally equivalent.

10BaseFL Ethernet Standards for Physical Media

The 10BaseFL Ethernet protocol requires 62.5/125-micron multimode fiber optic cable. There are two main types of fiber optic cable—multimode and single mode. Single mode fiber optic cable is capable of carrying information over much longer distances than multimode, but it is also much more expensive to install. Multimode fiber suffices for most LAN installations. The two measurements refer to the diameter of the inner fiber optic core (62.5 microns) and the outer protective sheath of the fiber (125 microns). While light waves do not travel much faster than electricity, they operate at higher frequencies and therefore can carry a great deal more information. (Light has a greater information density or bandwidth than electrical signals.) Some estimates indicate that a single fiber optic cable has a bandwidth between 50 and 75 terabits (trillion bits) per second. Unlike electrical signals, light waves are resistant to interference from external electromagnetic or radio wave sources. Single mode fiber has one additional virtue: It experiences much less signal loss (attenuation) than either multimode fiber or electrical signals on copper wire. (Single mode fiber is more expensive than multimode fiber for this reason.)

10BaseT and 10BaseFL Ethernet Standards for the Physical Shape of the Network

10BaseT and 10BaseFL require that a network assume a star topology. (Topology refers to the physical arrangement or overall shape of the network.) This means that each computer should be connected to a central point in the network. Star topologies are distinguished from bus topologies, in which all computers are connected in a long chain. There are other topologies such as ring and mesh as well. The central point of a star network usually consists of one or more hubs or switches, often (but not always) in a central wiring closet. Hubs and switches are special kinds of connecting equipment that help pass network information onto its destination.

To protect the integrity of the electrical signal, no signal on a 10BaseT or 10BaseFL network path (from the two computers at the farthest extremes of the network) may traverse more than four hubs before reaching its destination. Additionally, signals may not traverse more than five segments. A segment is a length of cable that is bounded by hubs, switches, routers, or some other kinds of network connecting equipment. Computers may only populate three of the five segments (the other two must lie between hubs or other network routing equipment). No segment may contain more than 1,024 devices.

For 10BaseT, the cable between the central wiring point and the wall jack for each computer may be no longer than 90 meters, and the cable from the wall jack to each computer (at the user's end) may be no more than 10 meters. For 10BaseFL, the maximum cable length is 2,000 meters.

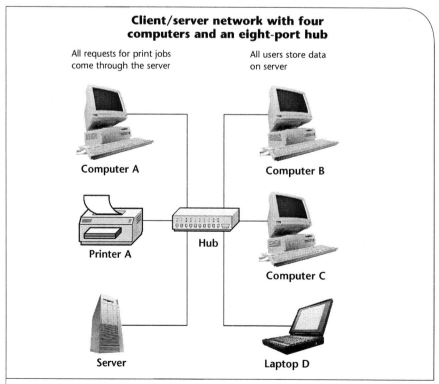

FIGURE 2.2

100BaseTX and 100BaseFX (IEEE 802.3u)

100BaseTX provides a transmission rate of 100 Mbps (10 times that of 10BaseT) and is rapidly becoming the standard installation for schools and businesses. 100BaseFX provides the same speed over fiber optic cable. The 100BaseTX and 100BaseFX Ethernet protocols provide sufficient speed for large databases, applications used by many people simultaneously, voice, and video.

100BaseTX and 100BaseFX Ethernet Standards for Data Format, Sending Data, Physical Media, and the Shape of the Network

Many of the requirements for data format such as sending data, cable, and the physical shape of the network are the same for the 100 Mbps branch of the Ethernet family as they were for the 10 Mbps branch. The most important difference concerns the cable required for 100BaseTX, which must consist of two twisted pairs of unshielded copper wire (one used for transmitting and the other for receiving signals) at or surpassing Category 5 for performance, or Category 1 shielded twisted pair (Category 3 cable is not acceptable). Additionally, the total length of cable connecting two client computers and their interconnecting switch must not exceed 205 meters, and the length of each cable may not exceed 100 meters.

Both 10BaseT and 100BaseTX versions of Ethernet may be run on the same network provided that the interconnecting equipment (hubs or switches) is designed to accommodate both protocols simultaneously.

Gigabit Ethernet

1000Base-T, 1000Base-LX, 1000Base-SX, 1000Base-CX (IEEE 802.3ab and IEEE 802.3z)

Gigabit Ethernet transmits information at 1,000 Mbps (1 gigabit per second), 100 times faster than 10BaseT Ethernet networks. Most schools take advantage of this speed in particular areas of their networks where it is needed most—to carry information between servers or between buildings. This area of the network is often termed its backbone. (The backbone of a network is distinguished from the wiring that connects desktop computers to the network. The backbone carries large amounts of data.)

Performance on network backbones is improved by installing Gigabit Ethernet. The Gigabit Ethernet backbone can be connected to the rest of a (presumably slower) network by interconnecting devices such as switches or routers that are designed to accommodate both Gigabit Ethernet and slower Ethernet protocols.

1000Base-T and 1000Base-CX use twisted pair copper wire, and 1000Base-SX and 1000Base-LX use fiber optic cable. 1000Base-SX is targeted at shorter, low-cost, in-building segments and 1000Base-LX at longer connections. Data, voice, and video information may be transmitted over a Gigabit Ethernet network. Here are some things to consider when adding Gigabit Ethernet to an existing network:

> Gigabit Ethernet network interfaces, hubs, and switches are necessary to build the network.

> Servers and desktop computers in the Gigabit Ethernet segment of the network must be fast enough to accommodate large volumes of data delivered at high speeds. Be sure to ask the server or connecting equipment manufacturer whether existing network components are compatible with Gigabit Ethernet.

> Minimize the initial installation cost by using Gigabit Ethernet components only where their power is truly needed—between servers and buildings.

1000Base-T, 1000Base-CX, 1000Base-SX, and 1000Base-LX Standards for Data Format, Sending Data, Physical Media, and the Shape of the Network

Many of the requirements for data format, sending data, cable, and the physical shape of the network are the same for the 1,000 Mbps branch of the Ethernet family as they were for the 10 Mbps branch, although there are a few important differences.

1000Base-T uses four pairs of twisted pair copper wire (as opposed to the two pairs used by 100Base-TX) as well as full duplex communications. In full duplex communications, two computers simultaneously transmit and receive data on each pair of wires. Full duplex communications are distinguished from half duplex, where transmitting and receiving occur at separate times. (Previous Ethernet standards also included full duplex communications as an option.) Finally, for Gigabit Ethernet segments using half duplex communications, only one repeater (a type of interconnecting equipment) may be included among the connected computers.

1000Base-T requires four twisted pairs of unshielded copper wire at or surpassing Category 5. If a Category 5 cable is used (most likely because Gigabit Ethernet is being added to an existing network), the cable installer should run additional tests for undesirable transmission characteristics such as crosstalk and signal return loss. (Be sure that the cable provider can fully explain the tests required by the current standards when installing Gigabit Ethernet.) Use Category 5E (or higher) cable for new installations.

1000Base-T covers distances as great as 100 meters or networks with a diameter of 200 meters. 1000Base-CX is used in computers rooms as a method of connecting central equipment over distances of 25 meters or less. 1000Base-SX uses 62.5-micron or 50-micron multimode fiber optic cable for distances between 220 and 550 meters. 1000Base-LX uses the same cable for distances up to 550 meters, or 9-micron single mode fiber optic cable for distances up to 5 kilometers.

Practical Advice

IMPROVING TRANSMISSION RATES

The actual transmission rate for any network can be dramatically affected by the quality of the cable (especially if twisted pair copper wire is used) and the physical plant through which it is run. Ethernet frames can become damaged (lose bits of information) if copper cabling runs near electromagnetic devices (such as power cables), or fluorescent lights, or if it is subjected to temperature extremes. When frames are damaged or lost during transmission, the sender retransmits them; these retransmissions increase network traffic and decrease total throughput. Be sure that the cable contractor runs high-quality cable through areas free of electromagnetic equipment or large variations in temperature and humidity.

A network's carrying capacity is also called its bandwidth. Expanding a network or adding new devices that allow for increased traffic can decrease network performance. Likewise, video, voice, graphics, and even Web surfing can require significant capacity and can saturate a network. (Other applications, such as electronic mail, require less network carrying capacity.) Using special devices such as switches and routers to interconnect the additional network segments can control the negative effects of network expansion. Be sure to work with the network manager or external network designers to ensure that any network expansion is carefully controlled.

Finally, a network can have plenty of bandwidth but still provide less-than-adequate performance. Latency, or the delay between sending and receiving data, can be induced by an incorrect configuration of routers and other connecting equipment. Network managers should routinely measure how much bandwidth is being used, error rates, lost frames, and latency. Network interconnecting devices such as network interfaces or switches and network operating systems such as Windows NT, Windows 2000, or Novell NetWare can provide this information.

ETHERNET

Ethernet is perhaps the most common physical and data link protocol used in school local area networks. There are several different varieties of Ethernet, with each variety delivering different speeds and using different types of cable and network equipment. One variety, called 10BaseT Ethernet, delivers information at 10 Mbps over twisted pair copper wire. Two other varieties of Ethernet, known as 100BaseTX and 100BaseFX, are perhaps the most common; they deliver information at 100 Mbps over twisted pair copper wire or fiber optic cable, respectively. The newest variety is Gigabit Ethernet, which delivers information at 1,000 Mpbs over both copper and fiber optic cable. Ethernet enforces stringent rules about the type and placement of equipment, length of cable allowed between computers, type of cable to be used, and many other characteristics of a network. Be sure that contractors abide by these rules precisely.

Wireless LANs

Wireless connections are useful in areas where wiring is expensive or dangerous to install, where computers change location frequently, or where people are housed temporarily. Wireless networks may include computers, laptops, bar code readers, scanners, handheld data entry devices that transmit information to and from a central database, and many other components.

To create a wireless network, each computer, printer, scanner, or other device must include a wireless network interface. For computers, printers, and scanners, the network interface often consists of a card that is inserted into one of the internal slots in the device. Handheld devices come with wireless interfaces built into their internal circuit boards.

If a wireless network is to use the resources of a wired LAN—for example its Internet connection or integrated learning system—then another device, called an access point, must be installed to bridge the gap between the wired and wireless portion of the networks. The access point is connected wirelessly to the computers and printers in the classroom and by copper wire or fiber optic cable to the rest of the network. Besides bridging between networks, access points also ensure that communication between the computers and printers within a classroom occurs in an orderly fashion, and they increase the distance across which clients can communicate by repeating their signals. At this time, wired connections are more stable and substantially faster than wireless connections.

Wireless LAN technologies have been used for several years, but until recently, there were no standards for their implementation. As a result, each manufacturer's equipment was not necessarily compatible with equipment from other manufacturers. With the appearance of one major standard, termed IEEE 802.11, in 1997, many incompatibilities were alleviated and the market for wireless networking grew rapidly. (When using proprietary technologies, always check the equipment specifications carefully before attempting to mix equipment from different manufacturers.)

Several other wireless standards have appeared recently to compete with IEEE 802.11, most notably Bluetooth, Wireless Application Protocol (WAP), HomeRF, HiperLAN/2, 3G, cellular, and several infrared methods. It is premature to predict which standards will eventually dominate the industry. Some combination of different standards will likely coexist; each standard will serve specific (and different) purposes. WAP provides information for mobile phones and other devices but is not widely deployed. HomeRF is a standard for home networking to connect, for example, cordless telephones; the European standard HiperLAN/2 provides very fast access but is not often used in the United States. 3G and cellular technologies are intended for mobile users, and infrared methods are quite limited in the distances they cover.

IEEE 802.11

Apple's newest iBooks, iMacs, PowerBooks, and Power Macs can all communicate wirelessly using IEEE 802.11 standards (with the proper components). They can share information with each other, or they can access traditional local area networks or Internet connections. Many Microsoft vendors have also implemented wireless connections. It is common to find schools with mobile computer labs—carts containing wirelessly connected laptops and printers; the carts are wheeled from classroom to classroom—having full network access.

The original IEEE 802.11 standards define communications at 1–2 Mbps. These standards were superseded in 2000 by a new standard, IEEE 802.11b, which improved transmission rates to 11 Mbps. Computers and equipment using both speeds (IEEE 802.11 and 802.11b) can coexist on the same local area network provided that the connecting equipment can manage both speeds.

TABLE 2.7: IEEE 802.11 TRANSMISSION RATES

Transmission rates	IEEE 802.11	IEEE 802.11b
1–2 Mbps	X	X
5.5 Mbps		X
11 Mbps		X

IEEE 802.11 and 802.11b Wireless Specifications for Physical Media and Transmission Rates

Wireless networks carry information on radio waves or infrared waves instead of copper or fiber cables. Waves impose special requirements on how networks are constructed:

> Waves vary in their capacity to carry data. Some waves (such as light waves that travel in fiber optic cable) can carry lots of data. Radio waves and infrared waves can carry less data (but they are still adequate to many LAN tasks).

> Waves tend to break apart when they pass through dense materials such as walls. Longer wavelengths are less susceptible to breakage. Radio waves, for example, can pass through quite dense materials, including most interior walls of buildings. Infrared waves are much more breakable, and cannot pass through cubicle walls.

> Radio waves are omnidirectional (travel like rays from a light bulb) while others, such as Infrared waves, can be concentrated into a beam. Infrared waves and some radio waves require the transmitter and receiver to have a direct (unobstructed) line of sight between each other.

TABLE 2.8: IEEE 802.11 TYPES OF ELECTROMAGNETIC WAVES

Electromagnetic Waves	IEEE 802.11	IEEE 802.11b
Diffuse Infrared	X	X
Direct Sequence Spread Spectrum		X
Frequency Hopping Spread Spectrum		X

The IEEE 802.11 standards define three types of carrier waves for your wireless network.

INFRARED WAVES. Infrared waves can be categorized into two types—direct infrared and diffuse infrared. Direct infrared waves travel in a beam, and they are used in many household remote control devices (such as TV or VCR remote controls). Diffuse infrared waves (DFIR) are omnidirectional and depend on bouncing off walls and ceilings to reach their target. The IEEE 802.11 specification includes diffuse infrared waves as a possible carrier at speeds of 1–2 Mbps.

For diffuse infrared waves, the transmitter and receiver must be within 10 meters of each other but need not have a direct line of sight. Because infrared rays cannot pass through walls, infrared LANs must be located within a single room. Many modern laptops and printers include (non-IEEE 802.11) infrared ports and are ready to communicate wirelessly.

SPREAD SPECTRUM RADIO WAVES. Spread spectrum radio waves occupy the 902–928 megahertz (MHz) and 2.4–2.4835 gigahertz (GHz) bands of the radio frequency spectrum. No Federal Communications Commission (FCC) license is required to operate within these bands. The phrase *spread spectrum* indicates that each wave includes many different frequencies.

The network signal hops among these different frequencies. Hopping has several benefits. First, it reduces potential electromagnetic and radio frequency interference because interference from a specific source usually distorts only a small range of frequencies. Second, hopping increases the number of clients that can share a physical space. When signals hop across frequencies, they are less likely to collide than if they all occupied the same frequency. Finally, snooping devices have more difficulty listening for signals that hop across multiple frequencies than signals on a single frequency.

There are two kinds of spread spectrum technologies: frequency hopping spread spectrum (FHSS) and direct sequence spread spectrum (DSSS). Frequency hopping spread spectrum signals hop from one frequency to another at a specified rate and sequence. Direct sequence spread spectrum signals hop from one frequency to another sequentially. Frequency hopping spread spectrum is more secure than direct sequence because it is more difficult for unauthorized users to determine the rate and order of its hops.

Both direct sequence and frequency hopping spread spectrum waves carry data omnidirectionally. For IEEE 802.11, they operate in the 2.4 GHz band with a transmission speed of either 1 or 2 Mbps. IEEE 802.11b uses direct sequence spread spectrum radio waves only, and transmits information at 11 Mbps whenever possible. If a computer moves beyond the range for high-speed transmission or if there is substantial interference, then communications proceed at lower speeds, falling back to 5.5 Mbps, 2 Mbps, and 1 Mbps. (The range for high-speed transmission varies depending on the physical shape of the room and its construction materials.) Both direct sequence and frequency hopping spread spectrum radio waves are able to pass through walls and both may be used outdoors. Most wireless LAN equipment implements spread spectrum technology rather than infrared technology because spread spectrum carries information farther.

IEEE 802.11 and 802.11b Wireless Standards for the Physical Shape of the Spread Spectrum Network

The IEEE standard for wireless networks supports two topologies. In the first topology, groups of computers communicate directly with each other. This topology is useful, for example, to share documents among laptops gathered in a classroom. In the second topology, client computers communicate with each other and also with clients on the rest of the (wired) network through the access point, which collects information from wireless clients and passes it on to another network.

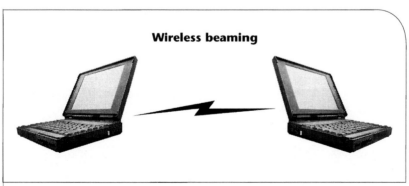

Wireless beaming

FIGURE 2.3

In the IEEE 802.11 and 802.11b standards, the area to be served by wireless connections is divided into cells. Think of each cell as a circle. Any computer within the circle can communicate with any other computer within the circle. However, if one computer moves outside the circle, it is no longer within communications range of the others.

Each of these cells is called a basic service set (BSS). A wireless LAN may consist of a single basic service set, with or without an access point. However, most wireless LANs include several basic service sets, usually arranged like overlapping circles. Each overlapping circle contains an access point. Wireless clients moving from one overlapping circle to the next always remain in contact with an access point and (therefore) with the main network and with each other.

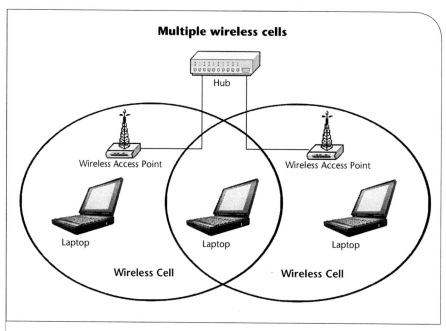

FIGURE 2.4

When a client computer enters a basic service set, it determines the presence of a wireless LAN in one of two ways—it sends a probe packet or it waits to receive a periodic transmission (called a beacon frame) from the access point. If it finds the access point, the wireless client and the access point exchange information and complete their LAN connection; in the absence of an access point, client computers perform these functions for each other. If more than one access point is available, the client chooses its access point based on signal strength and error rates. Once the client has chosen, it tunes to the radio channel for that access point; it also checks periodically to see whether a different access point might provide better service.

For IEEE 802.11b, the maximum distance from client to access point, or between clients without an access point, is 300 feet. Distance estimates are based on spaces containing absolutely no obstacles or interference. In reality, wireless networks will likely cover much less area. Maximum range for a network should be determined during the initial site survey (the analysis of the physical plant that is conducted before a wireless network is installed). A single access point can serve between 10 and 50 clients performing normal computer operations.

IEEE 802.11 and 802.11b Standards for Data Formats and Sending Data

The IEEE 802.11 family specifies a format for data traversing the network consisting of a header and a 2,048-byte frame body. Like the computers on Ethernet, each computer on an IEEE 802.11 or 802.11b network listens to the network for a pause in transmission before it sends data in an attempt to avoid overwriting other transmissions. The IEEE 802.11/802.11b scheme for listening is called Carrier Sense Multiple Access/Collision Avoidance (CSMA/CA) and differs from Ethernet's CSMA/CD in one important respect: After a computer sends its information, it does not listen to the network because collisions are difficult to detect over wireless media. Instead, the sending computer listens for an acknowledgment from the receiving computer and resends the information if no acknowledgment is received.

If an access point is present, these client-initiated communications exist side-by-side with more regulated communications. Access points under IEEE 802.11 and 802.11b poll each client to request transmission and ensure that each client gets a fair chance. (This polling may degrade network performance if the access point has too many wireless clients.) Finally, the IEEE 802.11/802.11b protocols support specific schemes for authentication (determining that only valid users are connected) and privacy (ensuring that data are available to the sender and receiver but not to anyone else); these schemes can be used in addition to different and often more robust authentication and privacy schemes implemented across wired and wireless networks as a whole.

Other 802.11 Standards

IEEE has also ratified a standard called 802.11a that offers transmission rates up to 20–24 Mbps at 300 feet or 54 Mbps at shorter distances. Standards for high-performance wireless networking are also in the wings from other organizations.

Practical Advice

THE IMPORTANCE OF A SITE SURVEY

The art of wireless networking involves determining where to place the overlapping circles (basic service sets) and access points. Wireless signals can penetrate walls of varying thickness (or sometimes several walls), but the reliability of the signals after they pass through such barriers depends on the material in the barrier and the shape of the building. For these reasons, it is not always easy to predict the reliability of wireless network connections, and it is advisable to engage in a site survey before installation. The site survey is critical to building a successful network.

One simple kind of site survey involves fitting two portable computers with wireless hardware so that they can communicate with each other. With the help of diagnostic software from the manufacturer, the coverage area for a potential access point can be determined by keeping one portable computer at the access point and moving the other computer around. Be sure to ask the manufacturers what tools they provide and what approach they recommend for deciding where to place access points.

Some network managers advise against purchasing equipment from more than one vendor. While the IEEE standards ensure that such equipment will interoperate, equipment must come from a single source to take advantage of built-in, vendor-specific enhancements for management or performance.

Access points require power and are sometimes located in areas where power outlets do not exist. Some access points can draw power over the Ethernet. Look for these access points specifically, if power is a problem.

After installing access points, configure both the access points and the client computer network interfaces. Look for vendors that supply tools to configure many access points simultaneously and whose access points can be configured using a variety of different venues—using Web browsers, TEL-NET, Simple Network Management Protocol (SNMP), or serial port connections.

Access points can be set to allow only specific Ethernet addresses or to require a network name or a security code. One or more of these settings can create a basic (if not entirely robust) security system for a wireless network. Access points may also be configured to encrypt information.

When setting up multiple access points, each should be tuned to a channel that does not overlap with channels being used by neighboring access points. IEEE 802.11 provides 14 partially overlapping channels, with three channels that do not overlap at all. These three nonoverlapping channels should be selected for neighboring access points.

IEEE 802.11b wireless LANs are sufficient for electronic mail, document sharing, Web browsing, and similar tasks. They should not be used to transfer large amounts of information—for example, downloading large documents from the Internet, supporting large numbers of simultaneous users, or transmitting video or voice.

Bluetooth

Bluetooth was developed by an industry consortium and named for a 10th century Danish king who united Denmark and Norway. It promises to provide a common networking scheme for a variety of disparate devices—including cell phones, computers, printers, servers, headphones, keyboards, and mice. In theory, Bluetooth would enable a group of students with laptops, graphing calculators, Web-enabled telephones, and handheld devices such as Palm Pilots to enter a classroom, beam information to one another, and work collaboratively to produce a team project. The projected cost of implementing Bluetooth is considerably lower than that for IEEE 802.11 wireless LANs, and the equipment installation substantially simpler and quicker.

Bluetooth devices use frequency hopping spread spectrum to communicate within a 10 meter distance at the 2.4 GHz range—the same unlicensed frequencies used by IEEE 802.11 and 802.11b. When Bluetooth-capable devices approach one another, they automatically initiate a conversation; if the negotiation is successful, they form a personal area network (PAN) or piconet that might be as small as the distance between two devices or as large as a good-sized room. Each set of communicating devices hops frequencies in synchrony to stay in contact with its peers. A piconet can include as many as eight devices, and as many as 10 piconets can overlap to create a scatternet, creating a maximum network size of 80 devices.

These networks can theoretically include many different kinds of communications, including voice, local area network, and Internet communications (among others). For voice communications, Bluetooth offers 64 kilobits per second (Kbps), roughly equivalent to ISDN lines. Network and Internet communications like those over modems occur quite a bit faster—723.2 Kbps in one direction and as fast as 57.6 Kbps in the other.

Bluetooth networks face several obstacles to implementation, not the least of which is that they are likely to interfere with communications on IEEE 802.11 networks. Bluetooth devices change frequencies much faster than IEEE 802.11 devices; as they cycle through different frequencies they are, therefore, somewhat likely to land on one that is in use by an IEEE 802.11 device. Because market forces drive new technologies faster than standards bodies can regulate their behavior, it is also possible that Bluetooth devices will appear among IEEE 802.11 networks before there are easy means to prevent such interference. At the moment, one way to manage these difficulties is to keep Bluetooth devices more than 50 feet from IEEE 802.11 networks.

Comparison of Bluetooth and IEEE 802.11

Speed is the most important difference between IEEE 802.11 and Bluetooth networks. At 11 Mbps, IEEE 802.11 networks operate almost 15 times faster than Bluetooth. They also operate over much longer distances (300 feet vs. 32 feet). IEEE 802.11 devices can also roam between different LANs. Bluetooth contains no such provision. Finally, configuring Bluetooth networks may present difficulties, at least for the present. Designed to prevent snooping, Bluetooth requires that communicating devices be registered with one another. In theory, for large networks, each device would have to be registered with each access point, and vice versa. IEEE 802.11 networks, on the other hand, use a more elegant system by which devices and access points, once configured, authenticate themselves to each other automatically. Nonetheless, Bluetooth is inexpensive and simple to use when just a few devices are involved. Bluetooth connects a wider variety of devices than IEEE 802.11.

Technical Information Summary

WIRELESS LANS

Computers can be interconnected without using cable by employing one of the relatively new wireless technologies. In a wireless LAN, each computer is fitted with a network interface that broadcasts infrared or radio waves. These broadcasts are received by other nearby computers (also fitted with the appropriate network interfaces) or by a connecting device called an access point. The access point connects the wireless network to the rest of a (wired or wireless) network.

New Standards for Wireless Technologies

Wireless LANs that conform to the IEEE 802.11b standards deliver information at 11 Mbps (about 10% of the speed of 100BaseTX Ethernet, currently a common school network technology). Be careful when purchasing spread spectrum wireless network equipment that is proprietary to a specific vendor. Make sure that it interconnects properly.

Bluetooth wireless networks connect a wider variety of devices than IEEE 802.11 (including handheld devices, computers, and cordless telephones). Bluetooth networks are also less expensive to implement and, on a small scale, easier to set up. However, Bluetooth delivers information at a maximum of 723.2 Kbps, almost 15 times slower than IEEE 802.11. They cover much smaller areas—32 feet vs. 300 feet for IEEE 802.11 LANs. Unlike IEEE 802.11 devices, Bluetooth devices are unable to roam from one area of the network to the next.

Other wireless connection methods have made their appearance recently, most notably Wireless Application Protocol, HomeRF, HiperLAN/2, 3G, cellular, and several infrared methods. None of these methods are likely to serve the specific needs of school networks in the near future, however.

Both IEEE 802.11 and Bluetooth use a type of radio wave called spread spectrum to communicate. Spread spectrum radio waves can penetrate walls of varying thickness (or sometimes several walls), but the reliability of the signals after they pass through such barriers depends on the material in the barrier and the shape of the building. For these reasons, it is not always easy to predict the reliability of wireless network connections, and it is advisable to engage in a site survey before installation. In a site survey, network professionals determine the optimal wireless communication paths for a site and, most important, select the placement of access points.

LocalTalk

Many generations of Macintosh prior to 1998 could be connected either by Ethernet or by a slow but simple kind of network protocol known as LocalTalk. Today, LocalTalk is no longer included with new Macintoshes. The ubiquitous Ethernet has far surpassed LocalTalk's paltry 230 Kbps transmission rate (about 1/400 the performance of the 100Base-TX Ethernet).

LocalTalk differs from Ethernet in its type of cabling, topology, and speed. In a LocalTalk network, each Macintosh is connected directly to the next by a small connector box and regular telephone wire. The first and last Macintosh computers on the network form the endpoints (they are not connected to each other) and are fitted with small devices called terminators, which absorb network signals so that they do not reflect back onto the network.

A network in which each computer is connected to the next is technically called a ring. (In the case of LocalTalk, the ring is referred to as open because the first and last Macintosh computers are not connected to each other.) This topology is also known as a daisy chain because it is constructed like the strings of flowers that children sometimes create. The topology used by LocalTalk is quite different from standards in which all computers are connected to a central point.

To enable LocalTalk networking, earlier-generation Macintosh computers included a LocalTalk network interface (the LocalTalk connector at the back of the computer was often marked with a picture of a printer). These early Macintoshes could be configured to use either their Ethernet or LocalTalk connections by choosing the appropriate settings in the Network or AppleTalk Control Panel. Small LocalTalk LANs could connect to an Ethernet network by installing a LocalTalk-Ethernet bridge (consisting of either hardware or software) between the two segments.

Routing and Protocols

There are many different protocols that govern how data travel across a network. These additional protocols fall into two major groups:

> **Network routing and transport protocols** (layers 3 and 4 in the OSI reference model) organize data into a logical stream, add destination and source addresses to the data, and append some error-checking codes to help ensure that the data arrive safely.

> **Session, presentation, and application protocols** (layers 5, 6, and 7 in the OSI reference model) initiate a network connection, prepare the text for transport, and, optionally, encrypt the electronic mail message.

While most desktop computers on a network agree upon a common protocol for the data link and physical layers of the OSI reference model (e.g., Ethernet), at the upper layers the story is quite different. Most computers include software to implement more than one upper-layer protocol stack, with each stack serving a slightly different purpose on the network. For example, Macintoshes will likely include software to implement the TCP/IP protocol stack for Internet communications and, simultaneously, the AppleTalk stack to manage communications with other Macintoshes, printers, and file servers. Likewise, Windows PCs run TCP/IP along with their proprietary stack.

TABLE 2.9: COMMON PROTOCOL STACKS OPERATING AT OSI LAYERS 3–7

Protocol Stack	Purpose
TCP/IP (Transmission Control Protocol/Internet Protocol)	The TCP/IP protocol stack provides Internet communications. Macintosh and Windows clients as well as Novell NetWare, UNIX, and Windows servers use TCP/IP.
IPX/SPX (Internet Packet Exchange/Sequenced Packet Exchange)	The IPX/SPX protocol stack is used in conjunction with one brand of server—a Novell NetWare server. If a network includes Novell, then all the Macintoshes and Windows PCs on the network may use the IPX/SPX protocol stack to communicate.
Windows (SMB [Server Message Block], NetBIOS [Network Basic Input/Output System], and, optionally, NetBEUI [NetBIOS Extended User Interface])	The Windows protocol stack provides communications among Windows PCs, or between Windows PCs and Windows NT or 2000 servers.
Macintosh (AppleTalk)	AppleTalk provides communications among Macintosh computers.

TCP/IP

TCP/IP (Transmission Control Protocol/Internet Protocol) provides Internet connectivity. Every computer that communicates directly over the Internet must include software to implement this protocol. In fact, now that Internet communications are critical to most organizations, modern computers are delivered with TCP/IP software as part of their standard configuration.

Components of the TCP/IP Protocol Stack

TCP/IP software includes many different components. The portion that manages address information for Internet-bound messages is referred to as the IP. IP also describes how data should be packaged into small units, called packets, for transmission across the Internet. The portion referred to as TCP ensures that IP packets are sent and received without error, and assembled into the proper sequence at both ends of the connection. These protocols (among others) carry out OSI network and transport (layers 3–4) services.

UDP (User Datagram Protocol) accomplishes many of the same tasks as TCP but does not check for errors. (UDP depends on higher-layer software to provide error checking.) While not checking for errors may seem counter-intuitive, omitting the error check makes UDP faster than TCP. Multimedia applications that deliver sound and video require a steady high-speed stream. These applications often use UDP instead of TCP.

Other protocols—including HTTP (HyperText Transport Protocol), FTP (File Transfer Protocol), TELNET (terminal emulation via a network), and SMTP (Simple Mail Transfer Protocol)—provide OSI application, presentation, and session services. For example, when a browser retrieves Web pages, it does so by making use of the procedures described in the HTTP. (This is why most Web page addresses begin with the letters http.) Programs such as Fetch or WS_FTP transfer documents to and from Internet sites using the FTP protocol. NCSA Telnet and Windows Telnet are two common software programs that implement the TELNET protocol. Finally, electronic mail programs make use of SMTP.

In addition to these protocols, there are many other protocols within the TCP/IP family whose names are less familiar but whose services are critical to your network nonetheless.

Internet Addresses, Host Names, and Domain Names

To make communications on the Internet possible, every computer connected to the Internet must have a unique numeric address, called its Internet Protocol address (or IP address). Be careful not to confuse the term IP address with Ethernet address. Each computer, printer, server, or other device on an Ethernet network has two unique addresses: its Ethernet address and its IP address. The Ethernet address is used for communication within a segment (small area) of a network. The IP address is used for communication across segments or along wider expanses including the Internet. There is good reason for using two different addresses. While Ethernet addresses provide a quick way for nearby computers to find each other, for two remote computers to find each other, local network equipment would have to keep a map of every Ethernet address in existence!

IP addresses provide a different and better way to route network information. IP addresses are hierarchical. They organize individual computers into groups so that other computers on the Internet need only keep track of these groups to route a message to its destination. Each group, in turn, receives messages on behalf of its members and then routes those messages to the appropriate individuals.

IP addresses consist of four numbers separated by periods. For example, one possible Internet address might be 2.38.10.11. Each of these four numbers represents 8 bits (on-off signals) of information, sometimes called an octet. Because 1 bit can communicate two distinct numbers (1 or 0 depending on whether the bit, or electrical impulse, is on or off), 8 bits can communicate 28 numbers (0 to 255). Each of the four numbers within the IP address therefore can assume a value from 0 to 255. A whole IP address is 32 bits long.

A portion of this number represents a unique network—for example, 2.38.10 might represent a district network. The remainder of the address represents a particular computer on that network. One particular computer might be number 11 on the 2.38.10 network. The computer's complete IP address would therefore be 2.38.10.11.

Just which portion of the address designates the network and which portion designates a particular computer varies a bit among different IP network addresses. In fact, IP addresses are divided into classes, each of which use different portions of the IP address to designate the network.

TABLE 2.10: NETWORK PORTIONS OF IP ADDRESS CLASSES A, B, C

IP Class	Portion of the Address That Designates the Network	Example
Class A	First octet	126.92.6.1
Class B	First two octets	128.16.55.29
Class C	First three octets	209.38.10.11

There are two additional Internet address classes—Classes D and E. These classes are reserved for uses other than assigning network numbers to an organization's computers and do not pertain to this discussion.

When an organization first connects to the Internet, it must lease Internet addresses from an Internet service provider (ISP). Most organizations lease a portion of a Class C Internet address. Each Class C license allows no more than 256 addresses for individual computers. (Actually, only 254 addresses are available; the addresses 0 and 255 are reserved for special purposes. No computer on the sample 209.38.10 network can be numbered 209.38.10.0 or 209.38.10.255.)

For some schools, a Class C license provides more addresses than they need; in fact, two schools might want to share the same license. In this case, each school subnets the Class C license, or divides its address space into smaller segments. To create the subnet, each school's network administrator defines a special number called a subnet mask and configures the school's network equipment and each desktop computer to remember it. A subnet mask looks something like an IP address. The subnet mask that divides an IP Class C license into two equal portions is 255.255.255.128. Once the subnet mask is defined and installed on each computer, then the first school on the Class C network can use addresses 193.38.10.1 through 193.38.10.126 and the second school can use addresses 193.38.10.129 through 193.38.10.254. Subnet masks work with IP addresses to define the portion of the address space that may be used for individual computers on a particular network.

While the Class C license may provide too many addresses for some schools, it may provide too few for others. These days, it is very difficult to get a Class C license. In fact, most schools get a few IP addresses from their Internet service providers (the organizations that connect each school to the Internet); these addresses are given out sparingly. Network address translation (NAT) can solve the problem of having too few IP addresses. To implement NAT, all computers on a network send Internet-bound traffic to one or more special network connection devices, most commonly proxy servers. The proxy server intercepts each network packet and repackages it with its own IP address instead of the sender's.

When the information requested by the packet returns from the Internet, the proxy server intercepts the information and redirects it to the originator. Only the proxy server needs to have a valid IP address; all other devices on the network can have unlicensed (but still unique) IP addresses.

Certain IP addresses are reserved especially for use on such private networks. Addresses beginning with 10 (Class A), or within the ranges 172.16.0.0 to 172.31.0.0 (Class B) or 192.168.0.0 to 192.168.255.0 (Class C) may be used behind proxy servers. (In fact, these addresses will fail to work if used with direct connections to the Internet.) Different schools can use addresses in the 192.168.0.0 to 192.168.255.0 range because the addresses are intercepted by each school's proxy server and replaced with valid addresses before the information reaches or returns from the Internet.

Once network administrators determine the valid IP addresses for their networks, they must assign each computer, printer, scanner, server, and network connecting device (hub, switch, router) its unique IP address. For small networks, they might visit each such computer and configure its TCP/IP software (usually through a Control Panel) with the address.

For networks consisting of dozens of clients, manual configuration is tedious and prone to error. Instead, most networks include servers whose purpose is to automatically assign addresses to computers as they start up. These servers are called Dynamic Host Control Protocol (DHCP) servers. Each computer, printer, scanner, or other device on a network usually contains software that seeks a DHCP server and sends a request for an address when it starts; the DHCP server responds with an IP address. The IP address is valid only for a time period specified by the network administrator, and when the time period expires, software on the client computer and DHCP server collaborate to assign a different IP address. Expiration enables administrators to remove IP numbers from a network when necessary and allocate them to other uses.

The DHCP server also sends other critical information, including the network subnet mask, default router, and Domain Name System (DNS) server. The default router is a connecting device to which each computer on a particular network segment sends information. The router forwards information if the information needs to be sent beyond the local segment.

While IP addresses enable network hardware and software to route information, they are cumbersome to use directly. (Imagine having to know someone's IP address to send electronic mail!) To simplify the situation, host names are used instead of IP addresses. For example, at Education Development Center, Inc., (EDC) the principal Web server is **www.edc.org** (its host name). A person seeking to view one of EDC's Web pages would type this host name into the Location or Address box of his or her Web browser software. When the person presses the Enter/Return key, a sophisticated set of computers called Domain Name System servers intercepts the request and determines the numeric Internet address to which the host name corresponds.

The host name of a computer is derived from another important name—one that an organization purchases at the same time that it secures its unique Internet addresses. This second name is called a domain name. A domain name represents one or more addresses (computers) on a network. At Education Development Center, Inc., the domain name is edc.org. This domain name refers to many computers at Education Development Center, Inc. The computers **www.edc.org** and **www2.edc.org** are host names of two of the computers within the domain. A domain name is purchased from an organization called an Internet registrar.

Each domain on the Internet is required to have a primary and a secondary DNS server within its network. The primary server maintains a master list known as the zone database, of the domains that it knows about or is responsible for. It updates this list constantly based on its own queries and on information provided by other domain name servers. The primary domain name server sends the secondary domain server a copy of its master list on a routine basis. If the primary domain name server is disabled or very busy, the secondary server responds to requests. In addition, secondary domain name servers can be placed in remote locations so that remote clients do not have to connect to the main network to find the information they need. Secondary domain name servers are also suitable for offices without technical staff. Once secondary domain name servers are set up they require very little maintenance.

The domain name edc.org belongs to a larger grouping of organizations on the Internet—those that make up the org domain. Internet addresses are divided into several major domains, including the United States domains edu, gov, mil, com, net, org, int, us, and many others.

IPv6

The system of IP addresses discussed thus far is technically called IPv4 (IP version 4). It is scheduled for replacement during the next few years because it does not provide enough addresses to accommodate the enormous increase in Internet users. (A 32-bit number like that used in IPv4 can represent 4,294,967,296 or 232 addresses.) The replacement system IPv6 (IP version 6—version 5 was skipped) increases the address length from 32 bits to 128 bits and can therefore supply many more Internet addresses. also includes additional features for privacy and performance.

IPX/SPX

Networks that were installed several years ago and include a file server using Novell NetWare software will likely have installed IPX/SPX (Internet Packet Exchange/Sequenced Packet Exchange). IPX/SPX software helps clients and servers manage communications, file sharing, printer sharing, and other network operations.

IPX describes how data should be packaged and carried across a Novell network. SPX ensures that the IPX packets are sent and received without error, and assembled into the proper sequence at both ends of the connection. (Notice that these protocols have analogous roles to IP and TCP, respectively, but differ in the particular ways they carry out these roles. For example, the identifying information for IP requires 20 bytes of space. The same information requires 30 bytes in IPX.) IPX and SPX (among other protocols) provide OSI layer network and transport layer services for Novell NetWare.

Application, presentation, and session services are provided by NCP (NetWare Core Protocol). When a desktop computer (client) wishes to save a document, it issues its request to the server using NCP, and the server acknowledges in kind.

IPX/SPX is being phased out. The current version of NetWare (version 5) uses TCP/IP rather than IPX/SPX as the default protocol for all network services. However, many sites continue to use IPX/SPX during the transition period.

Windows

If a network includes a Windows NT file server, the computers and connecting devices will likely run Windows network software, including NetBEUI (NetBIOS Extended User Interface), NetBIOS (Network Basic Input/Output System), SMB (Server Message Block), and WINS (Windows Internet Naming Service) protocols.

Within the Windows protocol stack, the NetBEUI protocol describes how data should be packaged and carried across a segment (portion) of a local area network. NetBEUI, however, suffers from not having the capacity to manage communications between different networks. NetBEUI cannot be used, therefore, in organizations of even modest size. Most organizations use the TCP/IP protocol stack to provide services at OSI layers 3 and 4 instead of NetBEUI.

The NetBIOS protocol provides services at OSI layers 1–5 and can work with TCP/IP at OSI layers 3 and 4 and Ethernet at layers 1 and 2. (Imagine different streams of activity occurring in layers. NetBIOS occupies the highest layer and rests upon TCP/IP; TCP/IP in turn rests upon Ethernet. Each stream of activity accomplishes one portion of a network's communications.)

One of NetBIOS' most important responsibilities involves tracking the Windows PC names on a network. (Windows names coexist with Internet host names. A computer may have one or both kinds of names.) For example, when browsing a Network Neighborhood to see a list of other Windows PCs or printers, NetBIOS helps to provide this information. Microsoft announced that it intends to eliminate NetBIOS with the release of Windows 2000 and move toward networks based entirely on TCP/IP.

Over the years, Windows has used several different schemes for mapping between Windows PC names and their associated IP addresses. (IP addresses are required for successful delivery of information across heterogeneous networks and the Internet.) In the mid-1990s, Windows networks introduced a scheme based on the WINS protocol. WINS allowed computers to register their names and IP addresses with a special shared computer called a WINS server. When one Windows PC needed to communicate with another, it queried the designated WINS server to find the recipient's IP address. More modern Windows networks based on Windows 2000 servers and clients use a different scheme. On these networks, Domain Name System servers resolve all computer names to their IP addresses. WINS, like NetBIOS, is scheduled to disappear over time.

The SMB protocol manages document sharing among Windows PCs. While WINS, NetBIOS, and DNS locate the computer that contains the document to be shared, SMB displays the folders and makes it possible to select and manipulate documents. SMB is used whenever a disk or folder is shared with another Windows user.

Macintosh (AppleTalk)

Like Novell NetWare and Windows, Macintosh computers are currently undergoing a transition from their legacy software, AppleTalk, to TCP/IP. At the time of this writing, most Macintoshes commonly found in schools still use AppleTalk to communicate with one another, print, and share documents. Ultimately, new Macintoshes (those that use the Macintosh OS X operating system) will make the transition to a system based mostly on TCP/IP. Because AppleTalk will persist for some years in school's older Macintoshes, it is worth a brief discussion.

Within the AppleTalk family, DDP (Datagram Delivery Protocol) describes how data should be packaged and carried across the Internet. ADSP (Apple Data Stream Protocol) ensures that the AppleTalk packets are sent and received without error, and assembled into the proper sequence at both ends of the connection. These protocols (among some others) carry out OSI network (layer 3) and transport (layer 4) services.

Other members of the AppleTalk family—including AFP (AppleTalk Filing Protocol), PAP (Printer Access Protocol), and ASP (AppleTalk Session Protocol)—allow Macintoshes to share documents and printers. These services fulfill the OSI session (layer 5), presentation (layer 6), and application (layer 7) services.

Macintosh OS X retains only a few members of the AppleTalk family—those used for printing and file sharing services. Otherwise, TCP/IP protocols have replaced the older AppleTalk protocols and now provide most of Macintosh OS X's network services.

Technical Information Summary

NETWORK ROUTING AND TRANSPORT PROTOCOLS AND APPLICATION, PRESENTATION, AND SESSION PROTOCOLS

The network routing and transport protocols (layers 3 and 4 in the OSI reference model) organize data into a logical stream, add destination and source addresses to the data, and append some error-checking codes to help ensure that the data arrive safely. The session, presentation, and application protocols (layers 5, 6, and 7 in the OSI reference model) initiate a network connection, prepare the text for transport, and, optionally, encrypt the electronic mail message.

Several common families of protocols (protocol stacks) provide services at OSI layers 3–7.

TCP/IP (Transmission Control Protocol/Internet Protocol) manages Internet communications.

AppleTalk manages communications between most Macintoshes on a local area network.

IPX/SPX (Internet Packet Exchange/Sequenced Packet Exchange) manages communications with older Novell NetWare servers.

Windows protocols manage communications among Windows PCs on a local area network. The Windows protocol stack includes NetBEUI (NetBIOS Extended User Interface), NetBIOS (Network Basic Input/Output System), SMB (Server Message Block), and WINS.

Each client, server, and many peripherals on a network include software that carries out the tasks specified by these protocol stacks. For example, on most networks, Macintosh computers include software for the TCP/IP and AppleTalk protocols, and Windows PCs include software for the TCP/IP and Windows protocols. A single client, server, or peripheral may include software to implement many different protocol stacks simultaneously.

Of all the protocol stacks, TCP/IP is most common. On a TCP/IP network, each computer or other communicating device receives a unique address—for example, 2.38.10.11. Optionally, the computer may also be associated with a host name. For example, one of the Web servers at Education Development Center, Inc., bears the host name **www.edc.org**. The host name includes an even more important name—edc.org, the domain name under which all of the computers on Education Development Center's network reside. When an organization wants to connect to the Internet, it purchases a set of Internet addresses from an Internet service provider (an organization that rents connections to the Internet) and a domain name from an Internet registrar (an organization that licenses unique names for Internet computers).

Other Protocols

Although this chapter is organized to explore the layers of the OSI reference model in sequence, two sets of protocols bears discussing in a different manner: Voice over Internet Protocol (VoIP)/IP telephony, and video.

Voice over Internet Protocol/IP Telephony

Voice over Internet Protocol (VoIP) defines a means for delivering voice signals over Internet Protocol-based networks. IP telephony includes VoIP services but also encompasses new technologies that replace the functions of traditional telephone switches and circuitry. VoIP and IP telephony depend upon many different protocols that work together at all layers of the OSI reference model to provide messaging services that include electronic mail, fax, and voice.

When a network supports IP telephony, it can route telephone calls through the network rather than through the telephone company's infrastructure (thereby eliminating telephone toll charges). Instead of using a PBX (private branch exchange) to manage calls, software is used on servers and client computers. People logged in to the network can place and receive telephone calls from their computers using microphones and special software. The software encodes the voice information and marks it so that it can be distinguished from other network traffic. Once it has been marked, hardware and software components on the network recognize and route the information properly between the calling parties.

A slew of protocols define VoIP and IP telephony services, but none has yet emerged as dominant. H.323 (developed by the International Telecommunications Union) was the first such protocol. Session Initiation Protocol (SIP, developed by the Internet Engineering Task Force, or IETF) improved upon H.323 by providing simpler call set-up mechanisms and better scalability. Media Gateway Control Protocol (MGCP, developed by Telcordia, Level 3, and Cisco) defines the way that media gateways—computers that connect voice components to the IP-based network—should be controlled. The International Telecommunications Union and IETF have collaborated to produce MEGACO, which is intended to supersede MGCP and, additionally, addresses multimedia conferencing (using graphics, for example, during a telephone call).

Video

Schools use video from a variety of sources—from their own libraries, from cable or satellite TV sources, from media distribution sources, or from live events transmitted through interactive television or videoconferencing. Traditionally, these video signals have been distributed over dedicated television circuits separate from the schools' data networks. However, data, voice, and video services are slowly converging so that they are handled on data networks using Internet Protocols.

For interactive television and teleconferencing, the H.323 and related standards describe ways video signals can be carried over IP networks. H.320, an older standard, describes the same functionality on traditional, digital telephone lines (such as ISDN). Each of the two standards enables synchronous, two-way communication among any devices that also adhere to the standard. The two standards also support sharing data in real time—for example, collaboratively writing a document (this capability is described by the protocol T.120). H.320 and H.323 can also communicate with each other using equipment such as gateways that are configured to translate between the two protocols.

H.323 and H.320, however, require very different hardware, and each protocol has different strengths and weaknesses. H.320 teleconferencing usually requires large, expensive equipment and telecommunications lines that provide dedicated, high-speed, two-way communications. In contrast, H.323 equipment can be small and much less expensive; it can also operate from any Ethernet connection. However, H.323 equipment shares the local area network with other applications; because it requires considerable bandwidth, its performance can be adversely affected by—or adversely affect—other network activity. To address this difficulty, data networks that carry video signals also implement quality of service (QoS)—their switches and routers demarcate video data and make sure these data receive priority over other traffic.

Video requires considerable bandwidth. Broadcast-quality television delivers 30 frames per second (fps); to achieve a frame rate of 20–22 fps—adequate if not seamless—a network needs to transmit 384–512 Kbps in both directions (384 Kbps x 2 = 768 Kbps). When a network cannot deliver this bandwidth, the video appears jerky and distracting. Less bandwidth is used if the video equipment uses compression or other special capabilities, if the number of frames per second being transmitted is reduced, or if the size of the video window on each participant's screen is reduced (although the last two alternatives may produce distracting results). Most systems retain acceptable audio quality even if the video degrades.

Although video delivery over IP networks does not yet work seamlessly, video services will likely move onto IP networks in the future. In planning for this eventuality, Ethernet networks should be capable of supporting 100 Mbps service (100BaseTX), leased line capabilities should be upgraded if possible, switches and routers that support H.323 and quality of service protocols should be installed, and desktop computers should be upgraded to the fastest possible speed.

For additional information, read the *eSchoolNews Special Report: Distance Education: Collapsing the Walls of the Traditional Classroom,* **www.eschoolnews.com/showstory. cfm?ArticleID=330**.

Protocols in Action

When two computers communicate, how do they marshal all these technologies to get the job done? To address this question, consider the following examples of computers communicating on a typical school local area network. This school network includes Macintosh computers and Windows PCs that are a couple of years old, a Windows NT 4.0 server, and a connection to the Internet.

From the point of view of protocols, here is what the network looks like: The Macintosh and Windows PCs were delivered from the manufacturer with an Ethernet network interface and the software necessary to manage it. They also included, as part of their standard configuration, the software that creates and manages network services for their particular protocol stacks. In the case of Macintosh, these protocols include AppleTalk and TCP/IP. For the Windows PCs, they include protocols such as NetBEUI and SMB. All this software is invisible to the end user; it works behind the scenes with electronic mail software, a Web browser, or other programs whenever these programs need to send or retrieve information. (Some of this behind-the-scenes software can be configured through Control Panels that adjust their behavior. The Macintoshes, for example, include AppleTalk and TCP/IP Control Panels, allowing users to see or change some of the Macintosh's network settings. Likewise, Windows users can manipulate the settings in the Network Control Panel.)

Sharing Electronic Mail between a Windows PC and a Macintosh

Sam (on Macintosh) and Jose (on Windows) want to exchange electronic mail. When Sam sends his message, electronic mail software calls upon the Macintosh's TCP/IP software (which implements rules defined in the TCP/IP protocol stack) to break the message into small, transportable sections called packets, to look up the Internet Protocol (IP) address of Jose's mailbox, and to send the message. In turn, the TCP/IP software calls upon Ethernet to place the message on the cable. At Jose's Windows PC, the reverse sequence occurs. His Ethernet software retrieves the message and hands it to his TCP/IP software to be reassembled; his TCP/IP software then passes the information along to his electronic mail program.

Sharing Documents on Similar Computers

Suppose that Sam and Maria, who both use Macintosh computers, want to see folders, copy, and change each other's documents. Maria adjusts her Macintosh's file sharing settings to assign a username and password for Sam, and to grant him access to the folder containing the documents he wants to see. (The actual details of setting up file sharing vary with different versions of the Macintosh operating system.) Sam then opens the Chooser on his Macintosh, clicks the AppleShare icon, and selects Maria's Macintosh from the list. After entering the username and password that Maria has given him, he sees the folder with the documents he needs.

Behind the scenes, the AppleTalk protocols on Sam's Macintosh communicate with those on Maria's to manage the login, folder, and document exchanges (the upper layers of the OSI reference model). They call upon Ethernet protocols to transmit the information they need for this management between the two computers (the lower layers of the OSI reference model). Software on both computers implements the same rules—the AppleTalk and Ethernet protocols. This sets up the exchange of information so that it can be successful.

If Sam and Maria both used Windows PCs, the procedure would be quite similar. Maria would grant Sam access. Sam would open Network Neighborhood (instead of the Chooser), select Maria's computer, and then enter the password she assigned. Behind the scenes, Windows protocols (instead of AppleTalk) would handle login, folder, and document exchanges. Ethernet protocols would still handle the data transmission.

Sharing Documents between a Windows PC and a Macintosh

What happens if a Macintosh wants to share a folder with a Windows PC? There are three possible ways to accomplish this task:

> The Macintosh owner can copy her folder onto the Windows NT 4.0 server, where the Windows PC owner can retrieve it. This occurs in part because the Windows NT 4.0 server has been configured with software that implements both AppleTalk and SMB protocols; in effect, the Windows server speaks AppleTalk to its Macintosh clients and SMB to its Windows clients.

> The Macintosh user might send the documents to the Windows PC user by electronic mail. In this case, the documents are not directly accessible between computers; instead they are packaged and sent using software that follows TCP/IP and Ethernet rules (protocols).

> If the Macintosh and Windows PC users want to share the folder directly from one computer to the other, things become a bit more complicated. To achieve folder sharing across different platforms (i.e., between Windows and Macintosh), the Windows PC must be capable of understanding AppleTalk, or the Macintosh must be capable of understanding Windows protocols. To enable a Windows PC to understand AppleTalk, install PC MACLAN (**www.miramar.com**) on the Windows PC. (PC MACLAN implements AppleTalk protocols on Windows PCs.) Macintosh computers can be made to understand Windows protocols by installing a program such as Dave (**www.thursby.com**).

The complexity of sharing information does not end when one computer accesses the other computer's documents. As many computer users know from weary experience, documents are often received that cannot be opened or used. Using the document requires one additional level of cooperation: The two computers must have common application software. They may both need to have, for example, compatible versions of Microsoft Word to exchange their word processing documents.

Recent computer operating systems interoperate more easily than those described here. Macintosh OS X Server, for example, allows sharing of documents among Windows, Macintosh, and UNIX clients with no additional software.

Technical Information Summary

PROTOCOLS IN ACTION

For two computers to communicate, they must use the same protocols. For example, for two Windows PCs to exchange electronic mail across the Internet, they must both use software that implements TCP/IP protocols. Likewise, one way for a Macintosh computer to save documents on a Windows NT 4.0 server involves installing software to implement AppleTalk protocols on the server.

Most computers include software that implements (puts into service) the rules described by more than one set of protocols. For example, Macintosh computers include software that implements AppleTalk, TCP/IP, and Ethernet protocols. These different software packages are active at the same time, each handling different kinds of tasks.

Network managers must define the tasks for which the network is intended, and then ensure that the network includes all the hardware and software necessary to implement the protocols to accomplish these tasks.

3.

Traffic Regulators

NETWORK INTERFACES, HUBS, SWITCHES, BRIDGES, ROUTERS, AND FIREWALLS

A network manager is like a city planner responsible for identifying and defining a city's resources—for example, public areas that sustain lots of traffic (computer laboratories), individual homes (teachers' desktop or laptop computers), large public gathering places (accounting and student systems), billboards (Web servers), telephone services (electronic mail systems), and so forth. A manager also decides where to locate these resources and the capacity of the roads leading to them. Just like a city's transportation system, computer networks contain small routes for areas with low traffic, large routes with traffic lights for areas of moderate traffic, and high-speed arteries with limited access for areas conveying long-distance, high-density traffic.

Network interfaces, hubs, bridges, switches, routers, and firewalls work together to create different kinds of network roadways.

Network interfaces, hubs, bridges, switches, routers, and firewalls are important for:

MANAGING NETWORK SPEED. These devices regulate the speed at which network information travels. Individual computers can be interconnected (like the spokes of a bicycle wheel) through the use of a device known as a hub. Depending on the speed of the hub, the computers may operate at 10 Mbps (relatively low) or 100 Mbps (moderate) or 1,000 Mbps (very high). Network interfaces, bridges, switches, routers, and firewalls offer the same speed options. (The actual speed at which network computers operate depends not only on hubs but also on all the other interconnecting devices in the path—network interfaces, routers, and so forth.)

MANAGING THE ROUTES FOR TRAFFIC. Devices known as routers suggest the most efficient route for network traffic to travel to its destination. These devices manage the flow of traffic, opening, closing, or directing it to specific streets as the need arises. Devices known as switches open circuits or connections directly between two communicating computers and keep other computers from interfering with the connection. Switches minimize contention by rotating connections among each pair of communicating computers. This makes for very efficient use of network roadways.

PROTECTING SENSITIVE INFORMATION. These devices help protect sensitive information. Routers and firewalls look at every bit of network information and decide whether to permit or deny it from reaching specific parts of a network.

Network Interfaces

A network interface is a device that connects a client computer, server, printer or other component to a network. In this respect, a network interface is like the driveway that connects individual homes to the streets they are located on. Network interfaces are also referred to as NICs (network interface cards) or adapters, or sometimes just cards. Most often, a network interface consists of a small electronic circuit board (the card) that is inserted into a slot inside a computer or printer. Alternatively, some computers, printers, or other devices include network interfaces as part of their main circuit boards (motherboards). In either case, the network interface provides two important services—it physically connects a computer to a network, and it converts information on a computer to and from signals for a network.

The network interface connects a computer to a network through a small receptacle called a port (sometimes called a jack). For wired networks, the network cable is inserted into this port. For wireless networks, the port includes a transmitter/receiver that sends/receives radio signals. Besides providing a physical connection to a network, network interfaces also convert information into signals of the appropriate shape and at the proper transmission speed.

All network interfaces must conform to a common physical and data link layer protocol for their signals to be compatible (and therefore to exchange information successfully). For example, on a 10BaseT Ethernet network, all of the computers, printers, and servers must contain 10BaseT Ethernet network interfaces. Likewise, all devices on a 100BaseTX Ethernet network must contain 100BaseTX Ethernet network interfaces. Some network interfaces accommodate more than one physical or data link protocol. 10/100 network interfaces can understand both 10BaseT and 100BaseTX protocols. They are useful for networks that are being upgraded from 10BaseT (10 Mbps transmission rate) to 100BaseTX (100 Mbps) or in networks for which the hardware in each computer or connecting device is being gradually changed over time. (Most 10/100 network interfaces automatically sense the appropriate speed they need to use.)

The network interface works closely with special software called drivers—software modules that control the network interface. Drivers are installed along with the network interface. They are usually available

> ❯ on the hard disk as part of the computer's standard software (operating system),

> ❯ on the operating system (Macintosh OS or Windows) master disks, or

> ❯ delivered by the manufacturer of the network interface by a CD-ROM or floppy disk or through their Web site.

The network interface usually includes instructions for installing both the interface and the drivers.

Each network interface is associated with a unique address called its media access control (MAC) address. (The term MAC address is technically the correct one to use, but many people use the phrase Ethernet address instead.) The MAC address helps route information within a local area network and is used by interconnecting devices such as switches and bridges. The exact role of network interfaces with regard to MAC addresses varies a bit among different networks. On Ethernet networks, each network interface receives a unique MAC address when it is manufactured. When the network interface is installed into a slot or onto the motherboard of a computer or printer, the interface's MAC address becomes the address for the computer or printer. Other types of networks use a more complex address-ing scheme that assigns each computer a MAC address dynamically when it connects to the network. In any case, assigning the MAC address is an important task executed by the net-work interface.

The MAC address is just one of several network addresses assigned to each network com-puter, server, or peripheral. Another network address is the device's internetwork address—its Internet Protocol (IP) address when sending information through the Internet or its IPX address if sending information between Novell NetWare servers. The MAC address is used to locate the next stop for the information within each network segment (small area of the network) through which it passes on its journey. The IP address is used to plan the overall route the information takes. Network connecting devices such as bridges and switches that route information within a network segment use the MAC address. Other connecting devices such as routers that send information between network segments use the IP address.

Technical Information Summary

NETWORK INTERFACES

Network interfaces connect clients, servers, and peripherals to the network. Most network interfaces consist of a small circuit board that is inserted into one of the computer's internal slots. Alternatively, modern computers sometimes include the network interface as part of their main circuit boards (motherboards).

Each network interface is associated with a unique address called its media access control address (sometimes referred to as the Ethernet address on Ethernet networks). The MAC address helps route information within a local area network and is used by connecting devices such as switches and bridges.

The MAC address is just one of several network addresses assigned to each networked client, server, or peripheral. Another network address is the device's internetwork address—its Internet Protocol address when it travels on the Internet. This address helps route information between networks. Every networked device maintains multiple, simultaneous network addresses that are used for different communication routes.

Practical Advice

PURCHASE CONSIDERATIONS FOR NETWORK INTERFACES

Consider the following guidelines when purchasing a network interface:

> Make sure that the network interfaces on all computers are compatible with the appropriate physical and data link protocol (e.g., when running a 100BaseTX Ethernet network, all network interfaces must also use this protocol).

> When installing a network interface card, make sure that it is compatible with the slot into which it will be inserted. Slots provide places on a computer's main circuit board (motherboard) where circuit boards can be inserted that add functionality (network interface cards, modems, and so forth). Before ordering a network interface card, check the computer to determine whether it has available slots, and then check the motherboard manual to ascertain the slot type.

> ❯ Purchase network interface cards from a known manufacturer with a proven track record of good customer support. Many managers used network interface cards from 3Com or Intel. Make sure the manufacturer provides a competitive warranty.

> ❯ Macintosh computers usually come with network interfaces as part of their main circuit boards. Some Windows PCs, however, still require a network interface card.

Hubs

On 10BaseT and 100BaseTX Ethernet networks larger than two computers, each computer or printer (or other networked device) is likely to be connected to a hub. The hub is a small box that gathers the signals from each individual device—computer, server, or printer—optionally amplifies each signal, and then sends the signal out to all other connected devices. Amplification helps to ensure that devices on the network receive reliable information. Hubs are also referred to as concentrators or repeaters. They come in various sizes, the most common being 12 port or 24 port (meaning they can connect to 12 or 24 computers/printers/hubs).

A simple 10BaseT or 100BaseTX Ethernet network may consist of a few dozen individual computers, printers, or servers connected to a single hub. In a more complex network, many hubs can be interconnected. The number of connections is limited by the ability of network servers to accommodate simultaneous users. Distance and repeater limitations imposed by the 10BaseT or 100BaseTX protocols also determine the size of a particular network.

All of the clients, servers, and peripherals connected to a hub (or to a set of interconnected hubs) share the same bandwidth (data delivery capacity). In Figure 3.1, arrows show that information sent from Laptop D eventually reaches all computers on the network, even though the information is addressed to only one of them (perhaps to the server).

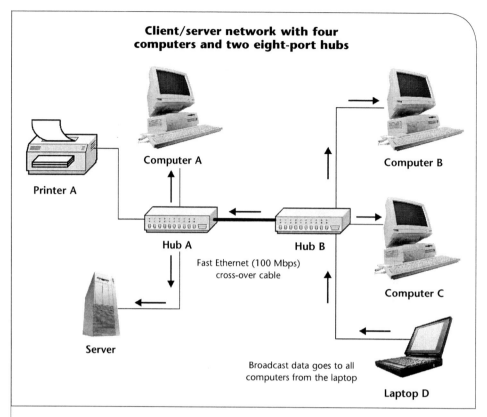

FIGURE 3.1

Technically, computers connected by hubs form a single collision domain—an area of an Ethernet network in which data sent to or from a device may potentially collide with the data from other devices. As more clients, servers, and peripherals are added to a collision domain, the performance of a network is degraded as the number of collisions increases. Performance can be improved by isolating network traffic into many smaller collision domains.

Unfortunately, hubs cannot divide a network in this fashion; they simply repeat every signal to all connected devices. Instead, switches, bridges, or routers can be used to divide networks into multiple collision domains. Each switch port, bridge port, or router port forms a new collision domain. Devices connected to a single port still share the network bandwidth, but are protected from the interfering signals of devices on other ports.

The optimal number of computers, printers, or servers in a collision domain varies greatly from one network to another and depends somewhat on whether a network carries voice, video, and graphical information. Some network managers believe that networks should be divided into smaller collision domains when collisions routinely exceed 10%; when utilization exceeds 80%; or when clients, servers, or peripherals have difficulty connecting to or retrieving information from the network. It is common for networks to run at 60–70% utilization before upgrades become necessary. (Keep in mind that approximately 30% of a network's bandwidth is already used for administrative housekeeping tasks.)

Like network interfaces, hubs must be compatible with the physical and data link protocol being used. Most hubs understand more than one physical and data link protocol, and 10/100 hubs (accommodating both 10BaseT and 100BaseTX networks) are common.

Hubs are referred to as layer 1 devices because they work at OSI layer 1 (the physical protocol layer that manages signal strength and propagation) directly with the network signal itself and not the data within the signal. In most modern networks, switches are replacing hubs. Switches provide the same basic services as hubs, but they also improve network performance in ways that hubs cannot.

Technical Information Summary

HUBS

A hub connects individual devices on an Ethernet network so that they can communicate with one another. The hub operates by gathering the signals from individual network devices, optionally amplifying the signals, and then sending them on to all other connected devices. If a network includes more than two clients, servers, or peripherals, they are likely to be connected to a hub or a switch.

Dozens of clients, peripherals, and servers can be connected through hubs; however, network performance may degrade if too many devices try to communicate within one area of the network. Performance is improved by adding switches, bridges, or routers to the network. Each switch port, bridge port, or router port regulates traffic so that devices on the port are protected from the interfering signals of devices on other ports.

Most hubs operate by examining incoming or outgoing signals for information at OSI layer 1, the physical layer. Switches are replacing hubs on most networks because they improve network performance in ways that hubs cannot.

PURCHASE CONSIDERATIONS FOR HUBS

Consider the following guidelines when purchasing hubs:

> Like network interfaces, hubs must be compatible with the network's physical and data link layer protocols. Some hubs, called multiprotocol hubs, can accommodate more than one physical and data link layer protocol. Make sure that the manufacturer certifies that they conform to other IEEE standards for performance. A multiprotocol hub should automatically sense which protocol is being used on each port. Autosensing hubs enable any part of the network to be connected to any hub port.

> Make sure that a hub includes an AUI port (connector). (AUI is an abbreviation for attachment unit interface.) AUI ports are intended to connect with a kind of cabling referred to as a thick coaxial cable (like that used for cable TV). While this cable is no longer used frequently for Ethernet networks, AUI ports are versatile in the sense that they can be fitted with adapters to connect to many different kinds of cable (for example, thin coaxial cable or fiber).

> Make sure that a hub includes a crossover port. Unlike regular hub ports, which connect hubs to clients, servers, or peripherals, a crossover port connects one hub to another. To understand this distinction, consider how network devices use the Ethernet cable to send and receive information:

> > All devices on 10BaseT or 100BaseTX Ethernet networks send their information over one particular pair of wires within the cable. This particular pair of wires is called the transmit pair. Similarly, all devices receive information from a different pair of wires, called the receive pair. The wiring standard that was selected when the network was installed specifies the location of each pair of wires within the cable.

> > When regular ports on hubs receive incoming information, they transfer it from the transmit pair of the sending device to the receive pair of the destination device. (If there were no hub, the receiving computer would get its signal on the transmit pair of wires—and would become very confused!) Crossover ports work in a different manner than regular ports. When crossover ports on hubs receive information, they simply pass it on without transferring it between transmit and receive pairs. By refraining from any change of pairs, crossover ports ensure that the next hub on the connection receives the original information intact, just as if the information came directly from a computer and not from an intervening hub.

Some modern hubs include one or more ports that toggle between regular and crossover modes (either manually or by autosensing the appropriate mode). Use these ports for regular connections to client computers or for connections to other hubs.

> Some hubs can be stacked or connected in sequence (daisy-chained). Stackable hubs look like one giant hub to the network. The Ethernet restriction on the number of hubs that can be traversed in a single network does not apply to stacked hubs.

> Purchase hubs from a known manufacturer with a proven track record of good customer support. Make sure the manufacturer provides a competitive warranty. Install hubs in a room that is cool and free of dust. Plug hubs into an uninterruptible power supply (UPS) to ensure that they receive clean power.

Switches

Switch Overview

Like a hub, an Ethernet switch is a device that gathers the signals from other devices that are connected to it and then regenerates a new copy of each signal. Switches, however, are more powerful than hubs and can substantially increase a network's performance. Switches can be divided into two groups. The first group, known as OSI layer 2 switches, are older and less capable but very simple to operate. The second group, known as OSI layer 3 switches, provides many additional network performance and management improvements.

The capacity of a switch is measured by the amount of data that can be processed by its backplane, the main circuit board into which the switch's component parts are plugged. If a switch has 12 ports that each process data at 100 Mbps, then under full duplex operation (transmitting and receiving information on each port simultaneously) the switch's backplane must process 2.4 Gbps of activity (12 ports x 100Mbps x 2 directions). Nonblocking switches accept packets even if their destination port is busy; the switch queues the incoming information until the appropriate port is free.

OSI layer 2 switches appeared in the early 1990s, and they bring benefits in environments where people communicate routinely with the same groups of colleagues in a relatively small local area. Modern networks have very different configurations. With the advent of Web-based intranets and centralized information systems (student record systems, financial systems, integrated learning or interactive curriculum systems) sometimes in different buildings, most people spend a good deal of time accessing information outside their local area. OSI layer 2 switches do not help much with this type of network.

A typical OSI layer 2 switch has one device connected to each of its ports (openings). The connected device may be a client, server, peripheral, hub, another switch, or router. The switch operates by learning the MAC addresses (Ethernet addresses) of all connected devices and associating each address with one of its ports. When a switch receives an incoming signal, it creates a temporary circuit between the port of the sender and the port of the receiver. (To understand the benefits of this temporary circuit, imagine a 12-way intersection without stop signs. The switch operates like a police officer who allows each vehicle in turn a moment to cross the intersection without interference from other traffic. The total traffic crossing the intersection within any given unit of time is greater than if all vehicles try to cross the intersection without assistance.)

Benefits

Switches offer the following benefits:

> The circuit allows the sender and receiver momentarily to exchange information without intrusion from other devices on the network. Each pair of communicating devices utilizes the full bandwidth (data carrying capacity) of the network instead of sharing that bandwidth, as they do in Ethernet network segments connected by hubs. In other words, each switch port defines a collision domain containing only two devices (the switch and the client computer) and thereby helps provide maximum performance for Ethernet networks.

> The circuit ensures that information travels directly between the communicating computers. This behavior differs markedly from nonswitched Ethernet networks. In nonswitched networks, data from a transmitting computer is sent by the nearest hub to all connected devices (not just to the recipient) and therefore congests parts of the network needlessly.

> Ethernet cable includes at least two pairs of copper wire—one to transmit data and the other to receive it. Within the switched circuit, sending and receiving can occur simultaneously on the two pairs if the switch and the network interfaces in the client computer are so configured. Termed full duplex communications, receiving and sending data simultaneously doubles the throughput of the network for that circuit. (Only some switches and some network interfaces are capable of full duplex communications.)

Besides creating circuits between sender and receiver, switches have other capabilities to manage and prioritize network traffic that hubs lack. Consider multicast traffic—network information that is sent from one computer to a designated group of other computers. Multicasting occurs, for example, when a concert, conference, or other event transmits audio or video of its proceedings over the Internet. In a multicast, intelligent switches send the audio or video information to ports connected to participating clients while sparing other ports from having to carry it.

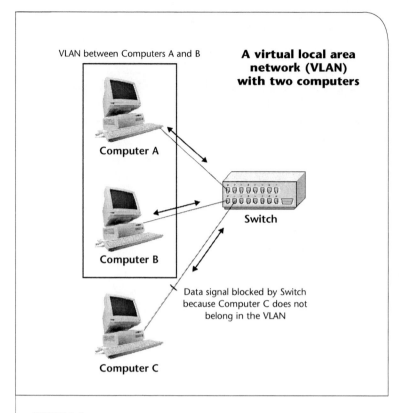

VLAN between Computers A and B

A virtual local area network (VLAN) with two computers

Computer A

Computer B

Switch

Computer C

Data signal blocked by Switch because Computer C does not belong in the VLAN

FIGURE 3.2

Virtual Local Area Networks

Switches can also give priority to network traffic based on a switch port or on a logical structure called a virtual local area network (VLAN). A VLAN consists of a group of client computers, servers, or peripherals located in any physical area of the network whose network communications are not transmitted outside their group unless the communications are specifically addressed to outside recipients.

To understand how VLANs work, it is necessary to know something about network traffic known as broadcasts. Network broadcasts are data sent to all computers for management purposes. As an example of broadcasts, a local area network using the TCP/IP protocol might receive a packet intended for one of its computers. Typically, the packet contains the recipient's IP address, but it does not include the one piece of information needed for delivery—the recipient's MAC address.

It is the responsibility of the local area network to map the IP address to the MAC address. To do this, the switch checks its list of known IP-MAC address mappings and, if it cannot find a match, it broadcasts a query to all devices on its network to locate the computer with the requested IP address. The intended recipient returns its MAC address. As another example of broadcasts, devices such as servers make their presence known by broadcasting their addresses and available services. Broadcast traffic on some networks is quite extensive. Switches that implement VLANs ensure that broadcast traffic remains within the VLAN instead of traveling to other parts of the network (as it normally would).

In the previous diagram, Computers A and B reside on one VLAN and Computer C on another. When Computers A and B send information, that information stays within their VLAN even if it is broadcast. Computer C receives information from the VLAN of Computers A and B only if it is directly addressed to Computer C.

VLANs are created by configuring switches to divide the devices connected to them into groups. Different identifiers should be used to define the group (VLAN) to which any device on a network should belong. The simplest identifier is the switch port. For example, a switch can be configured so that any devices connected to its ports 1–4 compose one VLAN and devices connected to ports 5–8 compose another. Grouping devices by port in this manner makes VLAN configuration simple, but it makes managing the network in general more difficult. If users move from one area of the network to another, each old and new switch port must be reconfigured so that the person's VLAN group membership does not change. For this reason, many network managers use identifiers other than ports. As an alternative to defining groups by port, provide the switch with the MAC address of each connected device and the VLAN it is assigned to. (When using OSI layer 3 switches, specify that different layer 3 protocols such as IP or IPX each get their own VLAN, or that the switch combine certain IP addresses into a VLAN.)

In any case, when a computer on the network starts up and connects to the switch, the switch can determine the appropriate VLAN by examining signals from the connecting device and then examining the configuration list. This type of dynamic VLAN addressing, which can adapt as users move from one place to another on the network, is more complex to set up than port addressing but easier to maintain over time.

Within your school district, separate VLANs can be created for administrative offices, students, library computers, or any other individuals who communicate frequently with each other. The members of the VLAN need not be located physically near each other and can in fact be connected to different switches.

Benefits

VLANs offer the following advantages:

> Managing broadcast traffic was once the province of routers. Now that switches have this capability, network managers can replace some routers with switches. Using switches instead of routers brings an immediate performance benefit to the network. Routers, which analyze traffic patterns and route information using software, add a delay called latency to the travel of each packet they examine. Switches, on the other hand, analyze traffic patterns in hardware (and often use much simpler—if less powerful—algorithms for analysis) and do not add latency.

> When confining broadcast traffic within each VLAN, network performance is improved by reducing traffic on the network at large.

> Because devices on one VLAN do not receive broadcasts from others, they do not know about the existence of servers and other resources on those VLANs. VLANs therefore provide a security benefit by hiding the resources on one VLAN from users on another. (Students on one VLAN, for example, are unable to see an administrative server located on another VLAN.)

> To confine network traffic among a group of computers on an older network, the computers would have to be physically located close together. Using VLANs, the same benefits are achieved even if users are housed in different physical locations. Users can also change physical locations and retain their VLAN membership.

VLAN implementations differ from vendor to vendor. For this reason, it is important to purchase switches from a single vendor.

Technical Information Summary

SWITCHES

Like a hub, a switch connects individual devices on an Ethernet network so that they can communicate with one another. A switch also has an additional capability: It momentarily connects the sending and receiving devices so that they can use the entire bandwidth of the network without interference. If used properly, switches can improve the performance of a network by reducing network interference. In most cases, a switch provides better performance at nearly the same price as a hub.

Switches can be divided into two groups. The first group, called OSI layer 2 switches, are older and less capable but very simple to operate; the second group, called OSI layer 3 switches, provide many additional network performance and management improvements. OSI layer 2 switches, obviously, examine network information at the data link layer (layer 2) of the OSI reference model.

OSI layer 2 switches have several benefits: (1) they provide each pair of communicating devices with a fast connection; (2) they keep information between the sender and the receiver so that it does not enter other portions of the network; (3) optionally, they can provide full duplex communications, in which sending and receiving occur simultaneously (doubling the effective throughput of the network); and (4) they can create virtual local area networks.

VLANs are groups of clients, servers, and peripherals whose communications do not traverse the network outside the VLAN unless they are specifically addressed to a recipient there. Keeping communications within the VLAN relieves the larger network of carrying the traffic and therefore improves general network performance. VLANs also make it easier to manage networks as people move from one physical location to another, and they provide additional security.

OSI layer 2 switches are particularly useful if a network is congested and traffic pools in predetermined local areas. If a network is not congested or if its traffic patterns do not create pools of local traffic, then use routers or OSI layer 3 switches to improve network performance.

Practical Advice

PURCHASE CONSIDERATIONS FOR SWITCHES

Apply the following criteria when purchasing and installing a switch:

> Switches must be compatible with the network's physical and data link layer protocols (e.g., when running a 100BaseTX Ethernet network, purchase a switch that handles 100BaseTX traffic).

> Some switches can accommodate more than one physical or data link layer protocol. Modern switches accommodate both 10BaseT and 100BaseTX protocols. It is wise to purchase a switch with at least one 100BaseTX port, because it can be interconnected to switches through their high-speed ports to improve network performance (even if the remainder of the network uses 10BaseT).

> If purchasing a switch that accommodates more than one protocol (for example, 10BaseT and 100BaseTX), make sure that it automatically senses which protocol is being used on each port. Autosensing switches ensure that any part of the network can connect to any switch port. Likewise, switches should autosense whether sender and receiver are using full duplex communications. (Older switches required that each segment of the network be attached to a port compatible with its physical and data link layer protocol and communications mode. Keeping the segments and ports straight presented a management headache.)

> Purchase switches from a known manufacturer with a proven track record of good customer support. For large switches, make sure the manufacturer provides a competitive warranty. Purchase a spare if a switch is located in a critical portion of a network.

> Install switches in a room that is cool and free of dust, if possible. Additionally, plug switches into an uninterruptible power supply (UPS) to ensure that they receive clean power.

> If implementing VLANs, be sure to purchase switches from a single vendor. VLAN implementations are proprietary, and switches from different vendors may not interoperate properly.

Bridges

Bridges are devices that connect two or more local area networks, or two or more segments of the same network, and filter information so that network traffic intended for one portion of the network does not congest the rest of the network. If a network includes both 10BaseT Ethernet and a lab using Apple's AirPort wireless connections, a bridge (known as an AirPort base station) can connect these two networks so that they can share information while still keeping traffic on one network from unnecessarily congesting the other.

Bridges may consist either of stand-alone hardware devices or of software running on a client or server. Like switches, bridges learn the MAC addresses of all connected clients, servers, and peripherals, and associate each address with a bridge port (network connection). Unlike switches, however, bridges often have many devices (all the devices in a wireless Macintosh lab, for example) connected to each port. When a bridge receives an incoming signal, it opens and reads its destination MAC address. If the port that will receive the signal is different from the port connected to the sender, then the bridge forwards the signal to the destination port. If the port that will receive the signal is the same as the port connected to the sender, the bridge drops the signal. (Since the bridge is by definition at the end of the network segment, the receiving computer presumably intercepted a copy of the signal on its way to the bridge.) If the bridge cannot determine which port is associated with a destination address, it passes the signal along to all ports.

Traditional bridges connect a single workgroup to another workgroup. More recently, however, manufacturers have produced multiport bridges. Multiport bridges allow network managers to connect more than two network segments to each other. Networks can be reconfigured or expanded simply by replacing one network interface card inside the multiport bridge with another (for example, adding a Token Ring interface to a multiport Ethernet bridge).

Like switches, bridges generally inspect information at the data link layer within a network signal—information such as the Ethernet (MAC) destination address. They do not attend to network routing or transport protocol information such as that carried within the TCP/IP, IPX/SPX, or AppleTalk portions of the signal. However, bridges can be fitted with custom filters that enable them to read this information—including network routing or transport source address, packet size, or type of protocol—and reject or forward information based on it. Custom filters enable network managers to isolate particular areas of the network and control which protocols enter or leave each area. For example, custom filters might allow requests from the Internet (outside the school district) not to enter certain areas of the network.

Because bridges (like switches) generally depend upon MAC addresses, they are referred to as layer 2 devices in the context of the OSI model. Bridges must be compatible with the physical network and its data link protocols.

Technical Information Summary

BRIDGES

A bridge connects two or more networks, or segments of the same network. These networks may use different physical and data link protocols. Most bridges operate by examining incoming or outgoing signals for information at OSI layer 2, the data link layer.

Bridges filter and reduce network traffic. They examine each set of data, transmitting only appropriate data to each connected segment. (Hubs broadcast all information to each connected computer, whether or not that computer is the intended recipient. Switches, like bridges, only transmit data intended for the other network.)

Bridges are relatively simple and efficient traffic regulators. However, in most circumstances, they have been replaced by less expensive or more powerful switches and routers.

Practical Advice

PURCHASE CONSIDERATIONS FOR BRIDGES

Consider the following guidelines when purchasing a bridge:

> Before deciding on a purchase, work with technical staff, manufacturers, and consultants to identify all possible configuration options. Each device brings a unique set of strengths and weaknesses to the job.

> Make sure that the bridge is compatible with the network's physical and data link protocols.

> Purchase bridges from a known manufacturer with a proven track record of good customer support. Make sure the manufacturer provides a competitive warranty.

> Install bridges in a room that is cool and free of dust, if possible. Additionally, plug large bridges into an uninterruptible power supply (UPS) to ensure that they receive clean power.

Routers

Routers are devices whose primary purpose is to connect two or more networks and to filter network signals so that only desired information travels between them. Routers are often used to regulate the flow of information between school networks and the Internet. They can inspect a good deal more information than bridges or OSI layer 2 switches, and therefore they can regulate network traffic more precisely. Routers also have another important capability. They are aware of many possible paths across the network and can choose the best one for each data packet to travel.

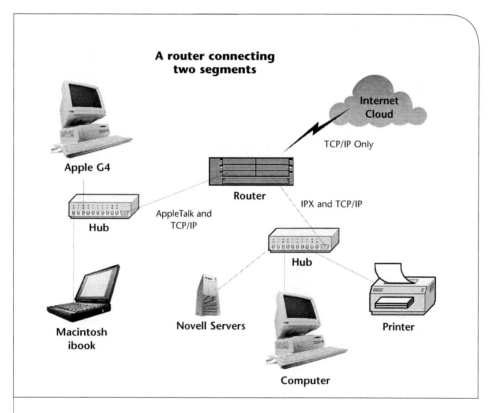

FIGURE 3.3

The local area network shown in the diagram includes two segments, one containing Macintosh computers and the other containing a Novell NetWare server and associated computers and printers. Each segment supports TCP/IP protocols. The Macintosh segment also runs AppleTalk to provide its document- and printer-sharing services; the Novell segments runs IPX/SPX. The router makes the link to the Internet, filtering the protocols so that only the particular protocol necessary for Internet communications—TCP/IP—reaches that connection.

Routers operate primarily by examining incoming data for its network routing and transport information—for example, information carried within the TCP/IP, IPX/SPX, or AppleTalk portions of the network signal. This information includes the source and destination network routing addresses. (Remember that every client, server, and peripheral on the network maintains multiple addresses—for example, both a MAC address and an IP address. The two addresses are used for different purposes. Among other things, on TCP/IP networks the IP address provides information on which routers base traffic management decisions.) Most routers also include the same functionality as bridges. That is, they can inspect the data link layer portions of the network signals for such information as the Ethernet destination address.

A router determines whether it knows how to forward the data packet toward its destination based on its compilation of complex, internal tables of network information. If the router has been configured with sufficient information to know which of its ports is en route to the destination, it transmits the packet. If the router has not been so configured, it typically drops the packet. Dropping unknown packets is an important method of eliminating restricted, wayward, or damaged information. Bridges and OSI layer 2 switches lack this capability (they forward unknown packets to all ports), and the information they forward often creates extra network traffic.

Routers can be programmed to prevent information from being sent to or received from certain networks or computers based on all or part of their network routing addresses. If sensitive student records are located on a server, for example, a router can filter packets headed for the server so that only authorized personnel can connect to it.

In addition to monitoring source and destination addresses, routers can permit or deny traffic to specified ports. (This type of port is different from the physical port, or opening, that connects a computer to a network or other external device.) A port in this context is a number encoded within a network packet that designates the software program that should process the packet upon its arrival. When electronic mail is sent, data packets are addressed to the recipient's electronic mail server. Software that implements the Simple Mail Transfer Protocol (SMTP) waits for this data, looking for packets marked with a particular port—port 25—and processes them. (This software is called a mail daemon or service.) When a Web browser requests a Web page, it marks its request for port 80 on the Web server; an HTTP daemon implementing HyperText Transfer Protocol (HTTP) waits for packets marked with port 80 and provides the Web pages they request. A program called TELNET directs its information to the telnet daemon on port 23 of a Web server.

Because these ports are quite predictable, routers can be instructed to allow or deny traffic associated with them. For example, a router could be configured to deny any traffic to or from TELNET port 23 if TELNET services are not wanted on a particular network (a common choice). Defining this set of rules for a router—the addresses and ports that it makes available—is known as configuring its access list. Denying access to traffic associated with a particular port is commonly referred to as blocking the port.

Routers also determine possible routes to the destination network and then choose the one that promises to be the fastest. As network traffic patterns change during a day, routers can adjust their route recommendations. (Very large routers route information across the Internet in this manner.) Routers must learn formidable amounts of information about a network to inspect network routing and data link layer portions of network packets and to route information along the best path to its destination. Unfortunately, routers do not learn this information without human intervention.

Installing routers is a complex task that involves configuring each network interface that connects the router to a network. First, enable support for the desired protocols on each network interface. Then, for each interface-protocol combination, either define routing tables or configure support for an automatic routing table update protocol. If user-defined enterprisewide policies for security (rules that define the kinds of information that must be restricted) are in place, define the filters that implement these policies for each interface-protocol combination. Needless to say, make sure that qualified personnel (either a network integrator or staff member) install and manage network routers.

Because routers play a key role in connecting networks, they can cause significant problems if they malfunction. As part of an overall network plan, consider how to deal with the potential (and seemingly inevitable) failure of key routers. Many sites include redundant connections—additional routers and network cable connections—configured to take over if one router or connection fails. The use of monitoring software (often provided by router vendors) is also a viable option. It can detect communication difficulties, provide an inventory of router configurations and changes, and help install router updates.

Because routers depend upon network routing addresses, they are referred to as layer 3 devices (layer 3 manages routing information between different networks) in the context of the OSI model.

Recently, network design experts have begun to replace routers with OSI layer 3 switches. These intelligent switches have many of the same capabilities as routers but are faster, cheaper, and easier to configure.

Technical Information Summary

ROUTERS

Routers connect two or more networks, as do bridges, but are much more powerful. Routers can filter traffic so that only authorized personnel can enter restricted areas, and so that unauthorized personnel cannot enter a network. They can permit or deny network communications with a particular Web site. Routers can recommend the best route for information to travel. As network traffic changes during the day, routers can redirect information to take less congested routes.

Schools connected to the Internet will most likely use a router to make the connection. Routers ensure that local area network traffic remains local, while passing on to the Internet all electronic mail, Web surfing connections, and other requests for Internet resources. They quickly become critical components of a network.

Routers are generally expensive to purchase and difficult to configure and maintain. If they fail, network services will be significantly impaired. When planning a network, consider how to deal with the possible failure of key routers. Many sites include redundant connections—additional routers and network cable connections—configured to take over if one router or connection fails. Routers operate by examining incoming or outgoing signals for information at OSI layer 3, the network address layer.

Recently, network designers have begun to replace routers with OSI layer 3 switches that have similar capabilities.

Practical Advice

PURCHASE CONSIDERATIONS FOR ROUTERS

Consider the following points when purchasing and installing a router:

> Purchase all routers from a single manufacturer. Purchasing routers from a single manufacturer ensures that the software used to configure, monitor, and manage the routers will be compatible across devices. (It is easier to learn about and operate devices that are relatively uniform because they come from a single source.)

> Make sure that the router manufacturer offers a wide variety of routers, including models for local area networks, dial-up connections, and wide area networks, so that the same manufacturer can continue to provide equipment and service the network as it expands.

> Consult with network administrators to see which router manufacturers they have used and liked.

> Before purchasing a router, determine the kind of cables to which the router must connect (twisted pair copper, fiber) as well as the protocols (for example, IP, IPX, AppleTalk) that will travel across the router to and from each network segment. (The router must accommodate all the cable types and must be compatible with all the protocols.)

> Routers allow traffic to cross from one segment to another only if it is specifically intended for a network address there. This traffic management helps to ensure that each segment of the network is used efficiently (only carries the necessary traffic). When arranging routers, try to keep traffic flows in mind. Put people who exchange information with each other frequently on one side of the router.

> Work with the router manufacturer or network integrator to choose the appropriate router model. Be sure that the manufacturer or integrator understands not only the protocols in use, but also the kind of information that will be exchanged on the attached network, the kinds of information that may be restricted, the number of users, and their patterns of usage.

> Routers are often expensive. They should be easily upgradeable so that they do not have to be replaced as the network incorporates additional kinds of cable or protocols. Ask the manufacturer about the particular expansion modules they offer, and what is involved in purchasing, installing, and maintaining them.

> Some managers plan to deliver multimedia applications over the network. These applications require a fast, steady stream of data to function properly. To deliver this increased performance, Internet standards organizations have defined options that allow routers and other network devices to reserve the bandwidth they need on the Internet. These bandwidth management techniques include quality of service (QoS) and class of service (CoS). Class of service provides a way for routers to group specific types of network traffic (for example, electronic mail or voice) and give each a different priority on the network. Quality of service creates similar classes and also ensures that certain classes always get the throughput that they need. Not all routers are capable of providing CoS or QoS services. Make sure that the routers are adequate for multimedia delivery.

> Price should not be the determining factor in purchasing a router. Routers, like servers, are key components of a network. It is far better to purchase durable equipment from premium manufacturers than to suffer equipment breakdowns or malfunctions.

Switches Revisited:
OSI Layer 3 Switches

Routers provide critical network services, but they do so at a cost. The calculations they make to determine the best path for traffic or to prevent unauthorized traffic from entering and leaving a network use up considerable processing assets. These calculations are performed by software running on small general-purpose computer chips not unlike those in the average personal computer. As networks get larger and traffic increases, the processing time (latency) introduced by routers creates performance bottlenecks.

OSI layer 3 switches combine the speed and simplicity of OSI layer 2 switches with most of the intelligence and power of routers. Using hardware called application-specific integrated circuits (ASICs) or digital signal processing (DSPs), OSI layer 3 switches inspect information at OSI layers 3 and higher, choose the best route, and filter information as necessary to prevent unauthorized packets from entering or leaving the network—and do so at wire speed (they match the speed of the incoming network without introducing latency, or delays).

There are as yet few standards governing the operations of OSI layer 3 switches. Given two important routing tasks—building a table of routes and forwarding packets along the best route to their destination—OSI layer 3 switches fall into several categories:

CUT-THROUGH SWITCHES. Cut-through switches calculate routing options for the first network packet (only) in a stream of incoming data. Succeeding packets, identified as part of the same stream, are switched at layer 2 (meaning that the switch looks at the MAC address and forwards the packet to the appropriate port without applying any fancy routing algorithms). Because layer 2 calculations are simpler and faster than those based on layer 3, these succeeding packets pass quickly through the switch. Cut-through switches do not exchange routing table information to help each other learn about routes through the network. They depend on a router or a route server for a list of available routes. Most cut-through switches support IP; a few support other network (layer 3) protocols such as IPX. Cut-through switches from different vendors are generally incompatible.

PACKET-BY-PACKET ROUTING SWITCHES. Packet-by-packet routing switches examine every packet the same way that traditional routers do. They inspect the internetwork address information (e.g., IP address) within the network packet and then choose the best route based on standard router protocols (OPSF, RIP, EIGRP, and so forth). Unlike routers, however, they perform these calculations using dedicated hardware (ASIC or DSP chips) at much greater speeds. Packet-routing switches share routing tables like routers do, and because they use standard protocols they can interoperate with equipment from other vendors. Packet-by-packet routing switches may also include other traditional router services—the ability to prevent unauthorized traffic from entering or leaving a network, contain broadcast traffic, and handle multicasts. They are more expensive than cut-through switches, but are preferable because of their flexibility and interoperability.

The discussion so far has involved OSI layer 3 information—particularly a packet's internetwork destination address. Multilayer switches can also make use of information at OSI layer

4, which includes the type of software that sent the information. Layer 4 switches can give priority to packets from these applications to ensure uninterrupted service. This is particularly useful for voice and video (which are sensitive to delays on the network). Layer 4 switches can also track the amount of data sent over the network by each application. Layer 4 switches include layer 2 and 3 capabilities.

While OSI layer 3 and multilayer switches surpass routers in terms of speed, many OSI layer 3 and multilayer switches have fewer ports than routers. Most support only TCP/IP networks (rather than IPX/SPX or AppleTalk networks, for example). OSI layer 3 and multilayer switches do not support as many different types of wide area network connections as routers do; and since WAN connections operate at speeds considerably slower than LANs, the switch's speed is wasted in this context. Most routers perform bridging functions, such as translating Token Ring (a type of local area network) to Ethernet frames, that multilayer switches cannot.

Practical Advice

PURCHASE CONSIDERATIONS FOR OSI LAYER 3 SWITCHES

Consider the following points when deciding when and where to deploy OSI layer 3 switches:

> Make sure that the switches routing the protocols (OSPF, EIGRP, RIP, etc.) are compatible with those used by other routers on the network. If they are not compatible, the switches and routers will not be able to exchange routing table information.

> Make sure that the switches' layer 3 protocols (IP, IPX, AppleTalk) accommodate all those in use on the network.

> Ask the vendor to describe the full set of tasks required to set up the switches and maintain them over time.

> Determine the packet-per-second speed of the switch and estimate whether it accommodates the current and future estimated throughput required by the network.

> Require that the vendor allow for interoperability testing of the switch on the network before the purchase. Insist on guarantees of stated performance for speed and latency.

> Look for advanced features such as support for VLANs, traffic prioritization for voice and video (CoS, QoS), multicast, and security.

Comparing Hubs, Switches, Bridges, and Routers

While hubs, switches, bridges, and routers overlap a great deal with regard to regulating network traffic, each of these devices possesses different strengths and weaknesses:

> Hubs, switches, bridges, and routers can interconnect two different kinds of networks such as 10BaseT Ethernet and 100BaseTX.

> Hubs (unlike switches, bridges, and routers) do not filter traffic between the two networks. Hubs simply pass all incoming information onto every device connected to each of its ports.

> Switches have the unique capability to utilize the full bandwidth (data carrying capacity) of the network by opening an unobstructed path between two communicating devices. Switches (and hubs) do not always accommodate the variety of protocols and cabling types that bridges or routers can.

> Routers are much more expensive and much more difficult to install and manage than hubs, switches, or bridges, but they can filter and route information quite precisely. They choose the best path to any destination, and they prevent unauthorized information from entering or leaving a network.

> OSI layer 3 switches can perform most of the functions of routers. They are easier to manage, cheaper to use, and faster than routers.

> While OSI layer 3 switches surpass routers in terms of speed, routers still have a place in the network. Many OSI layer 3 switches have fewer ports than routers and support fewer types of local area and wide area networks.

Security Systems

Even though school systems use a combination of security systems, no network is entirely secure. Security systems protect networks from unwanted intrusions or limit the Internet resources that network users can access. They include firewalls, proxy servers, intrusion detection systems, Internet filters, encryption, and authentication systems. Each provides a different kind of security.

All hardware devices and software programs have vulnerabilities, and there are many inventive people who practice exploiting them with some regularity. Network managers can only minimize potential security risks by identifying the types of threats they will be defending against, the hardware and software they will need to combat these threats, and the strategies they will use in employing their security-enhancing tools.

The job of protecting a network begins with a set of management decisions that identify school network assets and risks. Management must define the most valuable assets at the greatest risk at one end of a scale and the least valuable assets at lowest risk at the other; only then can the network manager deploy security resources proportionately.

Consider the following questions:

> What are the different types of hardware, software, and data on the network involved with sensitive information (student grades, attendance, payroll, student projects, Web pages, etc.)?

> Which of these resources are critical to school operations and which are less critical?

> Who are the different groups of people on the network (teachers, administrators, students, community members) and which sets of data should each be able to access? What kind of access should they have (ability to read but not write, ability to delete, weekend or 24-hour access, etc.)?

> Given these assets and types of access, what types of threats are posed? What actions need to be taken to counter each of these threats?

Once these policies have been defined, the next step is to consider the technical differences among different security devices and devise strategies for deploying them on the network. Keep in mind that the devices discussed in this section form only one aspect of network security. Physical security (placing servers in locked rooms), passwords, and enforcing appropriate use play important roles as well.

What Are You Protecting Against?

Computer crimes and security breaches include (but are not limited to)

> theft or destruction of computer equipment or data;

> guessing or otherwise learning another user's password and then using the password to access sensitive information (sometimes called social engineering);

> distributing self-replicating code such as viruses, Trojan horses, worms;

> unauthorized use of hardware or software to examine the data passing through cables or wireless connections on a network (also called sniffing);

> hijacking Internet Protocol (IP) packets so that information intended for one person is delivered to another, or impersonating another person using the telephone or electronic mail;

> logging in to systems without authorization and optionally installing software or data (for example, replacing a school's Web pages with unauthorized versions);

> unauthorized scanning of equipment on a network to determine its type and capabilities; scans make it easier to attack the network (also called probing); and

> flooding an organization's Web servers with so many requests that they become overwhelmed and do not permit further connections (denial of service attacks).

Statistics indicate that these threats are rising in number, increasing in severity, and becoming easier to perpetrate. Today, intruders can attack thousands of systems simultaneously and can hide their presence on a network with some sophistication. Many of the scripts that wreak this havoc are freely available on the Internet and require little knowledge to deploy. Network personnel must keep themselves aware of new security threats and apply security software updates and other changes to the network as a matter of routine.

Statistics also indicate that the majority of threats to an organization's information come from within. While this section primarily discusses strategies for protecting information from external intruders, remember that internal threats need to be addressed as well.

Firewalls and Proxy Servers

A firewall is a device that prevents unauthorized electronic access from outside a network. The term firewall is generic and includes many different kinds of protective hardware devices and software. Routers operate as firewalls when they control access based on source or destination address. Software firewalls are simple to install and usually found on home computers (especially those with a high-speed connection such as DSL or cable modem). Software firewalls can also be installed on network servers. Yet another firewall consists of a stand-alone box (a computer with no keyboard or monitor) that watches all the traffic on a network.

All firewalls have one thing in common: They guard networks by examining information inside every network packet. Based on a list of restrictions provided by the user, firewalls allow or prevent packets from traveling over a network.

To understand how firewalls restrict network traffic, consider what happens when an electronic mail message is sent and received. The sender's electronic mail program addresses a series of packets containing the contents of the electronic mail message to the recipient's electronic mail server. Each packet is marked with a port number—in this case, 25—so that the mail daemon (or service) on the recipient's electronic mail server can recognize and process the packet when it arrives. The first such packet that arrives contains a greeting called a SYN (synchronize) packet. The recipient's electronic mail server replies with an ACK (acknowledgment). After that, the sender's electronic mail server transmits packets containing the contents of the electronic mail message, and the recipient's electronic mail server acknowledges the receipt of each packet as it arrives.

Firewalls contain interfaces (connections) that can be independently configured to implement specific rules known as access lists. For example, one rule might allow incoming traffic to port 80 (HTTP or Web browsing) while a subsequent rule might deny login requests to port 23 (inbound TELNET requests). Other rules might allow outbound traffic to any port so long as it is a SYN packet (initiating a conversation) or block outbound traffic on port 80 to specific Internet Protocol addresses. (Some school districts block the addresses of external proxy servers that students use mischievously to bypass the school's own proxy or Internet filtering services.)

As a firewall intercepts each packet, it matches the packet against each of the instructions in its access list. If a packet gets to the end of the list without a match, it is dropped. In other words, access lists define every action that is permissible on a network. If an action is not defined, it is not permissible.

Sophisticated firewalls include additional capabilities such as inspecting incoming packets for application-specific information (for example, malicious Java program code), determining whether packets are part of a legitimate ongoing conversation, protecting against specific threats such as denial of service attacks, and providing virtual private network services.

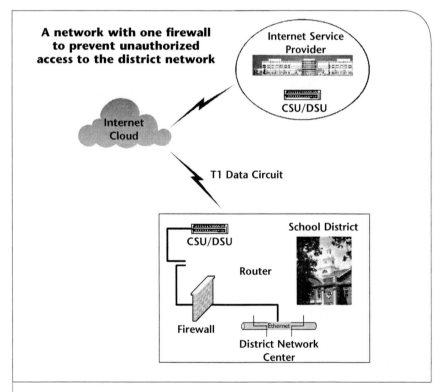

FIGURE 3.4

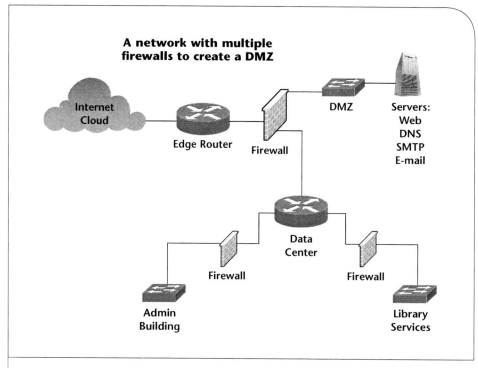

A network with multiple firewalls to create a DMZ

Internet Cloud — Edge Router — Firewall — DMZ — Servers: Web DNS SMTP E-mail

Data Center — Firewall — Admin Building — Firewall — Library Services

FIGURE 3.5

Firewall Placement and DMZs

The simplest kind of protection scheme involves placing a single firewall at the point where a network connects to the Internet. Diagram 3.4 depicts this scheme. Such a firewall can be configured to intercept any traffic coming from the Internet and to prevent it from reaching sensitive information kept on administrative or curriculum systems residing on the school's internal local area network. On the other hand, information that must be accessible from the Internet—such as the school's electronic mail, Web, FTP, proxy, and other public servers—must reside on the external side of the firewall. This configuration is simple and inexpensive, but it leaves the school's public servers vulnerable, as they are not protected by the firewall.

Installing more than one firewall improves security. Multiple firewall configurations are referred to as demilitarized zones (DMZs). A demilitarized zone is a section of a network that can be accessed both from inside and outside the district (e.g., through the Internet). Typically, a DMZ contains electronic mail, Web, and other public servers. It is distinguished from more private portions of a network, such as administrative or library systems.

To create a demilitarized zone, use (at least) two firewalls, and provide the outermost firewall with two interfaces (connections). The first interface connects to the electronic mail, Web, and other public servers and is configured to allow just enough access for inquiries from the Internet or from your internal network. The second interface connects to one or more internal firewalls.

These internal firewalls impose a high level of security by preventing access from the Internet except as part of an ongoing conversation (initiated from within the internal network as when a student requests a Web page). Within the private area of a network, additional firewalls can be installed to provide more protection for especially sensitive information.

Other Types of Firewalls

On large networks, firewalls generally consist of hardware devices that can be divided into three major categories: packet-screening firewalls, proxy servers, and stateful inspection proxies.

PACKET-SCREENING FIREWALLS. Packet-screening firewalls operate by examining incoming or outgoing signals for information at OSI layer 3, the layer responsible for internetwork addresses. For example, this firewall can examine incoming packets for their Internet (IP) source address (the place where the information originated); it can deny access to the network if the packet comes from a network or networks, or Web sites identified as unauthorized. Alternatively, this firewall can examine information leaving the network for its Internet (IP) destination address (where the information is being sent); it can deny access if users on the network attempt to connect to unauthorized sites.

Besides source and destination addresses, packet-screening firewalls can filter information based on the type of protocol used, the port number to which it is addressed, or content type (e.g., JavaScript, Java). These firewalls can control information that enters a local area network from the Internet, that leaves the network for the Internet, or that travels from one part of the network to another.

Packet-screening firewalls have traditionally been implemented as add-on services within routers. On the positive side, they are among the fastest firewalls (because they examine a more restricted set of information than other firewalls). On the negative side, they examine only network address and related information and therefore cannot implement complex security rules (e.g., allowing the use of Web browsers but restricting the use of video). Finally, packet-screening firewalls leave networks vulnerable to malicious information in portions of the packet that they do not examine—the data area beyond the packet's network address information.

PROXY SERVERS. Proxy servers (also known as application-layer gateways) operate by examining incoming or outgoing packets not only for their source or destination addresses but also for information carried within the data area (as opposed to the address area) of each network packet. The data area contains information written by the application program that created the packet (e.g., Web browser, FTP, or TELNET program). Because the proxy server knows how to examine this application-specific portion of the packet, it can permit or restrict the behavior of individual programs. A proxy server, for example, can be configured to allow Web browsing but deny requests from FTP programs such as Fetch or WS_FTP. Alternatively, a proxy server can permit FTP requests, but only if they read (not write) information. Moreover, proxy servers can deny Web browsers access to unauthorized Web sites.

A separate (software) proxy server must be configured for each application that needs to be screened. Proxy server (hardware) will include multiple proxy servers (multiple software programs) if the network intends to screen information based on the common Internet applications—Web browsers, FTP, TELNET, and electronic mail. Not all application programs can be proxied, however. Accounting systems or integrated learning systems may not be able to be proxied. For application programs without proxies, protect the program through packet-screening firewalls or other network services (i.e., passwords).

Besides filtering information, proxy servers perform several other useful tasks. First, proxies hide an organization's Internet (IP) addresses so that intruders cannot easily determine the addresses to attack. Second, proxies cache information. That is, if the proxy grants permission to retrieve an Internet resource such as a Web page, it also keeps a local copy. The next time that someone on the network wants to browse the same page, the proxy server checks its local cache. If the page is there, the proxy server checks with the originating Web server to see if the page has been updated. If not, the proxy delivers its local copy of the Web page to the user. This sequence of events is much faster than retrieving the Web page from the original server. Some school districts estimate that 40–70% of the Web pages requested by students and teachers can be drawn from cache, so the performance improvement provided by proxy servers can be substantial.

The specialized server that runs the proxy software is made as secure as possible by hardening it (i.e., stripping it of all but essential services). Regular network servers may offer login and file- and printer-sharing capabilities, but secure proxy servers (and, for that matter, secure firewall servers) allow none of these services; all unnecessary or risk-prone services are turned off. Additionally, operating system updates, which often contain security fixes, are applied religiously. Stripping the proxy server (or firewall server) of extraneous services and keeping its operating system updated hinders unauthorized access.

When using a proxy server, configure each client computer's Web browser software so that it connects to the proxy. This can be done manually by entering two pieces of information in the browser's preferences: the proxy server's IP address and the port the proxy uses for incoming requests. (The proxy server's instruction manual will suggest a port to use.) A proxy server's port is often a large number such as 8080. The well-known IP ports should not be used for proxy services because they are already in use for standard IP services.

New technologies allow automatic configuration of client browsers. Depending on how the network is set up, students may be able to circumvent the district's proxy server by typing the address of one of the thousands of other proxy servers on the Internet into their Web browsers (instead of using the district's proxy server). Work with the network manager to determine how to address this difficulty.

STATEFUL INSPECTION PROXIES. Stateful inspection proxies examine the data within network packets to ensure that they are a legitimate part of a sensible, ongoing conversation between computers rather than a random insertion of (possibly malicious) material. Stateful inspection proxies fall midway between packet filters and proxy servers in terms of security, but they offer relative ease of use and high performance. Like proxy servers, stateful inspection servers hide internal Internet (IP) addresses from would-be intruders.

Closing Points about Firewalls

Purchasing, configuring, and maintaining firewalls require great skill and considerable effort. It is important to rely on experienced staff and consultants to guide these actions. Given that caveat, here are some things to keep in mind when purchasing a firewall:

> Most managers recommend implementing a combination of packet screening and proxy or stateful inspection services. Packet-screening firewalls are the fastest performers but the least powerful in terms of the kinds of information they can filter. Proxy and stateful inspection servers are more powerful but slower.

> Firewalls (packet screening, proxy, and stateful inspection) provide traffic logs and summary reports that should be monitored frequently. Logs indicate the people and resources that are active on a network, and they often provide the first indications of suspicious behavior.

> If a network includes many firewalls or firewalls that are located at some distance, make sure they can be configured remotely (that is, from a central location). Be sure to ask about the hardware and setup time required for the remote management software.

> Avoid mixing security products from different manufacturers. Incompatibilities among equipment can cause unnecessary work and security risks.

> Test network security frequently by purchasing and using network discovery tools, similar to those used by intruders. These tools map each network firewall or server and indicate the services being run. Using these tools, locate and then update old or improperly configured software.

> Tight security policies will slow down a firewall's operation because of the quantity of information it must examine to enforce complex rules. These same policies will increase the cost of the network accordingly.

Intrusion Detection Systems

Intrusion detection systems (IDSs) identify suspicious network behavior from within or outside a network (based on a set of user-defined rules) and then take automatic action to terminate the behavior and trace its source. Intrusion detection systems also monitor and analyze user activity, audit system configuration vulnerabilities, and assess the integrity of critical system files.

Suspicious network behavior can arise in several ways—by the exploitation of security holes especially in operating system software. Java applets or other programs downloaded from the Internet can be used to commandeer a user's system. Password cracking (electronically guessing passwords) can also lead to serious breaches in network security. Intrusion detection software can be configured to recognize these difficulties and correct them automatically.

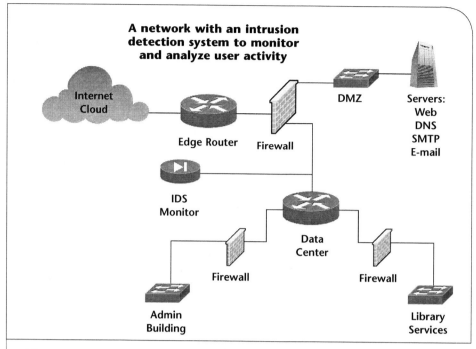

A network with an intrusion detection system to monitor and analyze user activity

Internet Cloud

Edge Router

Firewall

DMZ

Servers:
Web
DNS
SMTP
E-mail

IDS Monitor

Data Center

Firewall

Firewall

Admin Building

Library Services

FIGURE 3.6

Forms of IDS

HOST-BASED SYSTEMS. Host-based intrusion detection systems consist of software installed on servers that contain sensitive information. The IDS monitors event, security, and system logs for any suspicious changes; examines each packet entering the server for suspicious connection or login attempts; watches specific system files to see whether they have changed in worrisome ways; and performs other security checks. When the IDS detects suspicious activity, it sends a notice to a local screen or to a central system that collects security information.

Host-based systems are economical when dealing with a small number of servers and require little additional hardware, but they protect only the server they are installed on and do not scale well when a network expands.

NETWORK-BASED SYSTEMS. Network-based intrusion detection systems consist of two parts: hardware sensors that match each network packet against known signatures and a management console. Some vendors sell separate sensors and consoles, while others combine them into a single package.

Network-based intrusion detection systems should be placed at the perimeter (edge) of a network—the point where the network connects to the Internet or commercial carrier. They can also be placed in a central area containing many servers or on a network backbone (the network segment that interconnects all the subnets on a network). Some intrusion detection systems permit the distribution of many sensors on a network and coordinate their findings using a primary IDS.

Network-based intrusion detection systems can be difficult to implement on a switched network because there are no obvious places where IDS sensors can capture lots of information. Network sensors may be foiled by encrypted packets, which they may be unable to read. (Host-based systems do not encounter this difficulty because the host decrypts packets before the IDS sees them.) Network-based systems impose a flat (if substantial) cost regardless of the number of servers, but they involve proprietary hardware and cannot monitor specific files.

Intrusion detection systems detect suspicious behavior by using signature analysis and statistical profiling.

SIGNATURE ANALYSIS. Signature analysis examines network packets to see whether they indicate a pattern of suspicious activity. Examples of suspicious activity include sending inquiry packets to determine the IP addresses in use (an activity called pinging); the insertion of fraudulent information into network packets; searching for exploitable user accounts; searching for known weaknesses in software; and the overloading of servers by sending spurious information.

STATISTICAL PROFILING. Statistical profiling creates a picture of the average behavior of users after they have logged on to any server and reports any deviations from that average. The profile includes the user's IP address, connection times, protocols and software packages in use, amount of data transferred, and other characteristics.

No matter which type of system is being used, when the IDS notices unauthorized behavior it can notify the network manager, terminate the connection, and record the suspicious information.

To maximize the benefit of installing a network IDS, have a clearly articulated response plan in place before suffering an intrusion. Include the names of people (and agencies) to be notified in case of attack as well as the name of the person(s) with final authority to shut the system down if necessary. Detail the conditions under which an intruder's connection will be terminated or left open in order to gain intelligence as to the intruder's identity and methodology.

Intrusion detection systems by themselves do not provide complete network security; they merely complement other forms of security, including firewalls, encryption, and authentication. An IDS can be expensive and ineffective if not managed properly. No matter how well managed they are, they can still be foiled by hackers. For this reason, some managers question their usefulness. Balance the cost to purchase and manage an IDS against the potential cost of lost data and productivity to determine the right strategy for a particular network.

Internet Filters

Federal legislation now requires that schools receiving discounted rates for telecommunication services through E-rate, or funding through the Library Services & Technology Act or Title III, must adopt an Internet safety policy that is likely to include Internet filtering.

Internet filtering software prevents students from accessing unauthorized Web sites.

A canonical filtering software package checks every request for a Web page from a school or district against a set of restrictions that the vendor, and in some cases a school or district, has established. The set of restrictions may take several different forms. Some packages block all sites containing "objectionable" keywords. Unfortunately, such keyword scans result in blocking many sites that deserve to be seen; classic objections to keyword-based systems cite the inappropriate censorship of Web sites about breast cancer or chicken breasts simply because they contain the word "breast."

For other filtering software packages, the manufacturer compiles lists of Web sites (a database) that should be excluded from or included in a school's access. Most companies do not publish their list of the blocked sites—in part to guard proprietary data and in part to discourage those with malicious intent from circumventing the filter's protection—but most will provide guidelines about their selection criteria.

When selecting such a filtering system, match the system guidelines against those of the surrounding community. If the filtering system depends on a database, ask the vendor how the database is compiled, how frequently it is updated, and the procedures needed to apply the vendor's updates to the network.

No matter how the sites are blocked, filtering software should allow authorized users to override the system to access sites when necessary. Ideally, the software should accommodate students at different levels of sophistication by establishing unique filtering rules for different groups (e.g., teachers and students) or even individual users. It should also allow users to establish their own lists of permissible or restricted sites.

Filtering software can be configured to recognize sites marked with content ratings such as those provided by the Platform for Internet Content Selection (PICS). PICS ratings consist of a set of labels that Web site creators voluntarily select to describe their contents, register with a labeling service, and then embed on each page of the site. Web visitors can determine the level of violence, sexuality, or other characteristics of the site based on these labels. Unfortunately, relatively few Web site authors have chosen to implement them.

Filtering software can be installed on individual client computers or on centralized servers, often a proxy server. The latter solution is significantly easier to manage, scalable, and faster to operate. Placing filtering software on a proxy server simply adds a new layer of intelligence to the proxy. The filtering software validates each Web site destination for appropriate content and the proxy continues to check for valid Internet addresses, protocols, or types of applications.

Filtering services can be purchased directly from some Internet service providers (ISPs). (The cost is included as part of the monthly fee.) Alternatively, application service providers (ASPs) rent software such as Internet filters for a fee. Application service providers manage the servers and all the associated software. While this simplifies local management, it increases the overall cost of maintaining the network and removes some local control over software and configuration decisions.

In addition to software that checks Web sites, there is also filtering software available to check electronic mail. Electronic mail filters examine incoming and outbound mail against rules similar to those used for Web servers. Working in conjunction with the electronic mail server (often through the SMTP), electronic mail filters flag suspect messages and then take appropriate action as specified by the network. These actions can include reporting the incident to a system administrator, alerting the sender or recipient, blocking the transmission, or adding a disclaimer (among many possibilities).

Remote Access Security

Portions of a network (such as its Web server) are intended to allow external access from outside. Other resources, such as personal documents or student records, should be accessible only to specified individuals or groups of people. When authorized users work from remote locations, they can generally use two different methods to reach restricted areas of a network. They can either connect directly to network modems through public telephone lines, or they can connect to their Internet service provider and create a connection known as a virtual private network.

To create support for modem connections, usually one or more servers fitted with modems are installed to receive the calls. The telephone company installs a line to each modem, and authorized users connect to the network by configuring their personal computers and modems to dial the network modems. Some remote access servers are stand-alone devices designed especially to manage telephone calls; others are servers fitted with modems and software to manage them. Some remote access servers handle only inbound calls while others handle both inbound and outbound communications (the latter can be used for computer faxing). The telephone lines may be either plain old telephone service (POTS) lines or Integrated Services Digital Network (ISDN) lines.

Various security services are available for both the modems and the remote access servers. Modems with caller ID capabilities match the caller's telephone number against a list of authorized numbers. Caller ID services are simple to implement, but they are not universally available and, of course, they do not ensure that the person using the registered telephone is the authorized user. They also do not work for people who travel. Alternatively, call back services receive an incoming telephone call during which they request the user's login name and password; they then terminate this original call and dial the user at a previously registered number. Call back services have the same limitations as caller ID services.

Once a remote modem is connected to a network modem, the remote access server gathers information to authenticate the user. This information usually includes a login name and password that the server authenticates against its authorization list, a list provided by the network, or another centralized authentication database.

Remote access servers authenticate usernames in a number of different ways. Under Password Authentication Protocol (PAP), a user's login name and password are transmitted at the beginning of a connection and validated against known names and passwords in an encrypted database. Systems using PAP are often simple, inexpensive, and interoperable among equipment from multiple vendors, but PAP transmits unencrypted passwords and therefore provides only limited security. Systems using Challenge Handshake Authentication Protocol (CHAP) encrypt all communications and reauthenticate users periodically during a connection (thus limiting the period of vulnerability). Like PAP, CHAP systems are inexpensive and interoperable, but CHAP databases are not encrypted and must therefore be protected by other means.

In addition to these server-based authentication schemes, larger systems that provide a centralized authentication database are available. If a network has multiple remote access servers, these larger systems standardize and simplify remote access management (because there is a single source of authentication information instead of many). When a remote access server has authenticated a user, it assigns an IP address, at which point the user can access all the resources he or she is normally allowed to use on the network (e.g., electronic mail, documents, printing, etc).

The best-known systems include Terminal Access Concentrator Access Control Server (TACACS) and Remote Authentication Dial-In User Service (RADIUS). Cisco Systems uses a proprietary (and improved) version called TACACS+ in its equipment. RADIUS, a free system developed by Livingston Enterprises, provides a more robust standard that authenticates users, tracks any restrictions applied to their network access, and offers packet filtering (examination of packets like routers do) and accounting services.

Third parties offer solutions that improve upon standard password security. These systems often provide a wallet-sized security card that generates a key; the user must present both a predetermined password and the security card to be authenticated on the network. The key may be generated frequently (say, every minute) and be valid only for that duration, or may consist of an encrypted password that is valid only for a single use.

Some school districts implement several layers of authentication. External users are required to log in to a remote access server and then, if authenticated, to log in again to the network. Only if they complete both logins successfully can they see the network's data and resources.

Redundancy

Over time, a network becomes critical to a district's daily operations. Accordingly, it becomes important to take steps designed to minimize potential network failures. The best way to ensure a network stays up and running is to build redundancy into the system (i.e., having secondary sets of equipment and system software ready to take over if the primary set fails).

Figure 3.7 shows a school's data center. The data center contains two networks that are redundantly linked—Network A and Network B. Network A is the primary network. If any component on Network A becomes disabled, Network B automatically resumes operations.

The data center uses an Asynchronous Transfer Mode (ATM) wide area network running over two fiber optic cables (marked OC-12, designating a speed of 622 Mbps) to connect to the Internet.

Data traffic arriving at the school may come in on either of the OC-12 lines. It travels to the router and the switch connected to the incoming line—Router 1 and Switch 1, or Router 2 and Switch 2. If the traffic arrives at Switch 2, it is routed to Switch 1; this routing ensures that Network A serves as the primary network. From Switch 1, the data traffic travels through Network A on the left side of the diagram and ultimately reaches the server farm.

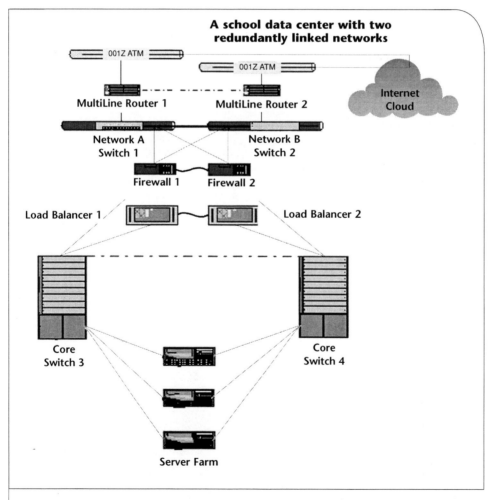

FIGURE 3.7

(i.e., a set of servers that are clustered, or joined, so that if one server fails another server can assume its tasks). As it travels through Network A, the data traffic traverses several switches, a firewall, and a load balancer (a computer that distributes network data to the least busy server).

Data traffic leaving the school travels from the server farm through Network A to the Internet.

If any component on Network A fails, Network B takes over automatically.

> If Router 1 fails, a special protocol called Border Gateway Protocol used by the Internet service provider detects the failure and reroutes traffic to Router 2.

> If any of the switches, firewalls, or load balancers on Network A fail, Router 1 detects the failure and reroutes traffic to Network B. Firewall 2 constantly talks with Firewall 1. If Firewall 1 fails, Firewall 2 alerts the routers that all traffic should now be routed toward Firewall 2. Likewise, Load Balancer 2 checks on Load Balancer 1 and alerts the routers if Load Balancer 1 fails.

> If one of the servers fails, a clustered server steps in. The load balancers automatically redistribute the workload.

Servers are connected to both Networks A and B (servers with dual connections are known as dual-homed). They can receive data from each network, and they return that data along the network from which they arrived.

Additional Forms of Security

Encryption

Encryption is the process of altering information so that it is unintelligible except to the sender and the recipient. Most common systems encrypt information by systematically applying a mathematical algorithm. This algorithm, called a key, comes in two forms—symmetric or asymmetric.

SYMMETRIC KEYS. Systems that use symmetric keys use the same key for encrypting and decrypting data (deciphering it to restore its original form). So long as the key is secret, the traffic is secure. Symmetric key encryption plays a role in the Secure Sockets Layer (SSL) protocol, a set of rules for managing the security of Internet messages and monetary transactions.

ASYMMETRIC KEYS. Asymmetric keys come in pairs known as public and private keys. The keys are issued by Certificate Authorities, agencies whose job is to verify the credentials of applicant organizations. Once an organization is certified, it publishes its public key, and anyone sending data to the organization can encrypt the data using the public key. The organization uses its private key to decrypt the data. Asymmetric keys require more computation than symmetric keys and are suited to small amounts of data. Asymmetric keys also play a role in SSL, which uses asymmetric keys to encrypt the symmetric key that is subsequently used to encrypt information. Asymmetric key encryption is also known as public key encryption.

Key length is measured in bits (on-off signals), and different encryption systems require different lengths to achieve the same security. The longer the key, the harder it is for an unauthorized user to decrypt the data. The asymmetric keys, like those used in Web browsers, commonly range from 40 to 512 bits long, with the latter length deemed quite secure. Symmetric keys, because they use a different mathematical algorithm, need not be as long; in fact, a 64-bit symmetric key achieves about the same level of security as a 512–bit asymmetric key.

Digital Signatures

A digital signature is a means of authenticating the sender and determining that data traffic has arrived intact and free of tampering. Like encryption, digital signatures use public and private keys, but the procedure for using them is somewhat different. In a digital signature exchange, three items are sent: (1) the original (unencrypted) data, (2) a code called a hash—the result of processing the original data through a mathematical formula—which is encrypted using the sender's private key, and (3) the mathematical algorithm itself. The recipient's software uses the sender's public key to decrypt the hash and then uses the same mathematical algorithm on the newly received unencrypted data. If the two hashes match, then the recipient can be sure that the traffic was not tampered with.

Secure Sockets Layer

For particularly sensitive data, Web servers can invoke the Secure Sockets Layer (SSL) protocol. SSL authenticates the server to the client, allows the client to select the mode of encryption, optionally authenticates the client to the server, and then establishes a secure connection. SSL uses both asymmetric (public) key encryption and symmetric key encryption during the connection. In the OSI reference model, SSL operates above TCP (layer 4) and below protocols such as HTTP (layer 7). Originally developed by Netscape, SSL is built into most Web browsers including both Netscape Navigator and Internet Explorer. When connecting to Web pages protected by SSL, the Web server and browser do all the work of authentication and encryption. (The small lock symbol in the lower corner of the Netscape Navigator window indicates that SSL is active.)

Final Comments on Security Systems

Recently some manufacturers have announced all-in-one software packages or suites that include the capabilities of firewalls, proxy servers, intrusion detection systems, remote access, and capabilities for virtual private networks (e.g., Microsoft's Internet Security and Acceleration Server 2000 or Novell's BorderManager).

Security equipment generally protects networks from intruders outside the network. However, statistics indicate that 80% of the damage done to an organization's network assets come from within the organization (theft, malicious destruction, viewing or tampering with restricted data). Big networks can use intrusion detection systems to help address this problem but all networks need other strategies as well, and these strategies should be outlined in an organization's acceptable use policy and security policy.

None of the security systems discussed in this section provides a full measure of protection unless an organization also has a security policy that prioritizes its assets, describes the possible threats to each of them, and outlines the actions to be taken if threats arise. These policies are less technical than political. Since there is an inverse relationship between security and convenience, policies need to be developed by consensus among administrators, teachers, students, and community members. Without a security policy, technical operations personnel are forced to guess at network priorities. This may not be sufficient to protect a school's management when (not if) security breaches occur and data are compromised.

Technical Information Summary

SECURITY SYSTEMS

A firewall is a device that prevents unauthorized electronic access from outside a network. The term firewall is generic, and includes many different kinds of protective hardware and software devices. Routers operate as firewalls when they control access based on source or destination address. Most firewalls operate by controlling access to a network based on information at OSI layer 3, the network-addressing layer, within incoming or outgoing packets.

Firewalls must be placed at one or more strategic points in a network to protect it. In the simplest case, a firewall can be placed at the point where the local area network meets with external services (e.g., an Internet connection). Many school districts install multiple firewalls. One common configuration known as a demilitarized zone places servers containing administrative and curriculum materials on an inner network with a firewall at its entrance; Web, proxy, electronic mail, and other servers that must be accessible from outside the school reside in front of this firewall and behind a second firewall that guards the entrance to the Internet. Demilitarized zones protect inner resources stringently but allow a bit more access to public servers.

Firewalls are divided into three general categories: packet-screening firewalls, proxy servers (or application-layer gateways), and stateful inspection proxies. Packet-screening firewalls examine incoming and outgoing packets for their network address information. They are used to restrict access to specific Web sites or to permit access to a network only from specific Internet sites. Proxy servers (also called application-layer gateways) operate by examining incoming or outgoing packets not only for their source or destination addresses but also for information carried within the data area (as opposed to the address area) of each network packet. The data area contains information written by the application program that created the packet (e.g., a Web browser, FTP, or TELNET program). Because the proxy server knows how to examine this application-specific portion of the packet, it can permit or restrict the behavior of individual programs. Stateful inspection proxies monitor network signals to ensure that they are part of a legitimate ongoing conversation (rather than malicious insertions).

Besides firewalls, other types of security software may also be useful. Intrusion detection systems identify suspicious network behavior based on a user-defined set of rules, and then take automatic action to terminate the behavior and trace its source. Filtering software maintains lists of Web sites that are permitted or restricted for students, and enforces those restrictions. Special-purpose security systems called remote access servers specialize in authenticating users who are accessing a network from outside a school or district. When purchasing large software systems such as student records or electronic mail systems, look for additional security capabilities including encryption, digital signatures recognition, and—especially for Web servers—Secure Sockets Layer software (SSL provides both encryption and authentication).

Building redundancy into a network ensures that critical systems will continue to operate if primary network equipment fails.

Many schools combine one or more of these solutions to create their network security system. Each solution has strengths and weaknesses. When assessing the needs of a network, begin by defining a security policy (e.g., personnel access to specific resources, actions to be taken in case of trouble, etc.). Once the assessment has been completed, work with vendors and technical personnel to ensure that the security solution meets the network's needs.

Travel Operations Centers

OPERATING SYSTEMS AND APPLICATION PROGRAMS

Operating systems (OS) provide the operations centers for the information highway. Operating systems monitor the destinations (clients, servers, or peripherals), highway performance, and traffic regulators, and they provide tools to understand or to change how those components work. Every computer has an operating system—software that determines every detail of how the computer interacts with the user. The operating system starts and shuts down the computer. It controls the way that folders and files look. It provides a way for users to copy and delete items. It also defines how dialog boxes look and operate, and how files are printed. The fundamental role of the operating system is to control every device—keyboard, monitor, disk drive, network interface, and so forth—that is directly connected to the computer and to provide various ways for users to interact with these devices. They provide the foundation upon which application programs operate. Modern operating systems include Windows (95, 98, Me, NT, XP, or 2000), Macintosh OS, and various versions of UNIX.

Application programs are the software packages used to perform most of the work on a computer. Application programs work cooperatively with operating systems, providing options for daily word processing, spreadsheets, and other tasks; operating systems perform behind-the-scenes tasks involving a computer's hardware or network services.

Operating Systems

An application program may offer options to save a document, but it does not carry out the task by itself. Instead, the application calls upon the operating system, and the operating system writes the information to the hard disk. In much the same manner, an application calls upon the operating system to print, send electronic mail, list documents in a folder, and perform some of the work associated with almost all of these activities.

Perhaps the most common operating system is Microsoft's Windows. Within the Windows family, there are Windows 3.11 (Windows for Workgroups), Windows 95, Windows 98, Windows Me (Millennium Edition), and Windows XP Home Edition, the newest member of the Windows family. Windows NT 4.0 and Windows 2000 are powerful operating systems that can be used by individuals but are primarily intended to manage shared resources on a large network and are generally classified as network operating systems.

The most common competitor to the Windows operating systems, of course, is the Macintosh operating system; Macintosh OS 8 and OS 9 run on most modern Macintoshes. Mac OS X (the "X" represents the Roman numeral for 10) officially joined the family in March 2001. Like Windows NT 4.0 or 2000, Macintosh OS X can be used by individuals but it also offers a variant called Macintosh OS X Server meant for large network management.

The UNIX family of operating systems forms another set of competitors to Windows and includes family members Linux (Red Hat), BSD (Berkeley Software Distribution), IRIX (SGI), Solaris (Sun Microsystems), and others. Still other operating systems include VMS (an operating system from Digital Equipment Corporation, now Compaq), OS/2, and OS/400 (IBM). In the world of education, Windows and Macintosh dominate the desktop.

The operating system software on a computer is tightly coupled with its hardware. For example, Windows requires special central processing units (Intel Pentium III or AMD K6, for instance), circuit boards, and other components. The Macintosh operating system requires different central processing units (PowerPC), circuit boards, and components than those used for Windows. Some versions of UNIX run on computers with Intel or compatible processors while other versions require different processors (e.g., Compaq's Alpha microprocessor).

Some software emulators allow foreign operating systems on a computer. VirtualPC is an emulator that allows Windows to run on a Macintosh computer. After installing VirtualPC on a Macintosh, any Windows application program will run on that Macintosh. (VirtualPC runs within the Macintosh operating system, and any Windows software runs within the environment created by VirtualPC.) Emulators are often useful in a situation when a Macintosh user must run a particular Windows-only application program but otherwise does not need Windows. There are drawbacks to using emulators, however. Installing, configuring, and maintaining emulation software is complex, and software running under emulation always runs more slowly than it does on its native hardware.

Operating systems also differ in the format or the manner in which electronic data (the encoded header information, the content, and the closing footer) is represented on disk.

Because of these differences, an operating system on one computer generally cannot read disks formatted on a differing operating system unless it has been fitted with special translation capabilities, usually in the form of translation/conversion software.

> Modern Macintoshes automatically include such special conversion software. This conversion capability is limited, however. Users can often see the names of documents on disk and copy or delete the documents, but they may not be allowed to open or edit the documents.

> Windows PCs cannot read Macintosh disks without installing additional software such as Conversions Plus (**www.dataviz.com**). Conversions Plus allows the user to see the contents of the disk and open and edit its documents.

When purchasing an application program, make sure that it is compatible with the operating system (otherwise the collaboration will fail). For example, a Macintosh lab using Macintosh operating system version 8.1 must use a version of AppleWorks that is compatible with Macintosh operating system 8.1.

Network Operating Systems

Network operating systems (NOS) are a special class of operating system that specializes in managing resources on a network. They make it possible for hundreds or even thousands of people to store their documents in shared folders, select a printer from dozens on their network, or use a shared electronic mail system. While the operating systems found on desktop and laptop computers have some of these capabilities, they normally do not serve as many people as quickly as network operating systems, and they lack many features for managing security, hardware, and services that network operating systems provide. Windows NT 3.51, Windows NT 4.0, Windows 2000, Novell NetWare, Macintosh OS X Server, AppleShare IP, and Linux are common network operating systems. Network servers always run network operating systems instead of standard operating systems.

The distinction between operating systems and network operating systems has been blurred in the last few years because many of the operating systems listed in the previous section also provide shared resources over the network. Most Macintosh computers since the mid-1980s and Windows PCs since the early 1990s have allowed users to share some of their resources. Operating systems generally lack other capabilities necessary to provide network services for hundreds or thousands of people. They may not allow the range of options for protecting documents and folders that network operating systems do, and they often slow to a crawl when moving large amounts of data.

Network operating systems manage the same basic services as operating systems—document storage, printing, the display of information and its input—but they are different in that they are specifically designed to allow large numbers of people to share resources. They provide tools for managing individuals and groups of users by creating separate user and group accounts. Network operating systems also monitor their own performance and operations. Most provide graphs of processor, memory, and disk usage on one or more servers so that users can locate, and perhaps relieve, the burdens on a network. It is common to find traffic analyzers on network operating systems checking for errors in transmissions and generally helping data to flow more smoothly.

The most common network operating systems are Windows NT 4.0 and its successor, Windows 2000; Novell NetWare; Macintosh OS X Server; AppleShare IP; and UNIX (especially the particular implementation of UNIX called Linux). Network operating systems require fast computers with large amounts of disk space and random access memory (RAM). For this reason, network operating systems usually run on servers rather than on client computers. Each network operating system, moreover, requires a specific type of hardware. Windows NT 4.0, Windows 2000, and NetWare all run on computers with processors from Intel and compatibles; Macintosh OS X Server and AppleShare, conversely, runs on Apple's PowerPC-based computers, while Linux runs on both types.

Windows NT 4.0

Windows NT 4.0 appeared in the late 1990s. It has recently been eclipsed by its successor, Windows 2000. Nonetheless, Windows NT 4.0 still forms the core of many networks. It organizes users and servers into domains. A domain is an arbitrary grouping of people, printers, and other network resources usually located in a single physical area of the network. An organization can have one domain or many. (Do not confuse Windows NT 4.0 domains with Internet domains. They are entirely separate and unrelated entities.)

Each domain has a single central database of information called the Security Accounts Manager (SAM) that resides on a special server called a primary domain controller (PDC). The SAM contains information about usernames and passwords, other computers within the domain, the names of groups (e.g., the Math Department) created by the network administrator, and the members of each group. In case the primary domain controller fails, a copy of the SAM is also stored on one or more backup domain controllers (BDC). All changes made to the SAM on the primary domain controller are copied periodically to the backup domain controllers. When users log in to an NT domain, the nearest primary or backup domain controller authenticates their username and password and allows them to log in (access network resources) if they are valid.

Besides primary and backup domain controllers, domains also include resource servers and clients. Users store their documents on and optionally run application software programs from the resource servers.

A Windows NT 4.0 network can be divided into domains according to several different models. For small districts that wish to centralize their network management, the single domain model groups all users, folders, printers, and other resources into one administrative unit. Larger districts may have multiple domains and may choose one of several ways of organizing them.

The master domain model divides the network into a master domain and one or more resource domains, with the master domain tracking all user accounts and the resource domains managing document and print services. Master and resource domains allow the district to distribute responsibility for network privileges. One set of network personnel can control the documents, folders, and printers in each resource domain while the central network administrator retains control of user access for the whole network. Alternatively, larger school districts may create multiple single domains or multiple master domains (domains that are functionally separate from each other).

When multiple domains are present, the domains share information using a series of trust relationships. Trust relationships define the resources on one domain that may be accessed by another. For example, imagine a network with three single domains: Emerson School, Fernald School, and Guilford School. If the Emerson School domain trusts the Fernald School domain, then the network administrator at Emerson School can confer access to its network resources on any members of Fernald's network. Trust relationships are not automatically mutual; Emerson trusts Fernald in our example, but Fernald may not necessarily trust Emerson. Trust relationships are also not transitive; if Emerson trusts Fernald and Fernald trusts Guilford, the network administrator at Emerson cannot grant access to Guilford's users.

On a Windows NT 4.0, Windows 95, or Windows 98, a user profile can store the way that each user's desktop is organized and the application programs available. User profiles are downloaded from the network server to each user's computer (Windows PC) only when the user logs on. This provides a way for teachers and students to move among different computers and still see the same desktop.

User profiles may also be used in conjunction with system policies—a more powerful tool for controlling users' access to their computers. System policies control whether users can access the Start menu's Run command, add items to the Start menu, access the Control Panel and Printers folders, view available drives on the computer, browse to see other computers on the network, and even shut down or reboot the computer. User profiles and system policies provide a starting place for reducing the complexity—and the support costs—associated with desktop computers. Many school districts use other tools as well.

In addition to its domain and desktop security services, Windows NT 4.0 enables Macintosh and Windows clients to share documents and printers; allows people to dial into the network from home or when traveling; enforces security to protect documents, client computers, and other network resources; and provides tools to monitor and optimize network and server performance. Windows NT 4.0 servers can host Web sites, automatically assign Internet Protocol (IP) addresses to clients, provide Domain Name System (DNS) services, and host large databases.

Over time, the Windows NT 4.0 Security Accounts Manager and domain architecture proved cumbersome for organizations with thousands of user accounts. Establishing trust relationships among multiple domains, tracking user rights, and maintaining the reliability and integrity of multiple primary domain controllers proved formidable tasks. Windows NT 4.0 also developed a reputation for instability and for security problems. Windows 2000 has tried to address these difficulties.

Windows 2000

Windows 2000 replaced the unwieldy domain controller and trust systems with a technology called Active Directory. Active Directory provides a single, centralized, networkwide listing of all resources on the network—including users, servers, clients, and printers. Active Directory provides a similar strategy for information to Novell's NetWare Directory Services eDirectory (NDS, available since in the mid-1990s).

Benefits

Termed global directories, Active Directory and NDS yield several benefits:

> Global directories allow users to log in to a network once and see all the other users, and printers and computers for which they are authorized, no matter where on the network those resources reside. If a network currently requires multiple logins for different servers, then global directories may hold significant benefits. (Under older directory schemes, each login connected users to only one domain or server and its particular resources; users sometimes had to log in multiple times to see the network's complete services.)

> Organizations can keep a single list of all their users, servers, and other resources instead of separate, partial lists on different servers. It is therefore easier to avoid duplications and to maintain consistent information about network resources.

> Resources within a school district can be organized according to a logical structure rather than simply by domain. If an Active Directory associates printers with a particular department (no matter where they are physically located), then users can locate all those printers easily instead of hunting through lists of printers attached to different servers. Active Directory's logical structure also provides a simpler way than Windows NT 4.0 to distribute the burdens of network management. It is no longer necessary to create a separate domain, for instance, to assign control of one building's computers and printers to a local administrator.

> Global directories can manage client computers based on their directory entries. They allow software to be installed or removed from a client computer, require that the user store documents on the server rather than the client, or determine which buttons and other options are available on a user's desktop based on the directory list. In the future, global directories may be able to identify specific users whose network traffic should receive higher priority than others.

The Active Directory stores information about every resource (user, printer, computer, and other device) on the network, including its characteristics and the people who can access that resource. It is not, however, stored centrally. In fact, each domain controller on the network contains only a portion of the Active Directory representing the objects within its particular domain. These different portions are synchronized routinely in a process called replication.

Windows 2000 networks no longer have primary and backup domain controllers. Because there is a single, distributed resource list, there is no need to keep master and backup copies as Windows NT 4.0 did. (In other words, while Windows 2000 networks still organize their resources into domains, they do not use primary and backup domain controllers to store the domain information. Instead, they distribute the domain information among one or more standard domain servers, each of which maintains just a portion of the domain information.)

Organizations with multiple domains can group them into structures called domain trees or forests. In a domain tree, each domain is the offspring of another. A domain forest consists of multiple domain trees that are not related directly to each other (like the family trees of different families). In a domain tree, the parent-child hierarchy simplifies the way that Windows 2000 shares resources. Any resource (person or object) that is part of the school domain is automatically available to participate in the child domains, and vice versa.

The Active Directory is expandable; network administrators can add objects (such as users, printers, or shared folders) or even define new types of objects. Some objects in the Active Directory update themselves. As domain controllers are added to or removed from the network, for example, they automatically make themselves known through an interesting technology called dynamic Domain Name System (dynamic DNS). Dynamic DNS notifies the organization's Domain Name System of the new domain controller. The Active Directory, in turn, uses the information in the Domain Name System to locate its Windows 2000 domain controllers on the network. Unlike Windows NT 4.0 domains, Windows 2000 domains are closely linked to Internet domains.

At the time of this writing Active Directory is a relatively new technology. Besides the Active Directory and the dynamic Domain Name System, Windows 2000 provides improved services for managing disks, system settings, users, and security policies (including the use of Kerberos authentication—a powerful means of recognizing legitimate network users and resources), and monitoring system usage.

Windows XP

The newest operating system from Microsoft (Windows XP) comes in a variety of editions, including Home and Professional (the desktop and server versions, respectively). Unlike previous versions of Windows, the Home and Professional product lines use a common software base known as the Windows 2000 common kernel. The Home Edition is intended for non-professional users. It includes a new look, additional entertainment options, and more help options. The Professional Edition includes all of the features of the Home Edition and with the added benefits of improved networking, security, and centralized management features. Windows XP promises to improve upon Windows 2000 in several ways. Among other new features, Windows XP

> has a new, simpler desktop that is reputed to make it easier to find commands or functions;

> provides a System Restore feature that returns the system to a previous, stable state without loss of data if difficulties occur;

> includes support for standards that govern connections to hardware devices such as DVD disks, infrared connections (from Infrared Data Association), and high-speed connections used for work with digital video—IEEE 1394 (also known as FireWire);

> automatically checks the Web for updates to the operating system and, with user consent, downloads them so that they can be installed (again, with user consent);

> allows a user to "clone" (make an exact duplicate) of the operating system and applications on one machine and install them on another machine (a handy feature when deploying lots of machines at one time);

> enables technical support personnel (or anyone else granted the privilege) to view and control another user's screen;

> assigns identical settings for security, appearance, and management options to groups of users; and

> provides security and enhanced performance for wireless networks.

Considerable attention has been paid to one new feature of Windows XP—its product activation requirements. Product activation is an antipiracy technology that allows Microsoft to determine whether a user is running legitimate copies of its software. Activation involves a two-step process. Windows XP creates a unique identification for each computer, based on the Windows XP installation ID (often found on the back of the CD-ROM jewel case that contains the original disks), the product key (Microsoft's unique number associated with each product), and a number generated by inspecting the particular hardware components of the computer on which XP is being installed. After an initial grace period of 30 days, Windows XP ceases to function unless this unique identification number is provided to Microsoft and combined with a specific activation code.

It is important to note that schools purchasing volume licenses for Windows XP—under Microsoft's School Agreement—are exempt from activation requirements. Volume purchasers receive a Volume License Product Key (VLK) used to bypass activation when installing Windows XP. Each VLK is assigned to a particular customer under a specific agreement. For School Agreement customers, the key is issued per enrollment agreement per product family. (In the future, separate keys will be needed for each of Microsoft's products.) Images (copies) of Windows XP using the VLK and volume licensing CD can be installed on any number of Windows PCs without requiring reactivation. For network installations, the system administrator can preapply the key to the image so that the installation can also proceed from the network without requiring a product key.

Novell NetWare

In the early 1980s, Novell provided the first successful network operating system for personal computers, and it continues to excel in both technology development and performance. Novell's NetWare Directory Services eDirectory (NDS), released in the mid-1990s, anticipated the shift from server-based to enterprisewide information services by providing a single list of all network resources no matter where they were located on the network. Most network managers and technical publications acknowledge that Novell's file and print services are the fastest available.

NDS, like Active Directory (its younger cousin), collects information about users, servers, printers, and all other network resources in a central store and then distributes portions of the information across servers at strategic locations on the network; these different copies are synchronized routinely. NDS (like Active Directory) maintains a hierarchical organization that makes it easy for users to locate the resources they need and for network administrators to keep information current and consistent throughout the organization. The internal implementations of NDS and Active Directory are somewhat different, and these differences affect their manageability and scalability. Neither of these architectures is clearly superior. Network managers and other technical personnel will need to make a determination about which technology will best serve the needs of a particular network.

NDS has certain advantages over Active Directory. It is several years older and therefore has been well tested. It runs on many different network operating systems (Windows NT, Windows 2000, and various versions of UNIX), all of which can fully participate in a NDS directory. Active Directory on the other hand is built into Windows 2000, and only Windows 2000 clients can fully participate in the directory. (Windows 95 and 98 clients can participate with nearly full capabilities once the appropriate update from Microsoft is applied.)

NetWare servers provide roughly the same range of capabilities as do Windows NT and 2000 servers: document and printer sharing; Web serving; database, DNS, and DHCP services; and management of Windows client computer desktops.

Like Microsoft, Novell has developed a product to manage Windows desktop computers from Novell NetWare servers.

AppleShare IP and Macintosh OS X Server

AppleShare IP is an easy-to-use server based on Macintosh OS 9 (a client operating system) that provides document and printer sharing as well as Web and electronic mail services for Windows and Macintosh clients.

Macintosh OS X Server extends the capabilities of AppleShare IP. It not only manages document and printer sharing and accesses Internet connections but also hosts Web sites and provides Web site development tools. In addition, it offers programming (scripting) languages to connect Web pages to database and electronic mail services, and provides DHCP and DNS services to Macintosh, Windows, and UNIX clients. Macintosh OS X also serves QuickTime streaming video (movies) to clients over the Web and manages client desktops—so long as they are Macintosh clients—by downloading standard configurations for users no matter where they log in to the network. Macintosh OS X is a radical departure from previous Macintosh operating systems; its core has been replaced by a version of UNIX, a mature operating system recognized for its speed, durability, and relative security. The UNIX core confers on Macintosh OS X memory and disk management features considerably more powerful than those in AppleShare IP. Unlike its UNIX server cousins, however, Macintosh OS X includes an easy-to-use graphical interface that simplifies server administration.

Macintosh OS X servers are especially designed for environments where servers are managed by nontechnical personnel and ease of use is paramount or where there are small groups of clients. While Macintosh OS X is considerably easier to install and manage than Windows or NetWare, it also lacks global directories and other management features required by large networks.

Application Programs

An application program offers a particular service beyond that provided by the operating system. Application programs include word processors such as Microsoft Word, spreadsheets such as Excel, electronic mail programs such as Eudora or Microsoft Exchange, presentation programs such as HyperStudio or PowerPoint, programs that combine many functions including AppleWorks, graphics programs such as Photoshop, Web browsers such as Netscape Navigator or Internet Explorer, and many others.

Practical Advice

SHARING DOCUMENTS

Sharing documents across different applications and different kinds of computers can be tricky. It may be helpful to keep the following information in mind when exchanging documents with others:

> Windows PCs require that documents be named in particular ways. For example, Windows expects that Microsoft Word documents end with a .doc extension. If a Word document name does not end in .doc, it is unrecognizable as a Word document and cannot be opened simply by double-clicking on its icon. Macintosh computers, on the other hand, look for a hidden internal setting in the document to determine what it is and whether a user can double-click the

icon to open it. When Macintosh users pass documents to Windows users, it is best if they name their files in the Windows fashion.

> The surest way to open a document sent from someone using a different operating system is to first open the application program that created the document, and then use its File menu and Open option to open the document.

> Documents created by different application programs may be difficult to share, even if they were created on the same kind of computer. (AppleWorks for Macintosh cannot open Photoshop for Macintosh documents.)

> Documents created by different versions of the same software may also be difficult to share. Often an earlier version of an application program is unable to open documents created by a more recent version.

OTHER SOLUTIONS

There are several ways to remedy difficulties in sharing documents. The simplest solution, but perhaps the least practical, involves providing everyone with the same hardware and software types and versions. Because that is not possible in most schools, other viable solutions are:

> Very often, the person originating the document can save the document in a special way to make it useful to recipients who use other kinds of computers or application programs. Most programs provide a Save As dialog box that offers a drop-down menu that lists alternative document formats.

> The manufacturer of an application may provide translation software. Microsoft provided a free translator for users of Word 6.0 (mid-1990s) so that they could translate documents received from Word 97 users (late 1990s).

> Purchase translation software (usually more powerful than that freely provided by manufacturers). Conversions Plus for Windows translates between hundreds of different software packages. Likewise, MacLinkPlus for Macintosh provides similar translation services.

Monitoring and Managing the Network

Managing hundreds or thousands of computers is expensive both in terms of money and staff time. Most organizations employ several software and hardware tools that help them to lower the overall cost of management, improve the performance and availability of their critical equipment, and consolidate the network tasks that must be done. A large percentage of schools have such a small support staff that they have no choice but to restrict network access. This limits the kinds of explorations and experiences that are central to higher learning.

Many tools are available to help make managing a network less costly and time-consuming. In the late 1990s, Microsoft created a set of system policies, scripts, and recommended strategies for minimizing the maintenance on Windows 95 clients connecting to Windows NT 4.0 servers. The Zero Administration Kit (ZAK) encompassed Microsoft's bid to lower a network's total cost of ownership. While these tools provide some control, many schools prefer to purchase third-party desktop security software such as Fortres 101 (**www.fortres.com**) or FoolProof (**www.smartstuff.com**) to strengthen Windows' native security capabilities. For Macintosh, schools often use FoolProof, At Ease (older Macintoshes), and Macintosh Manager (newer Macintoshes).

While system policies and desktop security programs help prevent difficulties, many schools find that they are not wholly sufficient. When computers are used frequently by many different students and teachers, they inevitably need to be restored to a standard, working configuration on a routine basis. Programs such as Symantec Ghost (**www.symantec.com/sabu/ghost/**) and Deep Freeze (**www.deepfreezeusa.com**) help shorten this task for Windows. For Macintosh OS 9 and later, these capabilities are built into the operating system.

Timbuktu Pro (**www.netopia.com/ebusiness/**) allows technical support personnel to view and fix both Windows PCs and Macintosh client computers (without having to visit them physically). Classified as remote-control software, Timbuktu and similar products allow one user to control the mouse, make menu selections, and change configuration settings on another person's computer (providing that person has granted the privilege to do so). Remote-control software can save hours of travel time and increase the speed at which support people resolve difficulties.

Several companies offer enterprisewide products that

> automate the installation of software upgrades and bug fixes on client computers;

> perform a detailed inventory of all the software and hardware devices on a network;

> monitor critical equipment, warn of impending or actual trouble, and take action to fix the problems; and

> provide remote-control access to users' desktops.

These systems include Microsoft's System Management Server or Windows 2000's built-in Intellimirror services (which are similar to but not as powerful as SMS), Computer Associates' Unicenter TNG, Tivoli, and Hewlett-Packard's OpenView. Apple Computer provides Network Assistant, software that can manage Macintosh computers in many of the same ways.

Enterprisewide systems promise great benefits, not the least of which is that they provide a unified interface from which heterogeneous network devices can be managed. Be aware, however, that SMS, Unicenter, Tivoli, and OpenView may be time-consuming to configure. Several years of planning and implementation may be required before a school system sees a return on its investment. Speak with colleagues who have worked successfully with these systems to gauge what will be required before employing them in a school district. Keep in mind that many schools manage their networks adequately by using smaller, simpler products—such as Fortres or Timbuktu—even though those products lack the scope of larger systems.

Technical Information Summary

OPERATING SYSTEMS AND APPLICATION PROGRAMS

Every computer has an operating system. The fundamental role of the operating system is to control every device—keyboard, monitor, disk drive, network interface, and so forth—that is connected to the computer and to provide various ways to interact with those devices. The most common operating systems are Windows (95, 98, Me, NT, 2000), Macintosh, and UNIX (including Linux).

Network operating systems manage the same basic services as operating systems. In addition, they make it possible to share resources such as documents, printers, CD-ROMs, and other devices. Network operating systems provide better security and performance than operating systems found on typical client computers. Some examples of network operating systems include Windows NT 4.0, Windows 2000, Novell NetWare, AppleShare IP, Macintosh OS X Server, and Linux. Network operating systems require fast computers with large amounts of disk space and random access memory (RAM). For this reason, network operating systems usually run on servers (rather than clients).

Modern network operating systems organize network resources so that they are easy for people to locate and use but still remain secure from tampering. To track this information, they use enterprisewide directories. Like telephone directories, network directories make it possible to look up a resource and find additional information about it. They store the resource location, users who have access, serial numbers, and a good deal of other information. While earlier network operating systems maintained this type of information by server (in effect, separate telephone directories for different servers), modern network operating systems offer a single directory for the whole network. Using a single directory allows people to find resources more easily and avoids duplication of information.

Application programs include word processors (e.g., Microsoft Word), spreadsheets (e.g., Excel), electronic mail programs (e.g., Eudora or Microsoft Exchange), presentation programs (e.g., HyperStudio or PowerPoint), programs that combine many functions (e.g., AppleWorks), Web browsers (e.g., Netscape Navigator), and many others.

Network managers must ensure that operating systems, network operating systems, and application programs enable people to share information as easily as possible. This includes making provisions for cross-platform communication.

Most organizations employ several software and hardware tools that help them to lower the overall cost of the network. Often, schools restrict students and teachers so that they cannot install software, save or delete documents on their desktop or laptop computers, or change a computer's configuration. Windows System policies, Fortres 101 (**www.fortres.com**), and FoolProof (**www.smartstuff.com**) strengthen Windows' native security capabilities. For Macintosh, FoolProof, At Ease (older Macintoshes), and Macintosh Manager (newer Macintoshes) perform similar tasks.

Remote-control software allows technical support staff to view and fix client computers over the network (without having to pay a visit). Enterprisewide management systems monitor the performance of critical equipment, keep inventory, automate routine software installations, and include remote-control capabilities. They are, however, time-consuming to implement and manage.

Technologies for Long-Distance Networks

MAN AND WAN TECHNOLOGIES

Information traveling over a wide area network (WAN) traverses longer distances and encounters a wider variety of physical and local environments than a M. WAN technologies resemble interstate highways that are intentionally built to limit access in order to provide greater durability and handle long-distance traffic with greater efficiency.

Metropolitan area networks (MANs) are sometimes considered to be hybrid networks occupying a space somewhere between LANs and WANS. MANs connect buildings in city-sized areas using a combination of LAN and WAN technologies (whichever is appropriate for the distance and conditions between the buildings). An organization connected by a MAN might use Ethernet to communicate between buildings that are a few kilometers apart and leased lines or frame relay for longer distances; the district owns the Ethernet infrastructure but leases the other parts. Large school districts are considered MANs.

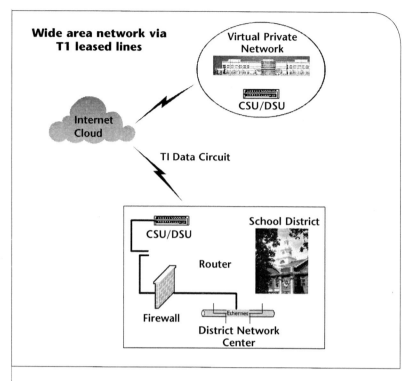

FIGURE 5.1

Metropolitan Area Networks and Wide Area Networks

Schools use WAN technologies (56 Kbps circuits, ISDN, leased lines including T1 lines, frame relay, DSL, and others) to connect to the Internet and to interconnect buildings at considerable distances. They generally lease, rather than own, these WAN connections although there is a growing trend toward privatization.

Ethernet is the predominant choice of LAN technologies. However, WAN technology comes with a host of confusing options. LAN technologies vary widely in the amount of data they can deliver, the speed at which they operate, their initial and recurring costs, their management requirements, and their flexibility to include new locations or new technologies such as voice or video. Metropolitan and wide area networks are likely to involve a mix of different WAN technologies—a practice that occurs less frequently on local area networks. For example, a MAN or WAN might use ISDN lines or T1 lines for some connections, wireless connections for others.

For the remainder of this chapter, the term WAN technologies is used to describe methods of carrying data over distances of several kilometers or greater with the understanding that these technologies can be used both on metropolitan area networks and wide area networks.

Planning a Long-Distance Network

Begin the planning process by drawing a sketch of the buildings that will become part of the network. For each building, draw a line connecting it to all the other buildings in this network. Label each line with the following information:

> The distance between buildings

> The kinds and volumes of information that will be exchanged, now and in the future. (For example, if School Building A is to exchange e-mail with School Building B, then draw a line between these two buildings and label the line electronic mail. If School Building A is also to receive cable TV transmissions, draw a line labeled TV to the cable provider.)

> The number of computers in each building

> The number of people who will use those computers at various times of the day

> The tasks that these people will engage in at various times of the day. Describe every action that will take place, including its duration and the number of participants. (For example, will staff and students primarily use electronic mail? Will they use the World Wide Web—and do so at certain times of the day more than others? Is there an integrated learning system in one building that must accommodate 30 simultaneous logins at the beginning of class periods during the day? Will classrooms collaborate on building Web pages, including large graphics? Is there a need to share video or voice transmissions?)

Once the drawing is completed, work with a network integrator to convert this functional description into a technical specification. Remember, the integrator's plan will be only as good as the initial description. If services are omitted or usage estimates off the mark, the finished network will likely be inadequate.

Investigating WAN Technologies

The following questions form the basis for any serious discussion involving the installation of WAN technologies:

Which WAN technologies are locally available?

To make wide area connections, a network must use the services of the local telephone company and other communications vendors such as MCI, Sprint, or AT&T. Different vendors offer different technologies. When planning a network, check with the local telephone company and other communications vendors to see what they support.

What are the installation and recurring costs for each technology?

WAN technologies vary in their startup and recurring costs. Startup costs include installation fees and equipment to be purchased. Recurring costs include service and maintenance contracts for the equipment and connections as well as communications line charges and per-call connection charges. Some technologies cost more as the distance between connections increases (just as long-distance telephone calls cost more than local calls); distance is irrelevant with others. Some technologies cost more as the amount of data being transmitted increases, while others charge a flat rate regardless of the amount of data. Consider the placement, frequency, and duration of network connections and choose a technology that provides a good balance of cost and performance.

What kinds of data does each technology carry?

Some technologies are suited for data such as electronic mail and documents only; others carry both data and video or voice transmissions. Determine what kinds of data will be exchanged and select the appropriate technology.

How fast is the connection?

WAN technologies vary significantly in their transmission rates. The slowest technologies run at about the same speed as fast modems—56 Kbps—and can provide connections for just a few simultaneous users to exchange data (not voice or video). The fastest technologies run many times faster than Ethernet and can service hundreds of simultaneous users exchanging any kind of information. Some WAN technologies carry data at two different transmission rates—they send downstream (to the user) faster than they send upstream (from the user). Make sure that the transmission rates accommodate the kinds of information the network will be sharing and the number of users it will eventually be supporting.

Are there distance limitations for the technology?

Some WAN technologies impose limits on the distances that they can carry data. Make sure that the network's WAN technology can negotiate the distances between its sites.

Does the technology support dial-up connections or permanent connections?

A permanent connection is one that is always available; a dial-up connection requires that a modem make a connection by dialing the specific number of equipment at another site on a periodic basis. Permanent connections between sites are preferable to dial-up connections because they are easier to manage and provide more durable service. Dial-up connections may be substantially less expensive than permanent connections but they are normally inadequate for large volumes of video, voice, and other kinds of data that must travel in continuous streams.

Common WAN Technologies

Plain Old Telephone Service

POTS (plain old telephone service) provides analog, dial-up connectivity over regular telephone wire. While POTS is woefully inadequate for use with moderate or even small-scale WANs, it may be cost effective when dealing with a network consisting of a very small number of simultaneous users.

To send information using POTS, attach a modem to the sending computer and a compatible modem to the receiving computer. The sending modem dials, and the receiving modem answers the call. The sending modem then converts digital signals from its computer into an analog representation, and sends them along the telephone line to the receiving computer. The receiving computer converts the incoming analog signals into digital representations, and passes them along to its computer.

Modems may be attached directly to an individual computer or to a local area network. If a modem is attached to an individual computer, then that computer (or anyone sharing its resources through a peer network) can initiate or receive calls from another computer or network. Most sites prefer to attach modems to their local area networks rather than to individual computers.

LAN modems may be stand-alone devices that connect directly to LAN wiring, or they may be attached to (or inside of) network servers. LAN modems can respond to connection requests from any user inside the LAN. They can also receive calls from an external computer or network. LAN modems enable students, teachers, and community members to dial into a network from home, download or upload files, and connect to electronic mail as if they were doing so within their school buildings.

Many schools find that supporting dial-up connections requires significant staff time. Network users calling from home often have trouble with connections and need technical assistance. Because of this, some school systems have chosen to offer connections to their networks only through the Internet. While Internet connections also involve connection problems, such problems occur less frequently. Internet connections are becoming more popular but they are inherently less secure than dial-up connections. Each dial-up connection occurs over an individual telephone line, whereas Internet connections travel over a public network.

Fast modems (56 Kbps to the user and 28.8–33.3 Kbps from the user) appeared a few years ago. Known as V.90, after the standard issued by the International Telecommunications Union, these modems have become commonplace and provide reasonable service. Recently, the new standard, V.92, emerged, offering significant improvements. V.92 modems are not yet in common use, so before installing them, make sure that the network Internet service provider supports them.

PLAIN OLD TELEPHONE SERVICE

POTS provides a way for computers to communicate over regular telephone lines. POTS connections are slow, however, and should not be used for moderate or small-sized WANs in most instances.

To create a POTS connection, install modems at each site. The modems can be attached to individual computers or to a LAN. Once the modems are installed, network users at each site can dial or receive calls from anywhere in the world.

Even the fastest modems (56 Kbps to the user and 48 Kbps from the user), known as V.92, are too slow to provide robust connections for wide area networks.

Integrated Services Digital Network

Integrated Services Digital Network (ISDN) connections provide half or full duplex digital data communications on a dial-up basis between two points over regular telephone wire. The term half duplex refers to a communications channel that can carry signals in only one direction at a time (although the direction may switch back and forth instantaneously, effectively transmitting data in both directions). The term full duplex refers to a communications channel that can carry signals in both directions simultaneously. (Regular telephone connections are full duplex.) Digital data are transmitted and received as a series of on-off signals. These signals are distinguished from analog signals composed of continuous variations in voltage. Digital connections generally incur a much lower error rate than analog connections.

ISDN Overview

ISDN services can be purchased at many different speeds, including 64 Kbps, 128 Kbps, 256 Kbps, and 512 Kbps. The most common ISDN service offers 128 Kbps and can support several dozen simultaneous users with reasonable response rates. ISDN services at 128 Kbps are now available in most areas of the country. ISDN carries both voice and data.

Basic rate ISDN provides two 64-Kbps channels (called B channels or bearer channels), which carry data between two callers, as well as a 16-Kbps channel (called a D or data channel) to carry control signals (e.g., "dial these digits," "ring the telephone"). Because the D channel initiates calls digitally, the time to establish the call is much shorter than that required by analog modems. The two B channels may be used separately for full duplex services, or they may be bonded (joined) to produce one half duplex 128-Kbps channel (which carries data in a single direction at any given moment).

When the B channels are bonded, the ISDN equipment allows users to accept incoming calls by switching one B channel to service the call temporarily; the equipment can automatically rejoin the channels when the incoming call is complete.

It is possible to achieve ISDN speeds approaching 230.4 Kbps if a modem and ISDN provider both support data compression. To take advantage of the speeds achieved through compression, purchase a high-speed serial card. High-speed serial cards fit inside a computer and connect to the external modem. The cards include a special chip, called a 16750 UART (Universal Asynchronous Receiver Transmitter), which includes a faster clock (to set the transmission rate), as well as more memory than the standard serial circuitry of new computers. While standard circuitry transmit data at a maximum rate of 115 Kbps, high-speed serial cards can transmit data at speeds of nearly 1 Mbps (1,000 Kbps).

Implementing ISDN

ISDN services require a special telephone connection. This connection, known as a U-loop, consists of two copper wires and has a maximum length of 5.5 kilometers (18,000 feet) between the network connection and the central telephone office (commonly referred to as the CO). The equipment on both sides of the U-loop has to be carefully designed to deal with the long length of the wire and the noisy environment.

The U-loop connects to an NT1 (network termination 1) device. The NT1 serves several purposes. First, it connects the two-wire twisted pairs used by telephone companies to the four-wire connectors commonly found in telephones, fax machines, and other telecommunications equipment. It also translates between the different signal encoding schemes used on the telephone company network and the local area network. The NT1 provides power for the telephone and fax machine if necessary, and allows more than one device to access the two B channels provided by ISDN (each device connects to one of the B channels when it identifies a message requesting its services).

The NT1 connects to an ISDN terminal device such as an ISDN router, digital telephone, or direct ISDN connection in a computer or server. Alternatively, the NT1 may connect to a terminal adapter; terminal adapters enable serial devices such as regular modems to connect to ISDN circuits. The terminal adapter translates the ISDN signals into a form that the serial device can use and adjusts the differing transmission rates between the two devices (usually according to a protocol termed V.120). Many terminal adapters have NT1 devices built in so that users can purchase a single piece of equipment to connect both ISDN-specific devices and generic serial devices (such as a fax machine) to the ISDN connection.

NT1 and terminal adapters may be internal or external to a computer or server. For PC-type computers, internal modems may be capable of reaching faster speeds than external modems (unless the external modem is connected through a special high-speed circuit board) because internal connections, or buses, that service the modem are faster than standard serial port connections that service external modems.

Regardless of whether the network uses an internal or an external modem, make sure that its switch type is the same as that used by the telephone company's central office. There are additional telecommunications provider compatibility requirements as well. Each piece of

ISDN equipment—fax machine, router, or digital telephone—is associated with a unique identifier that the provider may need to have specified in the equipment setup procedures. Likewise, a specified data link protocol, such as PPP (Point-to-Point Protocol), may need to be used atop the ISDN physical connection. To ensure compatibility, ask the telephone company to indicate which equipment (such as an NT1 or terminal adapter) must be purchased and the brands, models, and protocols they recommend.

Although most ISDN connections are dial up, some ISDN connections can be left on at all times (creating a permanent connection). If a permanent connection is needed, ask the ISDN provider about these services. ISDN technology is also called digital subscriber line technology. Its major competitors are more advanced, faster technologies known collectively as DSL. Cable modem is also a competitor.

Example

Suppose a school district consists of four interconnected buildings and each building has its own connection to the Internet. If these connections to the Internet are by ISDN, consider the following points:

> The local telephone company and Internet provider must support ISDN services.

> Each building must be no farther than 5.5 kilometers from the central telephone office, must procure ISDN services from the telephone company, and must purchase compatible equipment (NT1, terminal adapter). If a building is subsequently added to the ISDN WAN, it must also conform to these rules.

> Connections are billed as a monthly charge plus an additional per-minute connection charge. If the buildings are located in areas subject to long-distance rates, ISDN calls will also be charged at these higher rates.

Technical Information Summary

ISDN

Integrated Services Digital Network connections provide digital data communications on a dial-up basis between two points over regular telephone wire. ISDN services can be purchased at many different speeds, including 64 Kbps, 128 Kbps (230.4 Kbps with data compression), 256 Kbps, and 512 Kbps. The most common ISDN service offers 128 Kbps and can support several dozen simultaneous users with reasonable response rates. ISDN services at 128 Kbps carry both voice and data. Connections are billed as a monthly charge plus an additional per-minute connection charge. ISDN services are available in most areas of the country. The major competitors to ISDN are more advanced, faster technologies known collectively as DSL. Cable modem is also a competitor.

Leased Lines (Including T1)

Technical Definition

Leased lines are privately rented telephone communications lines that provide constant (as opposed to dial-up) digital connections between two sites over copper wire. Leased lines may be rented at many different speeds. The most common connections are T1 (1.544 Mbps) and fractional T1 (various speeds that are all multiples of 64 Kbps). Burstable T1 runs at speeds (as fast as 1.544 Mbps) that vary with the momentary demands of the network. T1 services provide very good response rates for hundreds of simultaneous users under average loads or a hundred users under heavy loads (e.g., many users surfing the Web simultaneously). Of all the LAN technologies in this chapter, T1 lines constitute the most common technology for connecting schools to the Internet.

Leased line communications are defined by a series of standards that the American National Standards Institute issued in the 1980s. Common standards include:

Standard	Transmission Rate
DS-0 (digital signal level 0)	64 Kbps
DS-1 (digital signal level 1)	1.544 Mbps
DS-3 (digital signal level 3)	44.736 Mbps

Telephone circuits implement these standards. For example, telephone lines called T1 lines conform to DS-1 standards, while T3 lines conform to DS-3 standards. Use these T-carrier circuits to transmit and receive data, voice, and video simultaneously.

Implementing Leased Lines

The leased line usually consists of two twisted pairs of copper conductors. These wires terminate at the network site in a jack. The jack is connected, in turn, to a Channel Service Unit/Data Service Unit (CSU/DSU), which provides digital connection services similar to those provided by a modem for analog connections. Generally, the CSU/DSU receives incoming signals from the telephone company's central office through one or two pairs of wires, processes the signals, and passes them on to a router on a local area network. (A router connects a local area network to other networks, such as the Internet.) For outgoing signals, the CSU/DSU receives information from the router, encodes it for travel over the telephone company line, and sends it on to its destination.

To provision a leased line, call the local telephone company or telecommunications carrier. Have the technicians install a leased line and a CSU/DSU between each pair of buildings on the network. The CSU/DSUs must be compatible with each other and with equipment at the telephone company central office (e.g., they must use the same encoding schemes when sending and receiving information). There are no restrictions on the distance between the two points connected by a leased line. However, leased line charges vary directly with the distance between connected points as well as with the speed of the line.

DSL, cable modem, and radio waves are competitor technologies to leased lines. They carry data, video, and voice information over long distances at reasonable rates. Frame relay services are also a competitor to T1 leased lines with regard to data, but frame relay cannot carry video with equivalent reliability. Other competitor technologies include Asynchronous Transfer Mode (ATM) and low-level satellite technologies.

Example

Suppose a school district consists of three school buildings that are connected to a district office (the fourth building in the network). In addition, the school buildings share a single Internet connection through the district office. If all of these connections are T1 leased lines:

> The school district's Internet service provider must support T1 services. In the district office, this means installing a leased line and CSU/DSU that are compatible with the Internet service provider's equipment.

> Provision three leased lines and purchase three pairs (that is, six total) CSU/DSUs to connect each school building to the district office. (One CSU/DSU resides in each school, and its matching CSU/DSU resides in the district office. In addition, the district office includes a CSU/DSU that connects to its partner at the ISP.) Install a router in the district office to connect the CSU/DSUs and bind the leased lines into a wide area network.

> Leased lines create a permanent connection between buildings. Charges are based on the distance between buildings and the speed of the connection.

Technical Information Summary

LEASED LINES (INCLUDING T1)

Leased lines are privately rented telephone communications lines that provide constant (as opposed to dial-up) digital connections between two sites over copper wire. Lease lines may be rented at many different speeds. The most common connections are T1 (1.544 Mbps) and fractional T1 (various speeds that are all multiples of 64 Kbps).

Leased lines provide very fast, robust communication services and are perhaps the most common way that schools connect to the Internet. They are also relatively expensive and require weeks of advance notice to provision. DSL, cable modem, and radio waves are competitor technologies to leased lines. They can carry data, video, and voice information over long distances at reasonable rates. Frame relay services are also a competitor to T1 leased lines with regard to data, but frame relay cannot carry video with equivalent reliability.

Digital Subscriber Lines (DSL and ADSL)

DSL Overview

Digital subscriber line technologies (DSL) use standard phone lines to deliver high-speed data communications. The fastest DSL transmissions are fast enough—as much as 52 Mbps downstream (to the user) and 2.3 Mbps upstream (from the user)—to support full motion video, IP telephony, and interactive multimedia applications delivered directly from the Internet. The most common form of DSL, called ADSL (Asynchronous Digital Subscriber Line), offers speeds similar to leased T1 lines and can support dozens of simultaneous users of voice and data communications.

The interest in DSL technology arose in part from the prohibitive cost of the competitive technologies. It also grew because of the Telecommunications Reform Act of 1996, which allowed local and long-distance carriers, cable companies, radio and television broadcasters, Internet and online service providers, and telecommunications equipment manufacturers to compete in one another's markets. Since late 1998, the number of telephone companies offering DSL services has increased significantly.

The DSL family includes several different technologies of increasing power, as shown in Table 5.1.

TABLE 5.1: DIGITAL SUBSCRIBER LINE (DSL) TECHNOLOGIES

DSL Technology	Speed	Cable	Distance	Application
Asynchronous Digital Subscriber Line (ADSL) G.DMT	7 Mbps downstream As fast as 1.544 Mbps upstream	1 pair copper	6,000 ft	Internet/intranet access, video on demand, remote LAN access, virtual private networks, voice telephony
Asynchronous Digital Subscriber Line (ADSL) G.Lite	1.5 Mbps downstream 500 Kbps upstream	1 pair copper	18,000 ft	Web surfing
High Bit-rate Digital Subscriber Line (HDSL)	1.544 Mbps (same speed as T1)	2 pairs copper	12,000–15,000 ft	PBX or LAN interconnect, frame relay
Single-line Digital Subscriber Line (SDSL)	1.544 Mbps (same speed as T1)	1 pair copper	10,000 ft	Collaborative computing, LAN interconnect traffic aggregator

Implementing DSL and ADSL

DSL services are not yet available in all areas of the United States. Check with the local telecommunications company to determine which services are available. If it offers DSL, inquire about the company's installation procedures, compatible brands of modems and other hardware, and rates. Like cable, DSL installations usually require that the telecommunications company install the connection at the network site.

Additionally, unless the telecommunications company has specific experience interconnecting buildings with DSL, plan to use DSL to connect school buildings to the Internet and not to each other. DSL lines suffer from the same security and shared bandwidth problems as cable modems when used to interconnect buildings. Current DSL technologies do not generally use dedicated (secure) connections between buildings. Instead, most DSL implementations send data from one school to the telecommunications carrier, where Internet-style routing directs the data onto another school building. Like all Internet connections, data on these connections travel on a public (insecure) network.

Because DSL data travel on a public network, network performance may also be adversely affected by other (public) traffic. Leased lines—the most common alternative to DSL—have the advantage of being private connections; they provide both security and reliable performance.

DSL connections carry both voice and data on the same copper wires that traditionally carried only voice. They accomplish this by sending data at frequencies other than those being used by voice transmissions (i.e., below 4 KHz). DSL is classified as a broadband connection because it carries data on multiple frequencies simultaneously. Cable connections are also broadband. At the telephone company central office, voice transmissions are routed to the regular telephone switch. Data are then passed directly to an Internet service provider, other Internet server, or internetwork. Happily, the voice portion of the signal remains active even if power is lost (unlike ISDN voice transmissions).

Asynchronous Digital Subscriber Line is a very common form of digital subscriber line technology. For data and voice to coexist peaceably, ADSL technologies make use of a device called a splitter. Splitters generally work in pairs, with one splitter in the telephone company central office and the other installed by the telephone company at the user's network site (e.g., home, school, or business). The splitter at the user's site connects the telephone company line to the telephone and, over separate wires, to the ADSL equipment. The splitter at the telephone company office channels telephone voice transmissions to the public telephone network, and data transmissions to ATM networks, Ethernets, T1 lines, serial lines, or frame relay (depending on the DSL services provided by the telecommunications carrier).

ADSL enthusiasts (and modem manufacturers), who would prefer that ADSL modems be as easy to install as regular modems, have agitated for a modification to the ADSL standard (technically called ADSL G.DMT) that would make it unnecessary for the telephone company to install each DSL connection. Accordingly, they proposed the G.Lite standard, which allows ADSL modems and telephones to share existing telephone lines without a splitter at speeds somewhat slower than ADSL. The G.Lite specification was formally endorsed by the International Telecommunications Union in October 1998 (a first step toward complete acceptance among manufacturers and telecommunications vendors). Some recent news reports indicate the G.Lite, splitterless technologies have not lived up to their potential, achieving neither robust connections nor telco-free installations. Because of these problems, and despite its potential, G.Lite has not developed a particularly large market share.

Like ISDN modems, DSL modems may be installed internally or externally. To install a DSL internal modem, simply insert the modem card into the computer and connect the modem card to the telephone company wall jack with an ADSL cable. External modems sport at least three connections: one for the DSL cable connected to the DSL telephone line, another for a plain old telephone connection, and a third for an Ethernet connection. If the external DSL modem will be used by just one person, connect the DSL modem's Ethernet port to the Ethernet network interface in the computer. Alternatively, to share an ADSL modem among a number of users, connect every user (including the DSL modem) to an Ethernet hub. As another alternative, employ a DSL router (instead of a DSL modem) to connect the local area network to the Internet.

Like T1 and cable technologies (and unlike ISDN), DSL connections are permanent, dedicated between two points, and billed at a flat rate for unlimited Internet access. In general, DSL connections are considerably cheaper than T1 connections at similar speeds.

Widespread use of DSL technologies depends on how well the telephone companies market and implement the services. The initial deployments have been uneven at best, and it is common to hear disgruntled customers complain about sporadic outages and difficult installations. Because ADSL is considered an "overlay" technology—one that uses existing telephone wires and whose other required components can be added quickly to the telephone company network as needed—most analysts expect rapid deployment.

Technical Information Summary

DIGITAL SUBSCRIBER LINES

Digital subscriber line technologies use standard phone lines to deliver high-speed data communications. The most common form of DSL, called ADSL (Asynchronous Digital Subscriber Line), offers speeds similar to leased T1 lines and can support dozens of simultaneous users of voice and data communications. Current DSL technologies do not generally use dedicated, and therefore secure, connections between buildings. Leased lines, the most common alternative to DSL, have the advantage of being private, secure connections. DSL technologies are relatively new and are not yet available in all areas of the United States. Where they are available, the user network must be within 12,000–18,000 feet of the telephone company central office.

Cable Modems

Cable Modem Overview

Cable modems deliver information as fast as 30 Mbps downstream and as fast as 10 Mbps upstream (although much slower rates of 10 Mbps downstream and 128 Kbps upstream are more common). They are primarily intended to provide residential Internet access.

Implementing Cable Modems

To implement cable modem connections, first determine whether the local cable company offers networking services. If it does, inquire whether it offers an interbuilding network (known as an institutional loop), Internet services, or both. An institutional loop is used to connect buildings within a network, and Internet services provide connections with the Internet. As with DSL technologies, use cable technologies only for interbuilding communication if your cable company has explicit experience with such installations. Otherwise, use cable connections only for traffic to and from the Internet.

To connect a site using cable, the cable company installs coaxial cable (just like the cable used to provide television cable service) and a cable modem (which the customer must rent). The coaxial cable is then connected to the cable modem, and the cable modem through an Ethernet cable to an Ethernet network interface in one of the customer's computers, servers, hubs, or routers. Like DSL, cable connections are also classified as broadband because they carry data on multiple frequencies simultaneously.

Like T1 and DSL, cable modems create a permanent connection to the Internet. They deliver data at remarkable speeds with high reliability, and many schools and individuals are queuing up for these services. Nonetheless, be cautious of implementing them for several reasons:

> ➤ Unlike leased lines, DSL, and ISDN, cable modems are shared among all users in a neighborhood, so that actual data delivery rates vary according to the number of users on the system. As the cable companies add subscribers, expect to see a decline in performance.

> ➤ Cable modem users essentially share a large public LAN with all other users on their subnet. Credit card information, personal information, and other sensitive data are vulnerable to malicious individuals who use electronic sniffers to watch the contents of each packet on the subnet. Only encrypted data are truly safe from other local cable users.

> ➤ The widespread introduction of cable modems depends on how well cable providers negotiate the learning curve involved with creating data networks. Upgrading such systems is very expensive, and many cable companies (already in debt) balk at spending large sums of money without knowing whether they will live to see an adequate return on their investment.

Frame Relay

Frame Relay Overview

Frame relay connections provide constant (as opposed to dial-up) digital data communications service within a network cloud (i.e., a network whose connections are not maintained by users and whose physical configuration is immaterial). In the case of frame relay networks, the telecommunications carrier maintains the frame relay connections between user sites. Frame relay networks span large areas of the country (e.g., whole states, in some cases).

Implementing Frame Relay

To create a frame relay network, connect each building in the WAN to a frame relay network cloud at the site maintained by the local telecommunications provider. These connections may use any WAN physical link technology. Once the connections to the frame relay network cloud are made, provision circuits (connections) within the cloud. For example, imagine a school district that consists of four buildings each connected to all others. Provision four connections (T1 lines, perhaps) to the frame relay network, and then six circuits within the network cloud to bind these connections into a wide area network.

Frame relay services can be purchased at many different speeds, including 56 Kbps, 128 Kbps, 1.544 Mbps, and 3 Mbps. Frame relay networks operate by sending data along a circuit—a path that is established for the duration of a connection. These circuits may be permanent virtual circuits (PVCs) or switched virtual circuits (SVCs). In a permanent virtual circuit, the path from one point on the WAN to every other point is defined at the time of configuration. In a switched virtual circuit, the path is defined when the connection is initiated (like a phone call). Switched paths may or may not traverse the same interim connections for each call. Permanent virtual circuits reduce call setup delays and other disturbances in data delivery, and they are the most common circuit offered by frame relay vendors.

Purchasers of frame relay services have the option to request a guaranteed level of service known as a committed information rate (CIR). The CIR may be exceeded by a second rate known as a committed burst rate (Bc), up to a maximum threshold specified by a third rate, the burst excess rate (Be). For example, a purchaser might select a CIR of 1.0 Mbps, a Bc of 1.25 Mbps, and a Be of 1.5 Mbps. If the CIR is exceeded when the frame relay network is congested (regardless of the other rates that may have been specified), the network may discard some of the traffic temporarily and signal the sending system to retransmit.

If network traffic consists mainly of electronic mail and shared documents—data that can tolerate small delays with no loss of integrity—frame relay may produce adequate throughput. However, if the network information consists mainly of services such as Web browsing or voice, describe the network operations to the frame relay vendor, get recommendations, and purchase the appropriate rates accordingly.

Frame relay and leased line networks are, perhaps, the most common WAN technologies in general use. Frame relay networks have some advantages when compared with leased line technologies:

> Under some circumstances, users will need to install and maintain fewer components for frame relay networks than for leased line networks. For example, a wide area network serving four buildings (each connected to all others) would require six leased lines and 12 CSU/DSUs—all maintained by the user. However, an equivalent frame relay network would require only four leased lines and eight CSU/DSUs. It would also require six frame relay circuits. In this case, the user would not be required to maintain the frame relay equipment or connections.

> It is easier to expand a frame relay network than a leased line network. If a fifth building were added to an existing four-building leased line network, four additional leased lines would have to be purchased to connect the four existing buildings to the new addition. If a fifth building were added to a frame relay network, only one leased line would be needed as well as four additional circuits within the cloud. Since it is considerably easier to provision circuits than leased lines, it is inherently easier to expand frame relay networks than leased line networks.

> Frame relay networks provide redundant paths for data. Unlike leased lines, if one path is damaged the network automatically switches to another path.

> Frame relay sets its price based on the network's average throughput rather than on the maximum throughput, as do most leased lines. Moreover, the costs of frame relay do not increase with distance. Frame relay services may be more expensive than leased lines at short distances (especially when purchasing a committed information rate), so check with local vendors to determine the distance and data rate at which they become cheaper.

Frame relay networks have some disadvantages with regard to leased line technologies as well:

> In a frame relay network, bandwidth (data delivery capacity) is shared with others, and their traffic may affect network throughput.

> Security is a greater issue because the frame relay is shared with other clients of the telecommunications vendor. While the network circuits are still private, discuss security issues with the frame relay vendor.

> Unpredictable retransmissions that sometimes occur with frame relay services make frame relay less desirable than leased lines if the WAN includes voice or video transmissions (which require dependable, steady delivery streams).

> Within any given cloud, the network connection is specified by standards for the user-to-network interface (UNI). However, complexities of connections between clouds are still being ironed out. Some of these complexities have been addressed in the network-to-network interface—NNI (which defines signal standards)—but billing and troubleshooting are not always compatible between different frame relay networks.

Technical Information Summary

CABLE MODEMS AND FRAME RELAY

Cable modems deliver information as fast as 30 Mbps downstream (to the user) and up to 10 Mbps upstream (from the user). Much slower rates of 10 Mbps downstream and 128 Kbps upstream are more common. Cable modems carry data on the same copper wires that traditionally carried only television signals. These wires have large capacities, servicing hundreds of simultaneous connections. Cable modem connections are faster than ISDN (roughly the same speed as ADSL), and they are permanent. Security breaches are possible if malicious users employ decoding devices to peer into private information.

Frame relay connections provide constant (as opposed to dial-up) digital data communications service within a network cloud. In the case of frame relay networks, the local telecommunications carrier maintains the frame relay connections between user sites. Frame relay services can be purchased at many different speeds, including 56 Kbps, 128 Kbps, and 1.544 Mbps. Frame relay is a proven WAN technology that may be less expensive to implement than leased lines. It is faster than ISDN, and more commonly available than DSL or cable modem. The costs for frame relay vary with usage (but are independent of distance).

Wireless

Wireless Overview

Schools have traditionally installed fiber optic cable to interconnect different school buildings, but there are circumstances in which fiber optics is not the optimum solution. Fiber is too expensive, for example, to be used for temporary buildings, and some buildings may be separated by prohibitive terrain. In these cases, wireless WAN connections are a potential replacement for fiber optics.

Many different technologies—including microwaves, lasers, and radio waves—can be used to create wireless WAN links. Of these technologies, radio waves have gained the most attention recently. Radio waves provide a relatively inexpensive kind of wide area network (connecting LANs as far as 25 miles apart) especially because the user owns rather than leases the components.

Wireless wide area networks use radio waves in the form of frequency hopping spread spectrum (FHSS) and direct sequence spread spectrum technologies (DSSS). Wireless WANs send information at transmission speeds as low as 1–2 MHz and as high as 100 MHz. They operate in the 2.4 GHz or 5.8 GHz wavelength band of the radio spectrum (reserved for unregulated industrial, scientific, and medical use) and do not need to be licensed by the Federal Communications Commission.

Implementing Wireless Connections

To create a wireless WAN, an organization typically purchases a wireless bridge and an antenna for each of its sites. The wireless bridge connects to the local area network, receives Ethernet data, filters the data intended for wide area transmission, and sends that data to its internal radio frequency modem. The radio modem changes the Ethernet data into a radio frequency suitable for wireless transmission and sends it by a cable to an antenna, which transmits the signal over long distances. In some bridges, the radio modem may be located on an interface card (a small, removable circuit board). Bridges that use interface cards can be easily upgraded to include multiple radios. Bridges with multiple radios, each broadcasting on a different frequency, are capable of point-to-multipoint transmissions that interconnect one central building to several other buildings (each with its own antenna and radio receiver). For some systems, the radio is located in the antenna rather than in the bridge.

When setting up a wireless WAN, be sure that the equipment is installed properly—particularly that the antennas are within radio line of sight and properly aligned to each other. Radio line of sight implies more than just visibility. Because obstacles on or near the transmission path can disturb radio waves, radio line of sight requires not only a clear direct path between sites but also an unobstructed swath above and below the center of the transmission line. One rule of thumb calls for 12 feet of clearance at the center of the path for every mile between the two points you are connecting. Some vendors offer charts that describe the relationship between the clearance required, the distance between the sites, and the height of obstacles in the path.

Ask the vendor to conduct a path analysis before purchasing wireless WAN equipment. A path analysis determines not only the line of sight, but also identifies potential obstacles, calculates the necessary power and requirements for repeaters, and selects the type of antenna that will best serve the network's needs. A path analysis also determines the location of the radio equipment, power, wiring and shelter requirements (if your equipment is located outdoors), the best antenna location, and expected signal strength.

When negotiating for services, look for systems that can be easily upgraded, perhaps by adding a circuit board or by applying software updates. Upgrades and routine maintenance can sometimes be negotiated as part of the initial purchase package. Finally, insist that the vendor supply equipment and set up a working prototype network to prove the wireless network's reliability before signing any purchase contract. Also, have professional installers set up the antennas, as line-of-sight positioning is critical to the success of a wireless network.

Virtual Private Networks

The Internet may seem to be an obvious example of a wide area network, but unlike other wide area networks, the Internet comes with a host of problems. (If it were easy to use the Internet to extend a district's network, many districts would already be doing it.) One of the major drawbacks to using the Internet is that it is inherently open to security risks. Sending private information—student records, payroll information, or financial data, for

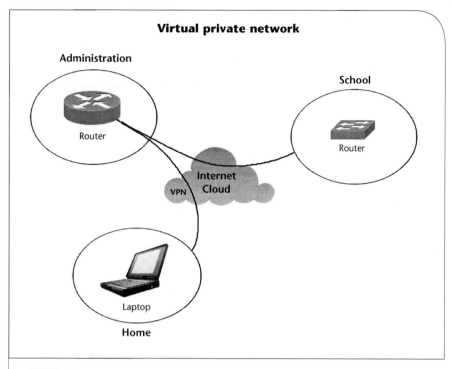

Virtual private network

Administration

Router

School

Router

Internet Cloud

VPN

Laptop

Home

FIGURE 5.2

example—across the Internet has the potential for creating enormous security problems. While local area networks provide ways to authenticate users (check their identities), prioritize and manage traffic, and secure information against tampering, the Internet provides few such mechanisms.

Virtual private network (VPN) technologies allow districts to use the Internet or other public networks as an extension of their local area networks. After installing VPN hardware and software, a network administrator can enforce security, user policies (definitions of the information on the network and who can access it), and quality of service (deciding which network traffic has priority) on these public networks just as if they were local area networks. In an Internet-based VPN, connections are made from each building or individual user to an Internet service provider. Data are encrypted at the sending site, transmitted along the public network, and then decrypted by the receiver.

VPN technologies have proven useful in solving three organizational needs:

INTERCONNECTING BUILDINGS OR SITES. VPN technologies replace traditional WAN connections. In a traditional MAN or WAN, school buildings are interconnected by leased lines or frame relay circuits. In a VPN, each building might connect only to its nearby Internet service provider (sometimes a much less expensive proposition). To communicate over the VPN, a sender transmits information to its assigned VPN server on the local area network. That VPN server in turn contacts the recipient's VPN server through an Internet service provider and Internet connections; the second VPN server receives the information and delivers it to users on the network.

CONNECTING PEOPLE FROM HOME OR TRAVEL TO THE SCHOOL NETWORK. VPNs allow teachers, students, and administrators to connect to a network from home and use all of the network resources—such as printers, servers, and shared documents—just as if they were accessing those resources from within the organization. To communicate over the VPN, software on the remote client computer (at the student's or teacher's home, for example) encrypts its data and contacts its local ISP. The ISP in turn contacts the school's VPN server.

PROTECTING SENSITIVE INFORMATION WITHIN THE SCHOOL NETWORK. VPN technologies within a network protect sensitive resources so that only specified people can access them (replacing security offered by VLANs and/or routers). By placing a VPN server between the sensitive information and those who want to access it, permission can be granted or denied on a user-by-user basis.

VPNs typically strengthen public network security by adding four types of services: authentication, access control, confidentiality, and data integrity. Authentication verifies that the senders are who they claim to be. Access control guarantees that only authorized users access the network. Confidentiality ensures that only intended recipients can view the data being sent. Data integrity ensures that the data arrive intact.

VPN systems depend on a number of protocols to provide access control, authentication, confidentiality, and data integrity services. The protocols vary among different implementations of VPNs. However, all VPNs, regardless of their method of securing data, depend on a general technology called tunneling. To create a tunnel, a VPN server receives the outgoing frames or packets (small packages of data) and encapsulates them within an envelope that is readable by the public network traversed by the VPN. (For VPNs on the Internet, the envelope makes the information look just like a standard Internet packet, even though within the envelope there is security-related information that is not normally part of an Internet packet.) The VPN server then sends the envelope on its way, and the public network treats the information as if it were native. At the recipient's end, a VPN client removes the envelope and delivers the data just as if it had never left the local area network. Depending on the public network, the envelope might be built according to Internet Protocols (for traversing the Internet), frame relay protocols (for traversing frame relay circuits), or other protocols.

Point-to-Point Tunneling Protocol (PPTP) is perhaps the most widely used VPN protocol, in large part because it has been incorporated into many versions of Microsoft Windows. PPTP builds its services on those of an earlier protocol, Point-to-Point Protocol (PPP), which has been used for many years to enable dial-up connections to the Internet. PPTP encapsulates and routes PPP packets for secure travel. PPTP also uses the authentication mechanisms previously defined for PPP, including Password Authentication Protocol (PAP) and Challenge Handshake Authentication Protocol (CHAP). PAP presents a client's password, sent as plain text (and therefore somewhat insecure), to the server for verification. CHAP presents a challenge (a special packet requesting information) from the server to the client. The client responds with a return packet that the server either validates or rejects.

CHAP challenges may be issued throughout the conversation to ensure that an authorized client is always connected. Beyond these authentication services, PPTP can use PPP to encrypt data. However, PPTP usually calls upon stronger encryption services, often those provided by yet another protocol—Microsoft point-to-point encryption (MPPE). PPTP has the great virtue of being able to carry multiple OSI layer 3 protocols—including IPX, IP, AppleTalk, and NetBEUI—over the VPN. In other words, if the local area network includes a Novell server using IPX and Macintoshes using AppleTalk, then these computers will be able to communicate over the VPN if PPTP is used to provide the connections.

Layer 2 Forwarding Protocol (L2F) improves upon PPTP in several senses. First, L2F can be used to create tunnels over networks other than the Internet. While L2F also depends on PPP to provide authentication, it also supports authentication through centralized servers, most-notably Terminal Access Controller Access Control System (TACACS) and Remote Authentication Dial-In User Service (RADIUS), or global directories such as Active Directory or Novell NetWare Directory Services eDirectory. Finally, L2F supports multiple tunnels for each connection.

Layer 2 Tunneling Protocol (L2TP) blends aspects of both PPTP and L2F to produce a protocol that many believe will become one of the most common standards for VPN connections. L2TP includes the authentication services of both PPTP and L2F along with L2F's ability to accommodate a variety of wide area network protocols other than IP. For encryption, L2TP uses the powerful services of the Internet Protocol Security (IPSec).

Internet Protocol Security can be used in combination with the VPN protocols described previously to supply encryption services, or it can be used to provide full VPN services including access control, authentication, confidentiality, and data integrity in its own right. IPSec embodies several technologies. These include Data Encryption Standard (DES), an encryption method that has been used for several decades; algorithms (recipes) to authenticate the packets that are being exchanged; and digital certificates (encoded electronic information) to validate each party's identity. Many network managers believe that IPSec offers the best solution for VPNs that run over the Internet. If the VPN crosses other types of public networks such as frame relay or Asynchronous Transfer Mode, then the network will be better served by PPTP or L2TP.

Beyond these protocols for access control, authentication, confidentiality, and data integrity, a VPN should also provide good tools for auditing network access. Auditing tools allow staff members to determine who is accessing the network, for how long, and using which resources.

To implement all these services, VPNs can include four components: the public network, security servers, user authentication servers, and certificate authorities.

Security servers sit between the public network and a district's private network, preventing intrusions and optionally providing encryption and tunneling services. Routers, firewalls, dedicated VPN hardware, and VPN software may all function as a security server. Because routers filter every packet bound for the Internet on many existing networks, they are the natural place to install a VPN. Vendors offer add-on software or hardware in the form of circuit boards that can be inserted into the existing router. The hardware solution provides the best performance.

Many firewalls also include VPN capabilities. Firewall-based VPNs are suitable for small networks, but routers provide better VPN performance for large networks. (Firewalls are taxed to perform a great many more functions besides routing and providing VPN services.) VPN software can also be added to existing servers, and these software-based VPNs are suitable for small networks or for managing dial-up connections.

User authentication servers list valid users and their access right for the network. TACACS, RADIUS, Active Directory, and Novell Netware Services eDirectory serve this purpose.

Certificate authorities keep track of digital certificates (electronic information that verifies the identity of individuals or entities exchanging information). A network can keep track of its own digital certificates on a certificate server. For small numbers of users, a third party certificate service will suffice. (IPSec includes digital certificates as part of its security technologies.)

Internet-based VPNs can sometimes provide substantial cost savings if connected buildings are far apart. Because distant buildings need not be connected directly to each other (but only to an ISP, which may be closer), leased line costs may be reduced. In some cases, the ISP assumes management responsibility for much of the VPN equipment. VPNs are also easier than WANs to expand as the network increases in size. Unlike WAN expansions, which require upgrades to communications lines and all associated equipment, VPN expansions require upgrades only to local area network equipment and network bandwidth.

When considering a VPN to replace an existing WAN, note that traditional WANs (using leased lines) provide greater security and stability because they involve private lines and proven technologies. VPNs, on the other hand, suffer if there are routing problems on the Internet, and may encounter difficulties with communications between various platforms (or with sophisticated encryption and other security technologies).

Address routing problems by selecting an ISP with care. If all buildings are in the same calling area, use a single ISP. If one or more buildings lie outside the local calling area, choose ISPs that are on the same backbone (e.g., BBNPlanet). VPNs add bandwidth overhead and management complexity to the network (if managing VPN equipment in-house). Undoubtedly, the stability, manageability, and security of VPNs will continue to improve, but for the moment, think carefully before replacing traditional WAN connections and employ VPNs with a clear sense of their strengths and weaknesses.

While VPNs have some liabilities when they replace traditional WANs, they have few such shortcomings when replacing remote access servers. VPNs are roughly as stable as remote access servers, but they provide increased security, manageability, and economy. Expanding remote access connections requires the substantial work of coordinating and installing new lines and hardware; expanding VPNs requires fewer equipment changes. Remote access modems have never been considered reliable, and long distance charges may be significant. With remote access servers, unauthorized access to a password can expose a network to attack. VPNs provide a more self-contained, secure solution.

Asynchronous Transfer Mode, SONet, and Fiber Distributed Data Interface

Asynchronous Transfer Mode (ATM), SONet (Synchronous Optical Network), and Fiber Distributed Data Interface (FDDI) provide powerful but expensive networks sufficient to convey voice, video, and data for large organizations.

ATM provides both LAN and WAN technology. The current price of installation makes its use on most LANs prohibitive, but it is frequently deployed for wide area connections. Running at speeds from 1.54 Mbps to 622 Mbps with additional capabilities for managing network congestion, ATM provides an astonishing potential to deliver high volumes of video, voice, and data.

ATM divides its operations into several levels (analogous to the levels of the OSI model). The upper levels describe how the network connects to ATM services. Intermediate levels describe how data is divided for the WAN transmission into small packages (53 bytes each, referred to as cells). The lowest level defines the connections between ATM and the physical network, including several possible alternative carrier signals with which ATM can be integrated—DS-3 (T3), SONet lines, and Fiber Distributed Data Interface. Although expensive, ATM is the technology of choice for combining video, data, and phone (voice) networks.

SONet defines a transmission scheme for fiber optic cable or copper wire. It is usually implemented on single mode fiber optic cable (rather than copper wire).

SONet operates at the speeds indicated in Table 5.2.

TABLE 5.2: SONET TRANSMISSION SPEEDS

| SONet | | |
Optical Fiber	Copper Wire	Transmission Rate (Mbps)
OC-1	STS-1	51.84
OC-3	STS-3	155.52
OC-12	STS-12	622.08
OC-48	STS-48	2,488.32

Fiber Distributed Data Interface defines 100 Mbps service over fiber optic cable. FDDI can provide data link and physical communications for ATM or, alternatively, it can provide full LAN or WAN services on its own. As a LAN technology, FDDI is expensive to implement. In some areas of the country, telecommunications carriers provide access to Fiber Network Services (FNS), a public FDDI network that provides very fast wide area connections.

Both SONet and FDDI are widely used. FDDI is more common with LANs; SONet is commonly found on large WANs (e.g., between Internet service providers).

Technical Information Summary

WIRELESS AND ASYNCHRONOUS TRANSFER MODE, SONET, AND FIBER DISTRIBUTED DATA INTERFACE

Many different technologies—including microwaves, lasers, and radio waves—can be used to create wireless WAN links. Of these technologies, radio waves have gained the most attention recently. Radio waves provide a relatively inexpensive wide area network and are able to connect LANs as far as 25 miles apart.

When setting up a wireless WAN, be sure that the equipment is installed properly—particularly that the antennas are within radio line of sight and properly aligned to each other. Ask the manufacturer to conduct a path analysis before purchasing wireless WAN equipment. A path analysis determines not only the line of sight, but also identifies potential obstacles, calculates the necessary power and requirements for repeaters, and selects the type of antenna that will best suit the network's needs. Have professionals install and align the network antennas.

Asynchronous Transfer Mode, SONet, and Fiber Distributed Data Interface provide powerful but expensive networks sufficient to carry voice, video, and data transmissions for large organizations. SONet defines a transmission scheme for fiber optic cable or copper wire. It operates at very high speeds, commonly 622 Mbps. ATM services at the upper levels of the OSI model are sometimes run over SONet at the lower levels. Fiber Distributed Data Interface defines 100 Mbps service over fiber optic cable. FDDI can provide data link and physical communications (lowest OSI levels) for ATM or, alternatively, it can provide full LAN or WAN services on its own.

WAN Technologies and the OSI Reference Model

Wide area network technologies implement the OSI reference model just as local area networks do but they generally focus on the physical and data link layers. Table 5.3 summarizes the most common wide area network technologies with regard to the OSI reference model.

TABLE 5.3: WAN TECHNOLOGIES AND THE OSI REFERENCE MODEL

WAN Technology	Physical Layer (Layer 1)	Data Link Layer (Layer 2)
POTS	POTS operates at the physical layer.	Point-to-Point Protocol (PPP) and Serial Line Internet Protocol (SLIP) work with POTS at the data link layer. PPP and SLIP receive information from the TCP/IP protocol stack on the network, encapsulate this information, and then pass it on to POTS connections.
ISDN	ISDN operates at the physical layer.	Point-to-Point Protocol and High-level Data Link Control protocol (HDLC) work with ISDN at the data link layer. PPP and HDLC receive information from the TCP/IP protocol stack on the network, encapsulate this information, and then pass it on to ISDN connections.
Leased Lines	Leased lines operate at the physical layer.	Point-to-Point Protocol, High-level Data Link Control protocol, and others are common carriers. The telecommunications provider will specify the data link protocol when provisioning the line. The links protocols (such as PPP and HDLC) receive information from the TCP/IP protocol stack on the network, encapsulate this information, and then pass it on to leased line connections.
Frame Relay	Frame relay uses leased lines or ATM at the physical layer.	Frame relay defines a data link layer protocol for conveying data over a variety of physical connections, including T1 or ATM. Frame relay receives information from the TCP/IP protocol stack on the network, encapsulates this information, and then passes it on to physical connections.
VPN	VPNs use the physical and data link layers of the public network over which they run (e.g., the Internet).	VPNs encapsulate information from a local area network within electronic envelopes suitable for a public network. The encapsulation can take place at OSI reference model layer 3 (IPSec produces IP packets suitable for the Internet) or layer 2 (PPTP, L2F, and L2TP produce a variety of frames suitable for different networks).

Comparison of WAN Technologies

Tables 5.4, 5.5, 5.6, and 5.7 summarize the most important distinctions among ISDN, leased lines, frame relay, and wireless technologies.

TABLE 5.4: ISDN

Cost	Monthly fee plus per minute charge
	Cost increases as the distance between points increases
Availability	Most urban areas of the United States
Bandwidth	64 Kbps to 128 Kbps (most common)
Uses	Voice, data, video
Advantages	Pay only for the time using the connection; ISDN is cost-effective if communications are infrequent
	Relatively inexpensive
	Simple installation
Disadvantages	Relatively slow
	Requires some time for installation

TABLE 5.5: LEASED LINES (T1)

Cost	Fixed cost
	Cost increases as the distance between points increases
Bandwidth	56 Kbps, 128 Kbps, 512 Kbps, 1.544 Mbps (T1)
Availability	Most urban areas of the United States
Uses	Voice, data, video (voice is carried on separate lines from data unless using Voice over IP)
Advantages	Pay a fixed rate; leased lines are useful if communications are continuous and expenses are budgeted to a fixed monthly sum
	Well-known and reliable technology
	Good security
	Easy to increase capacity from 128 Kbps to higher bandwidth
Disadvantages	Expensive
	Requires considerable time for installation

TABLE 5.6: WIRELESS

Cost	Purchase and installation plus maintenance agreement for repair
Bandwidth	1–100 Mbps
Availability	Anywhere
Uses	Voice, video, data
Advantages	The only recurring charge is the maintenance contract
	Connects buildings that are otherwise too expensive or physically difficult to connect
Disadvantages	Requires careful installation
	Distance limitations (for example, 10–12 Mbps WANs span 25 miles or fewer)

TABLE 5.7: FRAME RELAY

Cost	Varies with bandwidth used
	Cost does not increase as the distance between points increases
Bandwidth	Any (depending on the WAN technology—such as T1—that connects the network to the frame relay network and the frame relay bandwidth contracted for)
Availability	Most geographical areas
Uses	Voice, data
Advantages	Can expand to include numerous geographically dispersed locations
	Troubleshooting is handled by the frame relay provider instead of local staff
	Easy to increase bandwidth
Disadvantages	Costs vary, but can be expensive

Appendixes

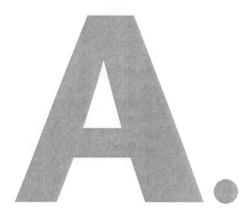

Designing Networks for Educational Environments

Harnessing technology to create a network capable of supporting educational environments requires four basic resources:

> Hardware
> Software
> Teacher professional development programs
> Support services, including maintenance, repair, and troubleshooting

If any of these resources is missing, an educational organization will be hard pressed to develop and maintain a network capable of handling its ongoing operations.

The actual design of educational networks is a matter of "form following function." The process is begun by having the organization outline the goals it wishes to achieve. It is important, therefore, that educators—not technicians or computer specialists—be involved in the planning from the very start. In general, every forward-looking network design should include provisions for supporting extensive use of distance learning technologies including the Internet and television (possibly interactive television). Moreover, to be a truly effective tool for learning, educational networks must support (i.e., have the bandwidth to comfortably handle) a combination of voice, video, and data (including multimedia) streams.

Network Infrastructure

Most schools install a combination of twisted pair copper, fiber optic, and coaxial (television) cable. Fiber optic cable provides significantly greater bandwidth (carrying capacity) than twisted pair copper and is free from electrical interference. It is also much more expensive. For these reasons, fiber is generally used where large amounts of data travel—in the (interbuilding) backbone of a network and sometimes also in portions of the network within each school building. Fiber optic cable that connects buildings should be rated for outdoor use; twisted pair copper wire is fine for use in the remaining sections of a local area network. The exact placement of twisted pair copper cable versus fiber cable is a balance between performance and cost. Coaxial cable is used both between and within buildings to carry television signals.

New networks should support connections at speeds of 100 Mbps throughout, with higher speeds available to connect servers. Because infrastructure will not be replaced for many years, network cabling should have sufficient bandwidth to handle future loads that are many times the network's current capacity. To gauge this capacity, describe the types, quantity, and pace of activity that the network now supports along with any foreseeable changes. Once this is accomplished, technical staff and cable installers should quadruple that capacity estimate and then determine the quantities and categories of cable to install.

Wiring contractors should test the cable installation according to the detailed standards required by the network and provide written verification of all such tests. Likewise, contractors should label all cables and provide cable maps and training on any equipment they install. Many networks fail because they are improperly installed. Because these failures sometimes appear in the weeks or months after the contractors are gone, secure the contractors' tests and warranties before paying for the work. The contract should indicate that the cable installer is responsible for all underestimates of materials and labor. That is, if a contractor identifies 90 "drops" (connections to a wall outlet, usually in a classroom) and later finds that 100 are needed—the contractor must absorb the additional costs. Finally, establish a policy governing "change orders," or requests to change the original wiring specification. Last-minute changes—especially those requested by nontechnical personnel—can significantly raise the cost of infrastructure installations.

Each building should provide (space permitting) a communications equipment room for servers, mainframes, and video or audio distribution systems. The communications equipment room provides the main connections to the district network infrastructure and the point from which all classroom connections emanate. It should include the following:

> Temperature and humidity controls

> Grounded power lines that include surge protection (wall outlets and equipment may require additional surge protection and backup batteries)

> Fire suppression and smoke evacuation devices

> A security system able to prevent intrusion and alert authorities

For obvious reasons, do not place communication rooms in proximity to general plumbing lines or facilities.

From the communications equipment room, the cabling system is likely to pass through a variety of structures. Some schools run connections directly to classrooms; others establish a hierarchical system with a communications equipment room and smaller intermediate distribution points. Certain schools use a system called zone cabling in which one or more fiber strands run to a switch (connecting box) in each classroom that allows multiple computers to share the strand. Each cabling system has its strengths and weaknesses. Throughout the building, any cable that is not enclosed in a conduit must be plenum rated. (Plenum-rated cable is enclosed in a fire-retardant jacket that does not release smoke when it burns.)

The network design should take into account the power needs of classrooms full of computers and peripherals. Plan to provide at least four amps of clean, grounded electrical power per computer. Arrange network and power connections in convenient places to accommodate all the different ways technology will be used in the classroom.

The New Jersey Department of Education has posted an example of thoughtful, comprehensive guidelines for designing schools and classrooms. Visit their work online at **www.state. nj.us/njded/techno/facstan/facstan2.htm**.

Network Policies, Procedures, and Standards

Policies and procedures for all major functions of the network, its staff, and users should be clearly defined. Make sure that the network's policies and procedures include the following areas (as a minimum):

> **Use of electronic mail.** Electronic mail is the property of the school or district and not of the user. Furthermore, electronic mail is an insecure medium and should never be used for sensitive communications, especially if such correspondence is sent in standard (unencrypted) form. Be sure that network policies include a section on electronic mail etiquette.

> **Salvage policy.** Establish guidelines for removing old equipment from the premises or distributing it for personal use.

> **Repurposing policy.** Computers are often reassigned to less demanding tasks as they are replaced by newer models. Define the point at which technical staff will no longer repair these older computers, whether the computers will be networked, and the point at which they'll be removed for good.

> **Standard software and hardware.** Establish standards for network hardware and software as a way of reducing training costs associated with new hires. Purchase computers in batches and establish purchasing guidelines that define how powerful the computers will be (their central processor speed, amount of memory, disk size,

etc.). Many sites establish lists of preferred vendors and manufacturers from whom all purchases are made.

> **Purchase of equipment and software.** Define the procedures by which teachers and administrators can purchase hardware or software.

> **Installation of hardware and software.** Consider requiring central approval before hardware is installed. (This is especially important because new hardware often requires coordination with other components on the network.)

Budgeting

Schools receive funding for technology from a variety of sources: bonds and other categorical sources that specify support for particular uses or groups of students only; school-based grants; school-based funds; district general funds; donations and parent support; business and education foundations; lottery; and other funds. Typically, schools project revenue for the coming year and then estimate the cost of providing the current levels of service. If extra money is available, they plan incremental improvements.

Setting aside funds for technology, or more specifically for constructing and maintaining a network, is a complex task that requires clear decision making. The realities of integrating technology into schools make the task even more difficult.

Many large expenses recur neither annually nor on long cycles, and these expenses may be sizeable rather than incremental. Desktop computers and many other network devices require routine replacement. If these components are not updated, they cannot run modern software and often cannot connect to the network. Programs that help teachers integrate technology into their classrooms may require large expenditures for several years to cover the costs of teacher professional development, consultants, and materials when they are starting up, and these programs may need to be repeated as new technologies appear.

Technology changes pay scales and job definitions. Even the smallest school networks require technicians to keep them running and technology curriculum integration specialists to help teachers use them. Districts often require help desk personnel and technology managers to supervise network activities. Furthermore, schools must often compete with the private sector for their technical talent. Although schools offer many benefits that the private sector cannot, salaries must still be competitive to retain technical staff.

Technology creates new expenditure categories that may not have a ready-made place in a district's budget. Teachers and technicians require an assortment of tools, training materials, and supplies such as CD-ROMs or floppy disks to make backup copies of their work; technical staff must maintain service contracts to help repair equipment.

Although school budgeting is often a top-down process, making technology work well requires direct input from the people on the front lines—teachers, students, and technology specialists. To determine the "best technology" for a site, administrative leaders, teachers, and students must all become involved in the process of determining their priorities well before budget time, and at least once a year.

Managing the Total Cost of Ownership

Living within a budget means that economic realities lie at the heart of every technology management decision. The pace of technological change accelerates constantly, demand for the technology intensifies, and per-unit prices fall consistently. Although technology has become less expensive over the years, the total cost of owning and maintaining the technology (TCO) continues to rise. This growth in TCO is due, at least in part, to the increasing complexity of the tasks that technology is being asked to perform. As the level of software and equipment sophistication rises, so does a network's infrastructure and management expenses each year.

Surprisingly, the cost of purchasing equipment constitutes only about 20% of the total cost of owning it each year. The Gartner Group (a consulting company) estimates that a typical business enterprise with 2,000 Windows computers currently spends an average of $9,500 per computer per year in direct and hidden costs for computing. In other words, while securing good purchase prices for equipment is important, it is more important over the long term to provide professional development and support services that help reduce the other 80% of the cost of owning computers.

The Consortium for School Networking (CoSN) has compiled a Web site (**www.cosn.org/ tco/**) that suggests how school districts might think about the costs associated with technology. In the 1999 version of *Taking TCO to the Classroom*, the CoSN site suggested that you allocate resources as depicted in Table A.1.

TABLE A.1: TOTAL COSTS OF OWNERSHIP (TCO)

Professional Development	15–30% of the technology budget according to various sources, including the U.S. Department of Education; or $15–35 per student per year according to a RAND study of pioneering high-tech schools; or $1,500 per year for each person requiring training according to Smart Valley
Technical Support	One staff member for every 100–250 users, according to the Northwest Regional Educational Technology Consortium; or one network manager at the county, one at the district, and 1/2 at each school, according to Smart Valley
Connectivity	4–8% of initial purchase price initially, and 7–15% ongoing
Retrofitting Buildings	Council of Educational Facility Planners International estimates $1,500 per "classroom equivalent" for infrastructure in new construction and $3,000 per "classroom equivalent" in renovation-modernization projects
Software Licenses	21–26% according to McKinsey & Company, Inc.
Replacement	Rolling replacement of a standard percentage of computers each year

The 2001 version of *Taking TCO to the Classroom* provides detailed charts describing the suggested total costs for two different models of school computing—the classroom model and the computer lab model. The report also summarizes information from many different studies of TCO and provides a budgetary checklist of items. The full CoSN report is available at **www.cosn.org/tco/tco2class.pdf**.

A special report from eSchoolNews titled *Network Administration* (**www.eschoolnews.com**) suggests many of the following strategies for minimizing the total cost of ownership:

1. Purchase top-of-the-line equipment, keeping network operations as simple and standardized as possible, and following preventive maintenance procedures religiously. Do not settle for inexpensive equipment or equipment will become obsolete in a few years, or that is not configured the way it was ordered. Know what is needed and get what is paid for.

2. Automate procedures wherever possible. Software packages such as Novell's ZENworks (**www.Novell.com/products/zenworks/**) or Apple's Network Assistant allow network managers to install and repair software from a central location (instead of visiting each computer). Most virus-detection programs offer similar centralized updates. Investigate tools for managing the creation and deletion of hundreds of student accounts in a single action. Use disk imaging programs such as Symantec Ghost (**www.symantec.com/sabu/ghost/**) when deploying hundreds of computers simultaneously. Use programs such as Deep Freeze (**www.deepfreezeusa.com**) to automate the process of rebuilding computer configurations on a regular basis.

3. Protect desktop computers from tampering by using system policies or software such as Fortres 101 (**www.fortres.com**), FoolProof (**www.smartstuff.com**), At Ease, or Macintosh Manager (available from Apple Computer). These products allow restrictions to be placed on teachers' and students' ability to boot from a floppy diskette, install or reconfigure software, change desktop settings, and save documents to their desktop computer. Bear in mind, however, that limiting teachers' access in this way also limits their ability to teach.

4. Insist that network staff develop a thorough knowledge of the baseline operations of all critical equipment, and that they share this knowledge with each other. When possible, purchase all equipment of one type from one manufacturer. Limit the software and hardware available to network users, but provide enough to get the job done.

5. Train network users about standard operations and calling for help when necessary (before they have spent hours on a problem). Respond quickly. Invent strategies for getting information into the hands of users and then get them to employ it. Work with the administration to ensure that network helpers are recognized and even compensated. Multiplying the number of reliable helping hands is one of the best ways to minimize the total cost of ownership.

6. Be selective about new technology. Ask whether the new technology really has the potential to make a difference in teaching and learning. When investing in a major improvement, make sure that the cost is justified by the potential benefit.

Infrastructure Installations—"The Project Manager"

When installing computers and network equipment on a large scale, count on planning and coordinating hundreds of separate actions and, at the same time, managing the activities (and expense) of several outside contractors. Because it is difficult for staff to tackle these responsibilities in addition to their regular work, many school districts hire project managers to direct these special projects. The project manager should report to the lead technology manager in the district, provide regular updates and warnings if milestones will be missed, and sometimes track the budget (especially if payments are keyed to milestones).

The project manager also serves as the single point of contact for administrators, principals, teachers, and community members who want to know how things are going (and when their work may be disrupted). When there are competing demands among these different groups, the project manager sets priorities and makes them clear. When demands arise that are not covered in the original plan, the project manager works with constituencies so that these demands do not arise often. This latter task requires a good deal of diplomacy. The most important role of the project manager is to align timelines and deliverables among all the various activities so that, overall, each task is completed in an orderly sequence.

Planning Professional Development

Adopting and implementing technology throughout a school district is a slow process that occurs in stages and can ultimately take years to effect. Plan your professional development programs to respect the following stages that most teachers and administrators go through as they accumulate technology:

1. **Familiarization.** During the familiarization phase, teachers learn how the technology operates, how to do basic tasks, and how to work around its peculiarities. The professional development program should provide opportunities for beginners, along with rewards, clear expectations of their participation, and consistent technical support afterward to get them past often-frustrating beginnings.

2. **Automation.** During the automation phase, teachers and administrators learn how to do what they already do better. They use spreadsheets to calculate budgets or schedules; they employ electronic grade books, report cards, and lesson planners; and they lecture with PowerPoint or use the Internet to provide selected teaching materials. In essence, however, they continue to do their jobs in much the same way as they always have.

3. **Innovation.** During the innovation phase, teachers and administrators break new ground. Their professional development involves asking questions and engaging colleagues in finding answers. Teachers need time and resources to explore (and possibly fail to answer) these questions. They need to discuss issues of pedagogy, student learning, and the technology tools themselves with colleagues who are also explorers.

For the first two phases, some districts offer summer workshops with follow-ups during the year; they employ teacher-mentors who coach and help spread technology into many classrooms; they offer Web-based discussions and courses; or they send teachers to conferences and institutes where they can brainstorm with teachers from other places. The only venues that educators usually warn against are single workshops that do not provide enough long-term support.

The following professional development examples show some successful strategies at each of these phases. Notice that these programs plan time for learning and for many types of follow-up support; they reward participants, scale to appreciable size, and ultimately aim to change the way teachers teach.

Mamaroneck Public Schools (New York) offered a 10-day summer program for middle school Unified Arts teachers to develop more learner-active, technology-infused classrooms. During the program, teachers developed inquiry-based problems that incorporated an authentic, open-ended task statement and rubric for each of their courses. (Often teachers designed the lessons as WebQuests with Internet resources.) They also addressed implementation issues including how to get started; facilitation issues; classroom management issues; assessment strategies; and differentiation of instruction. Instructors taught the classes in a manner that modeled the classroom management approaches they were presenting to teachers. For example, teachers made their own daily schedule, which included time for individual and small group activities as well as presentations. Teachers posted complete activities on the district's Web site where students could see them. During the following school year, the summer instructor continued to meet one day a month with each teacher.

Brookline Public Schools (Massachusetts) interviewed its K–8 principals to determine their curricular goals (not their technology goals) and developed a monthly seminar series that would help them understand how technology could be used to achieve those goals. The district provided the principals with laptops and a hands-on introduction to using them, information on making digital movies, demonstrations from teachers on how they use technology in their classrooms, exploration of programs such as Inspiration, overviews of a variety of assistive technologies, and information on other topics. The program succeeded in helping these principals become confident technology leaders (not experts) and to establish their priorities around technology and communicate them to teachers.

Teachers in Louisiana school districts working in collaboration with Education Development Center, Inc., participated in a series of Web-based courses about integrating technology into classrooms and, somewhat later, co-facilitated an online course with an experienced online instructor. Ultimately, these teachers led their own online courses based on EDC's curricula. The courses not only infuse new technology, but they also build district-level capacity and provide professional development in which teachers can participate from any place at any time.

In any school district, teachers and administrators move unevenly through the three stages. Only a small percentage of people eagerly adopt new practices (especially time-consuming and unproven ones). Use these individuals to make a persuasive case in favor of technology.

The following professional development resources provide additional information:

> Wasser, J. D., & McNamara, E. (1998). Professional development and full-school technology integration: A description of the professional development model of the Hanau Model Schools Partnership [online]. Available: **http://modelschools.terc. edu/modelschools/TEMPLATE/Publications/pdf/ProfDevPaper.pdf.**

> Wasser, J. D., McNamara, E., & Grant, C. M. (in press). Electronic networks and systemic school reform: Understanding the diverse roles and functions of telecommunications in changing school environments. *Journal of Educational Computing Research.*

> Grant, C. (1999). Beyond tool training: Professional development for elementary math teachers. *Learning & Leading with Technology, 27*(3), 42–47.

Disaster Recovery Planning

No matter how good a network maintenance program is, disasters can still occur. Planning for these eventualities is an important part of any comprehensive network operation. A disaster recovery plan is a document that describes the steps to be taken in the event a site and equipment are physically destroyed. Creating a disaster recovery plan is a joint activity involving a district's technical and administrative groups. Developing and implementing the plan takes considerable time and resources (especially if the plan includes an emergency operations center at another location). Balance the concern over disaster preparedness with the time and money available.

A disaster recovery plan usually contains the following parts:

> **Arrangements.** A description of how to set up operations at another site, if necessary

> **Procedures.** A description that details:

1. When the disaster plan should be invoked

2. The distribution list for the plan

3. The district's administrative structure and notification trees in case of emergency

4. How to mobilize staff

5. Backup resources (including descriptions of the off-site locations where all of the backup information is stored)

6. Emergency operations procedures for each functional unit in the district that outline which operations will be restored after the emergency, and in what order

7. Details of how network resources will be recovered—the servers where

documents are stored or that connect the network to the Internet, the desktop machines that teachers and students use, and the records system on which the administration depends

8. Testing and training for the disaster recovery plan including walk-through rehearsals and simulated real-time exercises

> **Inventory.** Lists of software and hardware at all sites (including serial numbers), passwords, support contract information, and insurance contract information

A disaster recovery plan may include the use of either a hot site or a cold site at which operations would be initiated after disaster occurs. At a hot site, all the equipment, furniture, telecommunications connections, power, supplies, and materials needed to conduct critical operations are set up permanently. No further work is required for operations to commence at the site. A cold site, on the other hand, provides space, but the responsibility for setting up the equipment, telecommunications lines, and the rest of the infrastructure still remains. Hot sites are more expensive to maintain than cold sites.

Ideally, a district should produce the plan in two formats—an extensive, detailed format to be used prior to disaster, and a brief format containing only essential information to be used after the disaster. When a disaster occurs, people will not have time to read lengthy details. They simply need index cards of contact names and charts of what to do and where to find the resources they need. Finally, store all the information needed to execute the plan (including the plan itself) at a remote location.

B.

Securing the Network

Security is an integral part of every comprehensive network design. Most organizations are vulnerable to malicious or inadvertent damage to hardware or software. Some even experience breaches that compromise the confidentially or integrity of their data. The costs associated with security breaches can be substantial, ranging from the price of restoring damaged data to stiff fines and other legal penalties. The first security-related task every organization needs to undertake is a five-step risk analysis.

1. **Define assets.** List all network components (desktops, laptops, servers, interconnecting devices such as routers, software) and data (student records, financial information, personnel, curriculum systems, etc.), and assign a value to each one. It is best if a team of people (not just technical personnel) collaborate on this task, because different team members will come up with somewhat different assessments of assets and value.

2. **Assess vulnerability.** Define all the ways that the network might be attacked. Include both electronic and physical attacks from outside and inside the school district. Assign probabilities to each type of attack.

3. **Evaluate controls.** A control is a countermeasure. Analyze the list of vulnerabilities and identify potential controls for each one. Since controls have a cost, evaluate whether the potential benefits outweigh the risk of exposure.

4. **Decide on strategies.** With each risk, there are three choices: accept the risk and do nothing, implement controls to diminish the risk, or transfer the risk (i.e., purchase insurance). Once a strategy has been determined for each risk, create a written security policy that outlines the security plans and procedures for administrators, students, teachers, and community members.

5. **Communicate and implement policies.** Teachers, students, administrators, and community members must understand and abide by security policies. Senior administrators must approve them. Set up an emergency response team and specific guidelines for actions to undertake if an emergency arises (i.e., defining whether a hacker will be allowed continued access in order to trace the source of the intrusion or whether security breaches are to be closed as soon as they are found).

Virus Protection

A virus is a malicious program that spreads from one computer to another through floppy disks, electronic mail, and Internet connections. Virus programs are intentionally written to damage data or internal components (such as the computer's hard drive). Some virus programs are simple nuisances; others can cause irreparable harm. Make virus protection a high priority. Install antivirus software on all desktop computers, network servers, firewalls, and electronic mail servers. Antivirus programs run silently in the background, checking documents as they are opened or copied. If a virus is detected, the protection program disinfects it (neutralizes its destructive power).

Other destructive virus-like programs are:

> **Trojan horse.** A program similar to a virus that exists solely for hiding destructive code within a system (just as the original Trojan horse hid warriors)

> **Worm.** A destructive program that reproduces itself and can spread across networks

> **Logic bomb.** A destructive program that is released on a specific date or after a specific action

When shopping for antivirus software, consult product reviews in computer periodicals. Most antivirus software manufacturers update their virus signatures as soon as each new virus is discovered. They distribute these updates over the Web every week or two. Servers should be configured to accept these signature updates, and desktop computers should be configured to receive them as soon as they start up and log in each day. Antivirus software should be upgraded frequently (at least once a year on all computers) because only up-to-date software can offer full protection.

There are many good virus protection software manufacturers, including Symantec (**www.symantec.com**) and Network Associates (**www.networkassociates.com**).

Passwords and Server Security

Passwords should be required for all servers, electronic mail, and any other systems that contain sensitive data. Insist that users create passwords that are hard to guess (many network systems are configurable to enforce such requirements) and instruct them as to the importance of securing the passwords. Here's a list of guidelines for creating good passwords:

> Make passwords at least seven characters long; the more characters they contain, the more secure they are.

> Include at least one special character—for example, digits, punctuation marks, or special characters such as !, $, and _ (for example: bully4you).

> Join two or more words with a special symbol (for example: rain$gear).

> Think of a common phrase and then use the first letter of each word as a password (for example: "Two heads are always better than one" becomes the password thaabto).

> Do not choose passwords that are the names of children, pets, or significant others.

> Do not include spaces in passwords.

Most servers provide tools besides passwords for restricting access. At the simplest level, the server requires that each user be granted permission (usually by a network manager) to access its documents, printers, and other services. Therefore, sensitive data such as student records or payroll information can be segregated onto separate servers. Carefully limit the number of users who have access to important data. Finally, as with most infrastructure decisions, it is important that users are partners in creating security system policies. Explain why it is necessary to impose security requirements, and ask for cooperation in carrying out the rules.

Backing Up the Network

Because computers (and software) are not 100% reliable, it is critical that secondary (backup) copies of network data and programs be kept on hand. There are wide varieties of hardware and software options that provide good backup services.

For small networks, a server can be outfitted with special backup software and a backup device called a magnetic tape drive. The tape drive is a small unit that sits inside the server and has a slot that holds a data tape cartridge. The software on the server can be configured to back up its own information automatically (without human intervention) on a preset schedule, usually at night when network traffic is lowest. One server may also back up information from other servers or, additionally, from desktop computers.

For larger networks with many servers, it is a good idea to purchase one or more specialized backup servers to orchestrate the backups. Each backup server is a separate computer outfitted with backup software and is responsible for backing up other servers and clients. Most often, backup servers do not have internal tape drives. Instead, they are connected to jukeboxes or tape libraries, devices that hold more than one tape cartridge. Tape libraries can improve backup speed by writing to more than one tape simultaneously. The backup servers control the selection of tapes and keep a catalog of precisely which documents are located on each tape so that they can be retrieved when needed.

It is a good practice on many large networks to locate all servers—both backup and other servers—in a single network segment (area). Backing up data creates substantial network traffic. Placing all backup devices on a single segment helps to segregate this traffic from the parts of the network that teachers, students, and administrators use for daily work.

If designed correctly, backups can be automated so that they occur after school hours with no human intervention. When designing backup services, consider the following:

> Select appropriate backup hardware and software.

> Establish a routine schedule for backup.

> Establish procedures for restoring files when users need them.

> Define the retention policy (the length of time that backup information will be kept before being overwritten).

> Identify services for off-site storage so that backup media are safe even if school buildings are physically harmed.

Tape backup drives (internal or external) utilize a number of different technologies. The most common network technology is digital linear tape (DLT). Newer technologies such as Quantum's S-DLT (Super Digital Linear Tape) and LTO (Linear Tape Open, developed by Hewlett-Packard, IBM, and Seagate Technology) are emerging and likely to be prevalent in the future. These technologies vary in the way that they write data to tape, the amount of data they can store on each tape, and the speed with which they copy the data onto tape. Digital audio tape (DAT), 8 millimeter (Exabyte Mammoth), and Sony's AIT (Advanced Intelligent Tape) are also available for networking use.

When selecting a tape technology, choose one that is compatible with the backup server (not all tape technologies are compatible with all servers) and that is widely used by other sites. (If data ever need to be restored at a remote site, it will be easier to do if the tape format is a common one.)

Common tape technologies such as DAT, DLT, and AIT each have variants that perform at different speeds. For example, DAT tapes come in DDS-3 and DDS-4 formats, and DLT tapes come in DLT4000, DLT8000, and other formats. The formats vary in their capacity, transfer speed, and sometimes their physical characteristics.

TABLE C.1: COMMON DATA TAPE TECHNOLOGIES

Technology	Capacity (native/compressed)	Format	Transfer Speed (native/compressed)
DAT (DDS-4)	20/40 Gb	4 mm removable cartridge	3/6 Mbps
DLT8000	40/80 Gb	DLTIV removable cartridge	6/12 Mbps
AIT-2	50/100 Gb	8 mm removable cartridge	6/12 Mbps
Mammoth	20/40 Gb	8 mm removable cartridge	3/6 Mbps

Along with different tape technologies, there are also many different kinds of backup software. Some well-known software packages include Computer Associates ARCserveIT and Veritas' Backup Exec. Because these packages will need to be installed on one or more servers, check to make sure that they are compatible with the server's network operating system. The software must also be compatible with the operating systems of the desktop client computers if these are to be backed up as well.

Backup software should provide a way to create disaster recovery disks or tapes—media that allow a server to start up and reconstruct all its data easily after a catastrophic failure. (Some packages do this more easily than others.) If the network contains servers at remote locations, find software that can back them up to a central office.

Support staff should check critical data backups to ensure that the original data can be restored from the backup media. At a minimum, the backup log indicating a successful backup should be checked each morning to ensure that all critical folders have been included in the backup. Moreover, support staff should periodically rebuild complete servers from backup tape, just to make sure that it can be done properly.

Some networks use storage devices other than magnetic tape to store their backups. While tape still provides the most cost-effective solution for backup, it is not always the most convenient format. Other data-protection alternatives are:

> **Network servers containing more than one set of primary hard disks.** (The server automatically writes data to both disks—a technique called mirroring.)

> **Network attached storage (NAS) devices.** NAS devices relieve servers of the burden of backup and provide scalability as the network expands. (Adding another NAS device to a network is easier than adding another disk or set of disks to a server.)

> **Storage area networks (SANs).** SANs provide a group of shared storage devices— computers devoted to storing data—which back up and restore documents continuously throughout the day and night. SANs provide fast, always-current storage and retrieval for large networks.

Case Studies in Student Participation

In some schools, students provide much-needed troubleshooting, technical support, and consulting services. Schools lend structure to student involvement by providing appropriate supervision and behavioral guidelines. They also define areas of support such as troubleshooting, Web site development, and teacher assistance that are appropriate for students. Assistance in areas such as networking, which involves access to critical equipment or sensitive data, may be circumscribed. Students prepare for these roles quite rigorously and generally perform their tasks with both creativity and responsibility.

Overview of Student Programs

To prepare students for technical work, high schools offer several semesters of classes that teach both technical and "soft" skills—nontechnical skills that include the ability to listen carefully to teachers' needs, explain clearly the technical tasks that will be undertaken, and work in a team. At the same time that students take classes, they also assume technical responsibilities in their schools or in local community organizations and businesses. They create Web sites, diagnose and repair school equipment, build computers for school use, and teach their teachers about technology, among many other tasks.

Several vendors including Cisco Systems, Inc., Nortel Networks, and Microsoft offer curricula that teach technical skills. Most schools, however, adapt these curricula substantially by reducing lecture-style modules, adding activities, and teaching customer-service skills. The vendor-provided curricula focus narrowly on developing competencies in those technologies associated with vendors' products, but success in the field of information technology requires equally the ability to research new questions, manage projects, think both deductively and creatively, and work well with clients and colleagues. (See, in part, information at **www.terc.edu** on the Networking Communities Project, a National Science Foundation supported program—grant DUE#9850311.)

Most schools that mount programs to prepare students for technical work encounter similar challenges:

> **Course content.** Technology changes rapidly, and curriculum must adapt. Put programs in place relatively quickly and make provisions for revising them routinely. Stress skills of lifelong learning—defining problems, researching their answers, managing projects, and collaborating—rather than simply amassing technical competencies, as the technical competencies become outmoded very quickly.

> **Faculty.** Find technical professionals to teach courses or to mentor faculty. If in-house faculty teach the courses, find time for them to learn the new material. As part of their preparation, send them to industry certification classes, provide job shadowing in industry, or have professional development workshops. Alternatively, promote a technician to be a teacher's assistant for the classes. In time, the technician may be able to take over the teaching load.

> **Course delivery.** Recruit students and solicit the support of other faculty such as counselors in this effort. Handle the logistics by scheduling the courses or finding rooms where students can work on equipment. Develop an admissions procedure.

> **Policies.** Acceptable use policies often prohibit the precise behaviors in which student technicians engage such as dismantling equipment or freely accessing the Internet. Develop a separate set of policies governing appropriate behavior and the consequences of inappropriate behavior.

> **Equipment, tools, software, and other supplies.** Locate all the resources that students and faculty need to practice their technical skills.

> › **Cultivating industry and employer support.** Work with community leaders to find internships for students and possibly employment after graduation as well as financial and in-kind support.

While this list might seem daunting, TERC's research indicates that schools create a variety of innovative solutions to these challenges, often with very few initial resources. (TERC's Networking Communities project, for example, provided just $6,000–$10,000 in seed money to each participating secondary school.) The best way to approach these programs is to engage their challenges and find a mix of answers that suits the school district's goals and resources.

Milwaukee Public Schools

Student Technology Services from Amy Fetherston, Teacher, Washington High School

At Milwaukee Public Schools (MPS), high school students will soon provide a variety of troubleshooting and support services for libraries, secondary, middle, and elementary schools. They will perform hardware maintenance (especially preventative maintenance) and emergency repairs, and they will assist teachers with classroom projects. In preparation, students complete several semesters of course work; they are then hired and assigned to local technical personnel (for example, technology coordinators in each school) for supervision.

The MPS program draws its technical curriculum from Cisco Systems Network Academy, a Web-based four-semester program that teaches students to design, build, and maintain computer networks. The curriculum also integrates soft skills modules from the student technician-training program at the University of Wisconsin, Milwaukee (UWM). MPS adapted both programs for their high school audience—particularly minimizing the lecture components, adding many more hands-on activities, and slowing the technical curriculum down somewhat to integrate soft skills training.

MPS teachers revise and deliver most of the curriculum and organize its classroom components; they meet monthly to see what is going well, to determine where they need improvement, and to provide mutual support. UWM students also provide periodic training for students on both technical issues and soft skills. Where possible, the same UWM team visits each building repeatedly; the students develop a rapport and, over time, MPS students begin asking questions of a more personal nature (e.g., "What is it really like to live in a dorm?"). For many MPS students, these connections form their first inkling that college life may be accessible to them. To strengthen these ties, MPS has negotiated special agreements with both the local technical college and UWM. Students who do not finish the entire Cisco curriculum in high school can do so at the technical college after they graduate, and UWM has agreed to hire MPS students into its technical support program at a higher-than-usual starting salary if they enroll there.

MPS assesses and supervises students in a number of ways. Students remain in classes throughout the program, and they are graded on their classroom work. Once they are assigned to a school, students report to the school's technology coordinator. (Schools without technology coordinators cannot participate in the program. MPS intends student assistants to supplement professional support, not to substitute for it.) The technology coordinator assigns tasks to the students, makes sure those tasks are attended to, checks when the students come in and leave, and signs their time cards. The program also employs a coordinator from UWM to serve as a liaison between the Cisco teachers and the technology coordinators; the coordinator provides a single point of contact for schools wishing to hire technicians or report difficulties.

Students may work as many as 20 hours per week providing technical support. They are paid $6.15–$7.00 per hour. MPS has implemented a pay schedule that involves reviews every three months so that students will be eligible for raises. For the next 18 months, student wages are covered by a TEACH grant. In the end, MPS hopes that schools will find the program so effective that they will be willing to hire the students directly.

Students find time for their on-site placements in a number of ways. Some students take release time before or after lunch. High schools release their students an hour or two earlier than middle schools, so other students will complete their assignments after school. Still other students will work in the summer, and students who work in libraries may work nights and weekends. Some students are employed at the schools they attend.

MPS began its Cisco Systems Network Academy program in 1998 and added the University of Wisconsin, Milwaukee, components in 2000. The first 20 students were ready for placement in spring 2001. Funding for the program comes in part from the school system and in part from a TEACH grant. The school system not only provides teacher salaries for the program but also provides funding for further training for teachers and release time so that teachers can meet once a month.

The MPS program has its eye on several simultaneous goals as do all the programs that engage students in technical support services. Providing support for needy schools is one of them. More important, every time students learn technical skills and realize they can do so, the program counts itself successful. Students' feelings of success are redoubled when they provide an essential community service to an appreciative audience. MPS' most important goal is to teach students about the value and the possibility of higher education—to help them see themselves connected with colleges and envision what they might be doing 5 to 10 years after they leave MPS.

Boston Public Schools

TechBoston from Mary Skipper, Director

TechBoston began in 1998 with 100 students. The program grew in 1999 to 700 students and in 2000 to 1,500 students with $480,000 in funding from federal, state, and private sources. Offering courses on networking, hardware repair, desktop publishing, Web design, database administration, and robotics (among others) in the Boston Public Schools, TechBoston describes itself as a teacher-centric program that builds students' confidence and prepares students both for careers and for post-secondary learning in areas such as computer science and engineering.

TechBoston teachers develop some of their own curricula—including a centralized curriculum for Web design, robotics, and Microsoft Office. They also adapt and implement curricula from many other sources, including Cisco Systems, 3Com Corporation, Microsoft

Corporation, Oracle Corporation, Sun Microsystems, and Adobe Systems, to include more hands-on activities and soft skills training. The first year that they use any curriculum, TechBoston pilots the program after school; they then talk to teachers about implementing and revising it (in collaboration with the vendors, where appropriate). They have also partnered with several vendors such as Cisco Systems to align curricula to the Massachusetts Curriculum Frameworks.

Each school within the district decides the program of studies it will offer. Students at each school generally take a course pathway—a series of skill-building courses—in their junior and senior years to prepare them for exams in their respective area of technology and to help prepare them for internships. Courses are also offered after school and on Saturdays to make it easier for students with scheduling problems to attend; some modules are also available in summer camp.

Internship plays an important role in the TechBoston experience. Students hired for an internship work directly under the supervision of a professional with technical expertise to screen calls at the desktop level; assist on help desks; diagnose and repair hardware and software problems; build Web sites; or troubleshoot network problems. Student coursework can lead to vendor certifications (especially useful for post-graduation employment). Students take one or two courses per year for up to three years, depending on the high school and particular program.

TechBoston built itself from the ground up and from the top down. At the base, it engages, asks opinions, keeps people informed, and gathers as broad an opinion as possible. It has worked collaboratively with major departments in the Boston Public Schools—especially the School-To-Career department and Instructional Technology. Teachers are involved at all levels: teaching courses, developing curriculum, and providing implementation strategies for all aspects of the program. It is also developing a student council including student representatives from each school involved in TechBoston.

At the top, TechBoston cultivates a "working group" of 40–50 representatives from their curriculum vendors, local industry and nonprofit businesses, community organizations, and school personnel to define strategies and initiatives. This group serves as an advisory board to consider, for example, how to recruit more women into the program or find internships for students. Additionally, Boston's Mayor Menino, Superintendent Thomas Payzant, and the Private Industry Council (the city's governance and policy-making body for workforce development) are staunch supporters of the program. TechBoston has also partnered with several local colleges, including the Massachusetts Institute of Technology, Harvard University, Simmons College, the University of Massachusetts (Boston), and Boston University on a variety of projects.

TechBoston was initially funded by a small Department of Education Technology Literacy Challenge grant; Boston's school superintendent and school department then funded the program generously as well. TechBoston now receives support from school, federal, state, and private sources; fundraising has been a continuous and successful effort.

TechBoston aims to help students feel like respected members of a larger community, and to instill the value of providing service to that community. They are also committed to including students of all skill levels, backgrounds, interests, and genders (it is not a program just for the technically talented, just for boys, or just for Boston's most select schools).

There are many success stories within TechBoston, but perhaps one anecdote summarizes best what its student participants feel. At a meeting with Boston's mayor, students were asked to submit comments or questions. One student wrote, "Thank you for this opportunity to learn. Thank you for this opportunity to learn *freely.*"

Generation www.Y

In Generation www.Y, students mentor teachers to help integrate technology into a curriculum-based project, lesson plan, or unit. Each Generation www.Y student completes an 18-week course (four hours per week) that teaches technology skills for Grades 6–12 as well as mentoring, leadership, research, writing, and project development skills.

Generation www.Y projects include creating or updating teachers' Web pages, helping fellow students search the Web, developing presentations in PowerPoint or HyperStudio, and tutoring teachers or students in technology skills. In some classrooms, students also deliver presentations that they created.

When their coursework is complete, students collaborate with teachers to develop a draft project proposal, which they submit to a Generation www.Y consultant who has both technical and content area expertise. The consultant assesses the proposal for its feasibility, educational value, quality of writing, and how well it aligns objectives with implementation strategies and assessment. The consultant may also suggest additional contacts or resources and may work with the team to help create a successful project. Once the project has been approved, students develop and deliver the project with their teacher's guidance. Students are expected to continue mentoring teachers throughout their career in the district, and some students return to the same classroom for more than one semester.

Each Generation www.Y program depends on a Generation www.Y supervising teacher, a teacher for the Generation www.Y class (who may be the same as the supervisor), to evaluate proposals, partner teachers who receiving mentoring, and students. Other than faculty salary, schools pay only small additional fees for classroom materials. Many Generation www.Y classes are held before school and some on Saturdays, with each school determining the credit they'll confer for the class. Teachers may take on their Generation www.Y projects as part of their regular work load or before or after school.

Generation www.Y began in 1996 at schools in Olympia, Washington, with support from a Technology Innovation Challenge grant from the U.S. Department of Education. Continuing support from state and local grants as well as corporate donations has provided additional materials development and dissemination. Two hundred schools currently participate in Generation www.Y programs.

As with the other programs mentioned in this section, Generation www.Y students gain poise, professionalism, and self-confidence as well as technical skills while at the same time providing professional development services for their districts.

Additional Information about Student Technology Programs

A comprehensive list of curricula and assessments, implementation tools, instructional resources, and additional Web links for schools developing information technology programs is located at the Educators' Web Site for Information Technology (**www.edc.org/ EWIT/index.htm**), developed by the Information Technology Career Cluster Initiative. Designed for teachers, business representatives, and students, the site focuses on integrating information technology across the curriculum—on involving all students and a variety of traditional subject areas in technology-related learning. It provides information to help link technology curricula to content standards. (The work of the Information Technology Career Cluster Initiative is supported by the U.S. Department of Education and co-managed by Education Development Center, Inc., the National Alliance of Business, and the Information Technology Association of America.)

The Information Technology Career Cluster Initiative participants have defined content areas for technology programs (**www.edc.org/EWIT/bltext.htm**). These contents areas include foundation skills on which all technical work builds—various academic subjects, communications, ethics, teamwork, and business concepts, among others. It also organizes technical coursework into four major areas: network systems, information support and services, programming and software development, and interactive media. These foundations and coursework are presented as part a process of lifelong learning that, the model makes clear, engages most technology professionals.

A list of pilot schools implementing the model is located at **www.edc.org/EWIT/ bltext.htm**. If a district is considering a similar program, district officials should contact a pilot school that is located nearby or one that is similar in size and demography. They should also contact The Information Technology Career Cluster Initiative, Education Development Center, Inc., 55 Chapel Street, Newton, MA 02458.

National Educational Technology Standards (NETS)

NETS AND PERFORMANCE INDICATORS FOR TEACHERS

All classroom teachers should be prepared to meet the following standards and performance indicators.

I. TECHNOLOGY OPERATIONS AND CONCEPTS

Teachers demonstrate a sound understanding of technology operations and concepts. Teachers:

A. demonstrate introductory knowledge, skills, and understanding of concepts related to technology (as described in the ISTE National Educational Technology Standards for Students).

B. demonstrate continual growth in technology knowledge and skills to stay abreast of current and emerging technologies.

II. PLANNING AND DESIGNING LEARNING ENVIRONMENTS AND EXPERIENCES

Teachers plan and design effective learning environments and experiences supported by technology. Teachers:

A. design developmentally appropriate learning opportunities that apply technology-enhanced instructional strategies to support the diverse needs of learners.

B. apply current research on teaching and learning with technology when planning learning environments and experiences.

C. identify and locate technology resources and evaluate them for accuracy and suitability.

D. plan for the management of technology resources within the context of learning activities.

E. plan strategies to manage student learning in a technology-enhanced environment.

III. TEACHING, LEARNING, AND THE CURRICULUM

Teachers implement curriculum plans that include methods and strategies for applying technology to maximize student learning. Teachers:

A. facilitate technology-enhanced experiences that address content standards and student technology standards.

B. use technology to support learner-centered strategies that address the diverse needs of students.

C. apply technology to develop students' higher-order skills and creativity.

D. manage student learning activities in a technology-enhanced environment.

IV. ASSESSMENT AND EVALUATION

Teachers apply technology to facilitate a variety of effective assessment and evaluation strategies. Teachers:

A. apply technology in assessing student learning of subject matter using a variety of assessment techniques.

B. use technology resources to collect and analyze data, interpret results, and communicate findings to improve instructional practice and maximize student learning.

C. apply multiple methods of evaluation to determine students' appropriate use of technology resources for learning, communication, and productivity.

V. PRODUCTIVITY AND PROFESSIONAL PRACTICE

Teachers use technology to enhance their productivity and professional practice. Teachers:

A. use technology resources to engage in ongoing professional development and life-long learning.

B. continually evaluate and reflect on professional practice to make informed decisions regarding the use of technology in support of student learning.

C. apply technology to increase productivity.

D. use technology to communicate and collaborate with peers, parents, and the larger community in order to nurture student learning.

VI. SOCIAL, ETHICAL, LEGAL, AND HUMAN ISSUES

Teachers understand the social, ethical, legal, and human issues surrounding the use of technology in PK–12 schools and apply that understanding in practice. Teachers:

A. model and teach legal and ethical practice related to technology use.

B. apply technology resources to enable and empower learners with diverse backgrounds, characteristics, and abilities.

C. identify and use technology resources that affirm diversity.

D. promote safe and healthy use of technology resources.

E. facilitate equitable access to technology resources for all students.

NETS AND PERFORMANCE INDICATORS FOR ADMINISTRATORS

I. LEADERSHIP AND VISION—Educational leaders inspire a shared vision for comprehensive integration of technology use and foster an environment and culture conducive to the realization of that vision.
Educational leaders:

   A. facilitate the shared development by all stakeholders of a vision for technology and widely communicate that vision.
   B. maintain an inclusive and cohesive process to develop, implement, and monitor a dynamic, long-range, and systemic technology plan to achieve the vision.
   C. foster and nurture a culture of responsible risk-taking that promotes continuous innovation with technology.
   D. use data in making leadership decisions.
   E. advocate for research-based effective practices in use of technology.

II. LEARNING AND TEACHING—Educational leaders ensure that curricular design, instructional strategies, and learning environments integrate appropriate technologies to maximize learning and teaching.
Educational leaders:

   A. identify, evaluate, and encourage use of appropriate technologies to enhance and support curriculum and instruction that lead to high levels of student achievement.
   B. facilitate and support collaborative technology-enriched learning environments that are conducive to innovation for improved learning.
   C. provide for student-centered learning environments that use technology to meet the individual and diverse needs of learners.
   D. facilitate the use of technologies to support and enhance instructional methods that enhance higher-level thinking, decision-making, and problem-solving skills.
   E. assure that faculty and staff take advantage of quality professional learning opportunities for improved learning and teaching with technology.

III. PRODUCTIVITY AND PROFESSIONAL PRACTICE—Educational leaders apply technology to enhance their professional practice and to increase their own productivity and that of others.
Educational leaders:

   A. use technology to enhance the efficiency of organizational improvement.
   B. model the routine, intentional, and effective use of technology.
   C. engage in sustained, job-related professional learning using technology resources..
   D. employ technology for communication and collaboration among peers, staff, parents, and the larger community.
   E. create and participate in a district-wide learning community that stimulates, nurtures, and supports faculty and staff in using technology for improved productivity

IV. SUPPORT, MANAGEMENT, AND OPERATIONS—Educational leaders provide direction to integrate technology tools into productive learning and administrative systems.
Educational leaders:

   A. ensure compatibility of technologies through development, implementation, and monitoring of policies and guidelines.

B. allocate financial and human resources to ensure full implementation of the technology plan.

C. integrate strategic plans, technology plans, other improvement plans, and policies to align efforts and leverage resources.

D. implement procedures to drive continuous system improvements and to support technology replacement cycles.

E. implement an effective data reporting and retrieval system that is easy to use and that is of immediate value to stakeholders.

V. ASSESSMENT AND EVALUATION—Educational leaders use technology to facilitate a comprehensive system of effective assessment and evaluation.
Educational leaders:

A. use technology in collecting and analyzing data, interpreting results, and communicating findings to improve instructional practice and student learning.

B. assess staff knowledge, skills, and performance in using technology and use results to facilitate quality professional development and to inform personnel decisions.

C. use technology to assess and evaluate managerial and operational systems.

D. use multiple methods to assess and evaluate appropriate uses of technology resources for learning, communication, and productivity.

E. publish positive technology evaluation results to stimulate improved learning, collaboration, communications, productivity, and technology integration.

VI. SOCIAL, LEGAL, AND ETHICAL ISSUES—Educational leaders understand the social, legal, and ethical issues related to technology and model responsible decision-making related to these issues.
Educational leaders:

A. ensure equity of access to technology resources that enable and empower all learners and educators.

B. identify, communicate, model, and enforce positive social, legal, and ethical practices to promote responsible use of technology.

C. promote and enforce security and online safety related to the use of technology.

D. promote and enforce environmentally safe and healthy practices in the use of technology.

E. participate in the development of policies that clearly assign ownership of intellectual property developed with district resources.

Glossary

A

10BaseFL: Ethernet standard for baseband LANs; provides a transmission speed of 10 Mbps over fiber optic cable.

10BaseT: The most common form of Ethernet network; provides a transmission speed of 10 Mbps using baseband signaling over twisted pair copper wire.

100BaseFX: Ethernet standard for baseband LANs; provides a transmission speed of 100 Mbps over fiber optic cable.

100BaseTX: Ethernet standard for baseband LANs; provides a transmission speed of 100 Mbps over twisted pair copper wire.

1000Base-CX: Ethernet standard for baseband LANs; provides a transmission speed of 1,000 Mbps (1 gigabit) over twisted pair copper wire for distances of 25 meters or less.

1000Base-LX: Ethernet standard for baseband LANs; provides a transmission speed of 1,000 Mbps (1 gigabit per second) over fiber optic cable for distances up to 5 kilometers.

1000Base-SX: Ethernet standard for baseband LANs; provides a transmission speed of 1,000 Mbps (1 gigabit per second) over fiber optic cable for distances of 220–550 meters.

1000Base-T: Ethernet standard for baseband LANs; provides a transmission speed of 1,000 Mbps (1 gigabit) over twisted pair copper wire.

access list: The list of addresses and ports that a router makes available or restricts to a network user.

access point: A device that connects a wireless local area network to the main (wired) network.

Active Directory: A global directory for a Windows 2000-based network that lists all the network's resources—usernames, passwords, disks, printers, servers, and so forth.

adapter: See *network interface*.

ADSL (Asynchronous Digital Subscriber Line): A member of the digital subscriber line family of wide area network technologies. ADSL delivers information at speeds of up to 7 Mbps downstream and 1.544 Mbps upstream over regular telephone wire.

analog signal: Data that travel a network as continuous changes in voltage rather than discreet binary units.

ANSI (American National Standards Institute): An organization that defines many different network standards. It is the American representative of ISO (International Standards Organization).

AppleTalk: The protocol stack (family of protocols) that describes how Macintosh computers communicate with each other.

application, presentation, and session protocols: Protocols that form part of the OSI reference model. They define how data moving to and from application programs are prepared for transmission across a network. See *OSI reference model, physical and data link protocols,* or *network routing and transport protocols*.

application program: A program designed to assist in performing a specific task such as word processing, database management, or accounting. Examples of application programs include Microsoft Word, Excel, AppleWorks, Eudora electronic mail, HyperStudio, and Netscape Navigator.

application server: A computer that specializes in providing application programs for use by network client computers.

ASP (application service provider): A service provider that rents software-based services (such as Internet filters) to schools, libraries, and other educational organizations.

asymmetric key encryption: A method of encrypting data on a network. Systems that use asymmetric key encryption employ two different keys, called public and private keys, to encrypt and decrypt their network data.

ATM (Asynchronous Transfer Mode): A network technology capable of transmitting information (data, voice, audio, and video) in data cells (packets consisting of 48 bytes of data and 5 bytes of routing information) at speeds ranging from 1.54 Mbps to 622 Mbps.

AUI (attachment unit interface): A 15-pin physical interface that connects a computer or other device to an Ethernet network.

B

backbone: The portion of a network that interconnects servers and/or buildings. Network backbones require speedier connections than other parts of the network.

backplane: The main circuit board of a computer, switch, or other device. A computer's component parts are plugged into the backplane.

backup server: A computer that specializes in making copies of network data for safekeeping.

bandwidth: The capacity of a network to handle data, or more specifically, the number of frequencies (or channels) over which data can be sent simultaneously.

baseband: A method of sending information that uses a single frequency (digital) along a cable or wireless path. Ethernet uses baseband signaling to send information.

Bc (committed burst rate): The amount by which a user may exceed a frame relay network's committed information rate over a specified period of time.

Be (burst excess): The maximum transmission rate above the committed burst rate.

block port: Denying access to traffic associated with a particular port. See *port.*

bridge: A device that connects two or more local area networks, or two or more segments of the same network. Bridges read the MAC addresses of the sending and receiving computers that are included in the network signal, and then send the signals on to the proper destinations. See *physical and data link protocols.*

broadband: A method of sending information that uses many frequencies along a single cable or wireless path.

broadcast: Sending data to all computers within listening range. Broadcasts are distinguished from multicasts, which send information to a specific group of listening computers.

BSS (basic service set): Stations (or nodes) that communicate within a LAN.

burstable T1: Provides wide area connections over T1 lines at variable speeds up to 1.544 Mbps (T1 speeds) based on the network's momentary demands.

bus: Set of electrical lines through which the internal components of a computer communicate. They are characterized by the number of bits they are able to simultaneously transfer.

bus topology: Computers are connected in a line or daisy chain configuration. A malfunctioning component of a bus topology ceases to communicate but it does not disrupt network operations.

byte: A group of eight electrical signals, each of which is interpreted as on or off. The eight signals, taken together, represent a single character such as an "A" or "1."

C

cable modem: Primarily intended for Internet access, cable modems deliver information as fast as 30 Mbps downstream and as fast as 10 Mbps upstream (although much slower rates of 10 Mbps downstream and 128 Kbps upstream are common).

cache: A storage place used to hold temporary information in a computer. Cache memory holds less information than random access memory but responds faster. See *level 1 cache* and *level 2 cache.*

card: A printed circuit board; an adapter (network interface, connector for an additional disk, etc.) that is inserted into one of the slots inside a computer to expand its capabilities. See *network interface.*

CD-ROM (Compact Disc-Read Only Memory): A storage device that holds data (roughly 650 Mb) placed on it by laser (light) rather than electromagnetic means.

CD-RW (Compact Disc-ReWriteable): Technology allowing data to be written to a CD multiple times.

CHAP (Challenge Handshake Authentication Protocol): Scheme for authenticating users when they log in to a network. This protocol encrypts all communications and reauthenticates users periodically during a connection.

CIR (committed information rate): The minimum level of service guaranteed to each permanent virtual circuit in a frame relay network.

client: A computer used to access shared network resources.

coaxial cable: Cable containing a copper core enclosed in a protective sheath.

collision domain: An area of an Ethernet network in which data sent to or from a device may potentially collide with data from other devices. Networks are commonly divided into multiple collision domains by deploying switches, bridges, or routers on the network. Each switch port, bridge port, or router port forms a new collision domain.

COM1: See *serial port.*

COM2: See *serial port.*

concentrator: See *hub.*

control: A countermeasure taken to guard against a network security breach.

CoS (class of service): A way for routers to group specific types of network traffic (e.g., electronic mail or voice) and give each a different priority on the network.

CPU (central processing unit): The chip that performs the principal calculations that control a computer's operations.

crossover port: A port on a hub that contains special wiring allowing it to connect to another hub rather than to a client, server, or peripheral on the network. Crossover ports provide convenient ways to connect hubs together.

CSMA/CD (Carrier Sense Multiple Access with Collision Detection): How computers on an Ethernet network determine when to transmit information. Each computer senses whether the cable is in use and transmits when it is not. After transmission, each computer can detect collisions (simultaneous transmissions by more than one computer) and retransmit if necessary.

CSU/DSU (Channel Service Unit/Data Service Unit): Provides connections between digital wide area network technologies such as T1 lines and a local area network.

D

database server: A dedicated server that specializes in storing and processing database-related information that is accessible to network users.

default router: A connecting device to which each computer on a particular network segment sends information.

DFIR (diffuse infrared): A form of electromagnetic radiation used to carry network information wirelessly.

DHCP (Dynamic Host Control Protocol): Enables client computers to receive Internet Protocol (IP) addresses automatically from a server on their local area network (instead of receiving them manually from a technician).

digital signal: Data that travel a network in digital form appear as chunks of information at discrete intervals. Most local area networks and many wide area networks use digital signals to represent data.

direct infrared: A form of electromagnetic radiation used to carry wireless information in many household remote control devices (such as a TV or VCR remote control).

disaster recovery plan: The procedure that outlines the exact steps an organization will take if there are major disruptions to its physical plant caused by fire, flood, or other catastrophe.

DMZ (demilitarized zone): An area of a network protected by multiple firewalls where Web, electronic mail, and other public servers are located. It is kept separate from portions of a network that contain private data.

DNS (Domain Name System): A way of mapping host (computer) names to Internet Protocol (IP) addresses. For example, when a Web address is entered in a browser, a DNS server maps that address to a number—the IP address—that the Internet requires to locate the Web page.

dock: A dock provides a laptop computer with connections to additional hard disks, monitor, keyboard, or other components.

domain name: A domain name represents one or more addresses (computers) on the network. A sample domain name might be greatschool.edu.

downstream: Downstream communications travel from the carrier's central office to the customer's site.

driver: A software module that manages the operations of hardware components.

DSL (digital subscriber line): Standard phone lines that deliver high-speed data communications for wide area networks and personal use. DSL transmissions are fast enough—up to 52 Mbps downstream (to the user) and 2.3 Mbps upstream (from the user)—to support full motion video, IP telephony, and interactive multimedia applications directly from the Internet.

DSSS (direct sequence spread spectrum): See *spread spectrum*.

dual-homed: A computer that is attached to more than one network simultaneously.

DVD (digital video disk): Optical discs that are able to store up to 17 GB (double-sided) of data.

E

EIA (Electronic Industries Association): An organization that defines many different network cabling standards.

electronic mail server: A dedicated server that specializes in handling electronic mail-related tasks for a network.

emulator: Software that enables a foreign operating system to run on a computer. For example,

VirtualPC lets Macintosh users run the Windows operating system on their computers.

Ethernet: The most common scheme for connecting computers in a local area network. Ethernet describes the rules for cabling and the kinds of network interfaces, hubs, switches, bridges, and routers that may be used on the network. Ethernet comes in various forms, including 10BaseT, 100BaseTX, 1000Base-T, and many others.

expansion slot: A slot inside a computer that accepts small circuit boards that add network connections, sound, and other capabilities.

F

far-end crosstalk: Interference along one cable caused by signals in an adjacent cable. When measuring far-end crosstalk, a signal is sent from one end of the cable and the crosstalk is measured at the opposite end.

FDDI (Fiber Distributed Data Interface): Defines 100 Mbps service over fiber optic cable. FDDI can provide data link and physical communications for ATM or, alternatively, it can provide full LAN or WAN services on its own. As a LAN technology, FDDI is expensive to implement and not widely deployed. In some areas, telecommunications carriers provide access to Fiber Network Services (FNS), a public FDDI network that provides very fast wide area connections.

FHSS (frequency hopping spread spectrum): See *spread spectrum*.

fiber optic cable: A glass or plastic core surrounded by a protective cable sheath that can carry signals at higher speeds, over longer distances, and with fewer errors than copper wiring.

file server: A computer that stores documents for people using the network.

firewall: A device that prevents unauthorized electronic access to the entire network. The term includes many different kinds of protective hardware and software devices.

floppy disks: Electromagnetic storage devices that hold a small amount of information.

format: Differences in the way various operating systems handle and store data (e.g., Windows format, Macintosh format).

fractional T1: A portion of standard T1 services for wide area networks.

frame: A small package of data. Physical and data link protocols on a computer receive outgoing packets and insert them into frames (sometimes dividing them to fit) for transport on the network cable or wireless path.

frame relay: Network connections that provide constant (as opposed to dial-up) digital data communications service within a network cloud. Frame relay services can be purchased at many different speeds, including 56 Kbps, 128 Kbps, and 1.544 Mbps.

FTP (File Transfer Protocol): Enables Web browsers or programs such as Fetch and WSFTP to transfer documents to and from the Internet. FTP is one of the protocols in the TCP/IP protocol stack (group of software modules).

full duplex: Communication between devices able to send signals and receive signals simultaneously. Telephone connections are full duplex.

G

Gbps: Gigabits (billions of bits) per second. The newest Ethernet standard delivers data at speeds near 1 Gbps.

Gigabit Ethernet: Provides a transmission speed of 1,000 megabits per second (1 Gbps) using baseband signaling over fiber optic cable. Gigabit Ethernet is used mainly to connect devices on the backbone of a network.

H

H.323: Defines one way that voice, data, and video can be carried over Internet Protocol (IP) networks.

half duplex: Communication between devices that can send signals or receive signals but cannot do both at the same time. To provide two-way communications, the channel switches back and forth between sending and receiving. 10BaseT Ethernet uses half duplex communications.

hard disk: A device with one or more inflexible platters that a computer uses to store data. Information is written to (and read from) the hard disk by manipulating the electromagnetically charged surface of the platters.

harden a server: The act of removing extraneous software, ensuring that the remaining software is configured properly and is up-to-date, and removing any back-door (hidden) access to the system. Hardening a server makes it more difficult for intruders to gain unauthorized access to a network.

HDLC (High-level Data Link Control): A data link level protocol according to the OSI reference model that carries information over a variety of wide area network physical connections, including ISDN and T1.

host name: For example, at Education Development Center, Inc. (EDC) the principal Web server is called www.edc.org (its host name).

HTTP (HyperText Transfer Protocol): Protocol that enables Web browsers to connect to Web servers. HTTP is one of the protocols in the TCP/IP protocol stack.

hub: An Ethernet hub connects and gathers the signals from several individual computers or several portions of a network. The hub regenerates each signal and then sends the new signal out to all other computers connected to the hub. By regenerating the signal, hubs ensure that clients on the network receive reliable information. Hubs are also called concentrators or repeaters.

I

I/O (input/output): Designates subsystems that are involved with moving data to or from the computer.

IDE/ATA (Integrated Drive Electronics/AT Attachment): A type of hard disk that is fast and inexpensive.

IDS (intrusion detection system): A system that identifies suspicious network behavior. An IDS may consist of software, hardware, or both.

IEEE (Institute of Electrical and Electronics Engineers): An organization that defines standards for many different network operations. Ethernet is sometimes referred to by the number of the IEEE working group that defined it—802.3.

IETF (Internet Engineering Task Force): An international community of network designers, operators, vendors, and researchers concerned with the evolution of the Internet architecture and its smooth operation.

incremental backup: An incremental backup copies all the data that have changed since the previous complete backup or since the previous incremental backup.

infrared: A form of electromagnetic radiation that can be used to carry information for wireless networks. See *DFIR* or *direct infrared*.

International Telecommunications Union: An organization that sets standards for many telecommunication operations.

Internet appliance: An inexpensive, limited-purpose device specialized for delivering electronic mail, Web browsing, video on demand, or other Internet-based services.

Internet filtering server: A computer that specializes in controlling the Web sites that students, teachers, and administrators may view.

Internet Protocol: See *TCP/IP.*

IP: See *TCP/IP.*

IP address: A numeric address that identifies the location of a client, server, or peripheral on the Internet.

IPX/SPX (Internet Packet Exchange/Sequenced Packet Exchange): A set of protocols that enables computers to connect to a Novell NetWare server.

ISDN (Integrated Services Digital Network): A type of wide area network connection that provides digital service at modest speeds and prices.

ISP (Internet service provider): An organization that rents connections to the Internet. Often, ISPs provide additional services such as space for Web sites and electronic mail.

K

Kbps: Kilobits (thousands of bits) per second. Modems carry data at speeds between 14.4 Kbps and 56 Kbps.

L

LAN (local area network): Local area networks connect hardware and software within one building or a few buildings in close proximity.

latency: The delay encountered by network data as they travel from source to destination. Many factors contribute to latency, including router processing time, characteristics of the transmission medium (cable or wireless path), time required to retrieve the data from disk, and so forth.

layer 1 device: Devices that operate at the OSI physical layer. Hubs are layer 1 devices. See *hub, physical and data link protocols.*

layer 2 device: Devices that operate at the OSI data link layer. Bridges and switches are layer 2 devices. See *bridge, physical and data link protocols.*

layer 3 device: Devices that operate at the OSI network routing layer. Routers are layer 3 devices. See *router, network routing and transport protocols.*

leased line: Telephone communications lines that are rented for private use. T1 lines are a common form of leased line.

level 1 cache: A type of computer memory that is built directly into the central processing unit. Level 1 cache responds very quickly when information needs to be sent or received.

level 2 cache: A type of computer memory that is slower than level 1 cache but faster than random access memory. Level 2 cache is located in a chip near the central processing unit.

LocalTalk: A physical and data link protocol that was at one time built into every Macintosh. LocalTalk enabled older Macintosh computers to share documents, printers, and other information in small groups. It has been replaced by Ethernet.

M

MAC (media access control): A unique network address that helps route information to and from a computer within its local network segment. On an Ethernet network, each network interface receives a unique MAC address from its manufacturer.

mail daemon: A computer program on a mail server that waits for mail to arrive and then processes the information.

MAN (metropolitan area network): A hybrid network configuration somewhere between a local area network (LAN) and a wide area network (WAN). Metropolitan area networks connect buildings over city-sized areas and generally combine the technologies found in both LANs and WANs.

Mbps: Megabits (millions of bits) per second. Ethernet networks convey data at 10 Mbps or 100 Mbps (depending on the form of Ethernet).

media access method: Defines the procedure used by computers on a network so that they can share a cable (or wireless path) without interrupting and overwriting each other's messages.

MEGACO: A standard for videoconferencing that combines H.323 and MGCP and addresses multimedia conferencing.

MGCP (Media Gateway Control Protocol): Describes one way to govern the behavior of a media gateway on a network that supports videoconferencing.

microprocessor: See *CPU.*

mirroring: The process of writing exactly the same data to two disks that share the same disk controller (the circuitry that connects the disks to a computer's main circuit board). Mirroring is distinguished from duplexing, in which the disks are attached to two different controllers.

motherboard: A computer's main electrical circuit board.

multicast: The act of sending information from one computer to a designated group of other computers.

N

NAS (network attached storage): Computers that connect directly to a network for the sole purpose of backing up data.

NAT (network address translation): The process of substituting IP addresses.

NetBEUI (NetBIOS Extended User Interface): Enables Windows computers to communicate with each other within a single network. (When Windows computers communicate across different networks, they usually use TCI/IP.)

NetBIOS (Network Basic Input/Output System): A standard that permits Windows computers to communicate directly at OSI layer 4, the transport level.

network computer: A client computer that lacks a hard or floppy disk and therefore uses a server to store its information.

network interface: The hardware that connects your computer to its network. The network interface may be a special card (also called a network interface card [NIC] or adapter), or it may be built into a computer's main circuit board.

network operating system: A specialized kind of operating system that manages services involving document sharing, printing, and communications. All network servers run networking operating systems. The most common network operating systems are Windows NT 4.0, Windows 2000, UNIX (including Linux), and Novell NetWare.

network routing and transport protocols: Describe the way that data travel from one network to another. The network routing and transport protocols (layers 3 and 4 in the OSI model) organize data into a logical stream, add destination and source addresses to the data, and append some error-checking codes to help ensure that the data arrive safely. In the OSI model, network routing and transport protocols form the middle levels. See *OSI reference model; physical and data link protocols;* or *application, presentation, and session protocols.*

NIC: See *network interface.*

nonblocking switch: A switch that accepts network data even if the destination port to which the data are headed is busy; the switch queues the incoming information until the designated port is free.

Novell NetWare Directory Services eDirectory: A global directory for a Novell NetWare-based network that lists all the network's resources—usernames, passwords, disks, printers, servers, and so forth.

octet: In an Internet Protocol address such as 2.38.10.11, each number separated by a period represents 8 bits (on-offs) of information.

operating system: Software that determines every facet of user interaction with a computer. The most common are Windows and Macintosh operating systems.

OSI layer 2 switch: Determines the port to which it will send data on the basis of the media access control address (MAC) within the data.

OSI layer 3 switch: Determines the port to which it will send data on the basis of its internetwork address (for example, its Internet Protocol address).

OSI (Open Systems Interconnect) reference model: Describes many different protocols, or standards of behavior, that are required in order for computers to communicate on a network. The OSI reference model divides these protocols into categories, or layers, based on the kinds of activities they perform.

P

packet: A small package of data. Network routing and transport protocols receive outgoing information from a computer and break it into packets for its journey. They also receive incoming network packets and reassemble them for use by application programs.

PAP (Password Authentication Protocol): Provides a scheme for authenticating users when they log in to a network. The user's login name and password are transmitted at the beginning of the connection and validated against known names and passwords in an encrypted database.

parallel port: An opening on a computer used to connect printers or other peripheral devices.

patch: See *hotfix.*

peer-to-peer network: A network that includes clients and/or peripherals but does not include servers (computers whose primary function is to provide shared documents, printing, and other services to clients).

peripheral: Devices such as printers, fax machines, scanners, CD-ROM towers, external hard disk drives, external Zip or Jaz drives, external modems, and so forth. Peripherals may be attached to a computer, server, or network.

physical and data link protocols: Describe how to convert outgoing information from a computer into signals for the network, and how to convert incoming network signals into information for applications. See *OSI reference model; network routing and transport protocols;* or *application, presentation, and session protocols.*

PICS (Platform for Internet Content Selection): Ratings that consist of a set of labels that Web sites voluntarily select to describe their contents, register with a labeling service, and then embed on each of the pages of the site. Web visitors can determine the level of violence, sexuality, or other characteristics of the site on the basis of the labels.

pinging: Sending a particular type of Internet packet to the network to determine the Internet Protocol (IP) addresses and other information related to computers on the network.

port: An opening on a computer that allows it to connect a device such as a printer, external hard drive, or network cable. A port number is assigned to each packet on the Internet or other IP network. It designates which program on the receiving computer should process the packet.

POTS: "Plain old telephone service."

PPP (Point-to-Point Protocol): A data link level protocol according to the OSI reference model; carries information over a variety of wide area physical connections such as POTS or ISDN.

print server: A dedicated computer that specializes in printing-related tasks.

processor slot: A slot inside a computer that accepts new or additional central processing units.

protocol: A standard of behavior by which network hardware and software must abide. Protocols can be divided into categories based on the kind of network service they specify. See *OSI reference model; physical and data link protocols; network routing and transport protocols;* and *application, presentation, and session protocols.*

protocol stack: A group of software modules that work together (like a family) to provide network services. Some common protocol stacks include TCP/IP, NetBEUI, IPX/SPX, and AppleTalk.

proxy server: A computer that manages several tasks related to Internet connections: (1) Proxy servers determine the Web sites and other Internet sites that students, faculty, and administrators can visit as well as the application programs they can use to do so. (2) Proxy servers hide the Internet addresses (IP addresses) of computers on a network to discourage tampering.

public key encryption: See *asymmetric key encryption.*

PVC (permanent virtual circuit): Circuits that reduce delays and other disturbances in data delivery. They are the most common circuit offered by frame relay vendors.

Q

QoS (quality of service): Options that allow a network to reserve a certain amount of its carrying capacity to ensure that time-critical data get first priority.

R

RADIUS (Remote Authentication Dial-In User Service): Provides a central database from which the network can authenticate users when they log in.

RAID (redundant array of inexpensive disks): Groups of hard disks that work together to protect the integrity of network data. Each RAID disk contains a portion of data along with information about how to reconstruct the data in the event of a network disaster.

RAM (random access memory): A type of computer memory that temporarily stores the information. Computers use RAM for temporary storage because RAM sends and receives information faster than it can be read from a hard disk.

RAM slot: A slot inside a computer that accepts additional random access memory.

repeater: See *hub.*

replicator: Provides a laptop computer with connections to a network, keyboard, or other devices.

return loss: A measure of the reflected energy caused by impedance mismatches (resistance to flow) in the cable.

ring topology: A physical network configuration in which each computer passes its information to the next computer in line. LocalTalk networks use a ring topology.

risk analysis: A security audit of network assets accompanied by a plan of action in the event the network is compromised.

ROM (read-only memory): A type of computer memory that cannot be changed easily and that stores part of the computer's startup programs.

router: A device that connects two or more networks. Routers examine the internetwork address for all data on the network and forward them to the appropriate destinations. They also provide powerful means to filter data and to determine its shortest path to a destination.

S

SAN (storage area network): A group of shared storage devices—computers devoted to storing data—that back up and restore documents continuously throughout the day and night. SANs provide fast, always-current storage and retrieval for large networks.

SCSI (Small Computer Systems Interface): A type of hard disk that offers expandability and performance enhancements over IDE/ATA disks.

segment: A length of cable that is bounded by hubs or some other kinds of network equipment.

serial port: An opening in the computer for modems and other devices that communicate through serial connections. The serial ports on Windows computers are labeled COM1 and COM2.

server: (1) Computers whose primary function is to store information for many clients to use simultaneously and provide access to application programs, (2) a particular software program within a shared computer.

server-based network: A network that includes clients, peripherals, and computers whose primary function is to provide shared documents, printing, and other services to clients (servers).

session, presentation, and application protocols: Describe how outgoing information from application programs should be prepared for its Internet journey, or how incoming Internet information should be prepared so that applications can read it. The session, presentation, and application protocols (layers 5, 6, and 7 in the OSI model) initiate a network connection, prepare the text for transport, and, optionally, encrypt information. See *OSI reference model, physical and data link protocols*, or *network routing and transport protocols*.

signature analysis: A method used by intrusion detection systems to examine network packets and see whether they indicate a pattern of suspicious activity.

single mode fiber optic cable: See *fiber optic cable*.

SIP (Session Initiation Protocol): Defines one way that telephone calls can be established on Internet Protocol (IP) networks.

slot: A place on a computer's main circuit board where daughter circuit boards are inserted to add functionality.

SMB (Server Message Block): Protocol that describes the proper method for Windows computers to share documents and folders. SMB is one of the protocols in the NetBEUI protocol stack.

SMTP (Simple Mail Transfer Protocol): Helps to convey electronic mail messages on the Internet. SMTP is a one of the protocols in the TCP/IP protocol stack.

SONet (Synchronous Optical Network): Defines a transmission scheme for fiber optic cable or copper wire. SONet operates at speeds between 51.84 Mbps and 2.488 Gbps. SONet often carries ATM signals.

splitter: Devices that enable Asynchronous Digital Subscriber Line (ADSL) transmissions to include telephone voice and computer data on the same pair of regular telephone (copper) wires.

spread spectrum: A method of sending information over radio waves. In spread spectrum communications, each radio wave includes many different frequencies. There are two kinds of spread spectrum technologies: frequency hopping spread spectrum (FHSS) and direct sequence spread spectrum (DSSS). Frequency hopping spread spectrum signals hop from one frequency to another at a specified rate and sequence. Direct sequence spread spectrum signals hop from one frequency to another sequentially.

SSL (Secure Sockets Layer): Protocol that authenticates the server to the client, allows the client to select the mode of encryption, optionally authenticates the client to the server, and then establishes a secure connection. SSL uses both asymmetric (public) key encryption and symmetric key encryption during the connection.

stackable hub: A set of interconnected hubs that enables a network to bypass the Ethernet restriction on the number of hubs traversed in a single network.

star topology: A physical network configuration in which a length of cable connects each computer to a central point in the network. This central point usually consists of one or more hubs or switches in a communications equipment room or central wiring closet.

stateful inspection proxy servers: Servers that examine the data within network packets to ensure that they are a legitimate part of a sensible, ongoing conversation between computers rather than a random insertion of (possibly malicious) material.

statistical profiling: A method used by intrusion detection systems to create a picture of the average behavior of users after they have logged on to any server on a network.

subnet mask: An Internet Protocol address that is used in conjunction with the IP address on a particular computer to determine the subnet on which that computer resides.

subnets: A portion of a network.

super disks: Electromagnetic storage devices that hold 120 Mb of information.

switch: Device that connects and gathers signals from several individual computers or several portions of the network. Switches regenerate these signals and create a temporary connection or circuit between each pair of communicating computers.

switched virtual circuit: A path within a frame relay network that is defined when a connection is initiated (such as a phone call). Switched paths may or may not traverse the same interim connections for each call.

symmetric key encryption: A method of encrypting data on a network. Systems that use symmetric key encryption use the same key for encrypting and decrypting data (deciphering it).

T

T.120: A family of standards describing how data can be shared among a synchronous (real-time) collaborating team.

T1 line: A network connection that provides wide area network connections at high speeds. See *leased line*.

TACACS (Terminal Access Controller Access Control System): Provides a central database of usernames and passwords from which the network can authenticate users who are trying to log in.

TCP/IP (Transmission Control Protocol/Internet Protocol): A protocol stack that enables computers to communicate over the Internet. TCP (Transmission Control Protocol) and IP (Internet Protocol) are individual protocols, or standards of behavior, within the family.

TELNET (Terminal EmuLation via a NETwork): Enables one person to log in to a remote computer through the Internet. TELNET is one of the protocols in the TCP/IP protocol stack.

terminator: A small device fitted at the ends of some networks to absorb network signals and prevent them from reflecting back onto the network.

TIA (Telecommunications Industries Association): An organization that defines many different standards for telecommunications and network cable.

Token Ring: A common scheme for connecting computers in a local area network. On a Token Ring network, a "token" (or special electronic signal) is passed among the computers on the network. The computer in possession of the token may send information, and other computers must refrain from sending until they possess the token. IBM's particular version of Token Ring has been standardized as IEEE 802.5. Fiber Distributed Data Interface (FDDI) networks also use a Token Ring scheme.

twisted pair copper wire: Network cable that contains four pairs of wires, with the partners in each pair twisted around one another to reduce signal interference between pairs.

U

UDP (User Datagram Protocol): Part of the TCP/IP family of protocols that helps transmit information on the Internet.

U-loop: A two-wire connection used for ISDN services that connects a site and the central telephone office.

upstream: Communications that travel from the customer's site to the carrier's central office.

USB (Universal Serial Bus): A relatively new type of connector that is used for add-on devices such as keyboards, scanners, and printers.

V

V.90: Standard for modem communications that specifies rates of 56 Kbps to the user and 28.8–33.3 Kbps from the user.

V.92: Standard for modem communications that specifies rates of 56 Kbps to the user and 48 Kbps from the user.

V.120: Standard that defines how data from devices such as modems (serial devices) may be transmitted over ISDN connections.

video slot: A slot inside a computer that accepts video circuit boards.

VLAN (virtual local area network): A group of client computers, servers, or peripherals that may be located in any physical area of the network and whose network communications are not transmitted outside their group unless the communications are specifically addressed to outside recipients.

VoIP (Voice over IP): A scheme for delivering telephone services over a network based on the Transmission Control Protocol/Internet Protocol family.

VPN (virtual private network): A private extension of a network that allows an organization to use the Internet or other public network.

W

WAN (wide area network): A network that connects several local area networks over significant distances. WANs use technologies such as ISDN, frame relay, or T1 leased lines to enable users on different LANs to communicate.

Web server: A computer that contains Web pages and displays them when people type its Web address (for example, **http://www.edc.org**).

Windows terminal: A computer that lacks a hard or floppy disk and uses a server to store and process information.

Z

Zip disks: Electromagnetic storage devices that hold 100–250 Mb of information.

zone database: The master list of Internet domains that a particular Domain Name System server knows about.

Index

digital signature 109

digital subscriber line (DSL) 37, 132, 135-137

direct infrared 48

direct sequence spread spectrum (DSSS) 48-49, 141

directory 116, 120, 123, 145
    Active Directory 116-117, 119, 145-146
    global 116, 120, 145
    Novell NetWare Directory Services eDirectory (NDS) 116, 119, 145-146

disaster recovery plan 163-164

disks 11, 13, 23, 27, 71, 166, 171. See also *CD-ROM, CD-RW, DVD*
    disaster recovery disks 171
    floppy disks 13, 27, 71, 158, 166
    hard disks 11-13, 15, 18-20, 22, 23, 27, 71, 171
    Integrated Drive Electronics/AT Attachment (IDE/ATA) 13
    mirroring 171
    optical discs 13
    redundant array of inexpensive disks (RAID) 20, 22
    Small Computer Systems Interface (SCSI) 13
    super disks 13
    Zip disks 13

distance learning 155

dock 15

document sharing 25, 66-67, 120-121

domain
    forest 117
    single domain model 114
    tree 117
    Windows 2000 116-117
    Windows NT 114-115, 117

domain controller 114-117. See also *backup, backup domain controller*

domain name 59-60, 63

domain name server 60

Domain Name System (DNS) 59, 61, 115, 117

downstream 128, 135, 138, 141

driver 71

dual-homed 106

DVD 13, 118

E

Electronic Industries Association (EIA) 40

electronic mail server 20, 86, 94, 166
    sharing 66, 68

emulator 112

encryption 30, 33, 92, 106, 109, 145, 146

Enhanced IGRP (EIGRP) 90-91

Ethernet 2, 3, 4, 29, 34-46, 51-52, 54-57, 61, 65-68, 70-78, 81-83, 86, 91, 92. See also *address*
    1000Base-CX 38, 43-44
    1000Base-LX 38, 43-44
    1000Base-SX 43-44
    1000Base-T 37, 38, 40, 43-44
    100BaseFX 38, 43, 46
    100BaseTX 37, 38, 40, 43, 46, 54, 65, 70-73, 75-76, 82, 92
    10BaseFL 37-39, 41, 42
    10BaseT 37-43, 46, 70, 71, 73, 75-76, 82-83, 92
    data format 39, 43-44
    frame 39, 45, 91
    Gigabit Ethernet 43-44, 46
    long-distance networks 125-126, 128, 136-137
    media access method 39
    physical media 30, 32
    topology 42

evergreening 22

expansion slot 12

Extended Industry Standard Architecture (EISA) 12

F

Fiber Distributed Data Interface (FDDI) 36, 147-148

File Transfer Protocol (FTP) 10, 32-33, 57, 96-98, 109

filtering 20-21, 23, 85, 95, 98, 102, 109

firewall 3, 4, 69-70, 92, 94-100, 105, 108-109, 145-146, 166
    packet screening 99
    proxy server 94-95, 97-98, 108
    stateful inspection proxies 97

fractional T1 133-134

frame 32, 45, 50-51, 65, 144

frame relay 3, 126, 134-136, 139-141, 143-145, 149-151

frequency hopping spread spectrum (FHSS) 48-49, 53, 141

full duplex 44, 77-78, 81-82, 130